Golden Oldies

STORIES OF HOCKEY'S HEROES

BRIAN MCFARLANE

ecw

This book is written with two of my all-time favourites in mind—softspoken Jean Beliveau and outspoken Ted Lindsay.

With thanks to all the former NHL Oldtimers who adopted me in the 1960s—a rank amateur—and allowed me to play a hundred games with them over the next two decades. From them came the genesis of this book.

With thanks to individuals who encouraged me and assisted me in this effort: Dave Batson, Bob Graham, Dan Sandford, Mike Robitaille, Clint Malarchuk, Bob Baun, Bob and Sheila McNeil, Ray Bradley, Norah Perez, Red Kelly, Len Thornson, Eddie Shack, Pat MacAdam, Scotty Bowman, Paul Patskou and my wife Joan McFarlane.

With thanks to Michael Holmes and Jack David at ECW Press for having faith in *Golden Oldies*.

INTRODUCTION

Hockey's fascinating history is filled with facts and stats that are familiar to most fans of the game. Who hasn't heard the story of One-Eyed Frank McGee and the record 14 goals he scored in a Stanley Cup playoff game in 1905? Who doesn't know that goalie Georges Vezina's nickname was "the Chicoutimi Cucumber" or that goalie Glenn Hall played in 502 consecutive games—without a mask or helmet! These stories, like Wayne Gretzky's 92-goal season or Paul Henderson's magical goal against the Soviets in 1972, are oft-repeated and have become part of the game's fabulous lore.

But the thirst for more tales from hockey's history appears to be unquenchable.

The game has been enriched by the actions of colourful stalwarts who were the best on ice 50, 75 and 100 years ago, men like King Clancy, who played every position on the ice in a Stanley Cup game; Sprague Cleghorn, the league bad man who was involved in dozens of "stretcher case" incidents and who once taught a Broadway beauty queen how to ice skate; and Ace Bailey, who was brutally attacked by Eddie Shore in a career-ending game in Boston. Others of more recent vintage, like Eddie

"Clear the Track" Shack, who claims he was "better than Frank Mahovlich and Bobby Hull" as a junior star, and Mike Robitaille, who sued and won an incredible lawsuit against his own team, the Vancouver Canucks, never achieved superstardom or Hall of Fame heights like others who appear in these pages. But they grab your interest. As does little Patsy Guzzo, who reveals the story of the Laughingstock Hockey Team, a saga passed on to me by my friend Pat MacAdam of Ottawa. Ridiculed at the outset, Patsy and his pals silenced critics by winning Olympic glory in 1948. Even a glimpse at Rocket Richard's bizarre 1956 contract, written in pencil, will fascinate readers.

Before we begin, allow me to dedicate this book to one of the greatest individuals in hockey—and Canada's—history, Jean Beliveau. Here's a letter written on the day of his death.

Dear Jean:

I hope I can find the right words to describe how I feel about you. It will be a challenge. And you know all about challenges.

In Toronto, even the most rabid of Leaf fans, or fans of any NHL team, will agree that, throughout your glorious career, you were above reproach and exempt from criticism, even when you and your mates were vanquishing Leaf playoff hopes and dashing Stanley Cup aspirations.

How was it possible, they wondered, for you personally to garner 10 Stanley Cups while their favourite Leafs, after 1967, won none? The answer is clear. You earned them. And I can hear you protesting: "No, no, no, not me. The team earned them."

Point acknowledged, Jean. We all know that hockey is a team game. But you were the peerless leader of the team. In Leaf history, one may have to reach back as far as Syl Apps in the late 1930s and early '40s to find a comparable leader.

Obviously, Leaf fans—like hockey fans everywhere—recognized class and greatness when they saw it. They may have snarled at Ferguson and hooted at Savard and Lapointe. But they never booed Beliveau. Not that I remember.

The aura, Jean— that's what people noticed. You created the aura that surrounded you. Give your parents credit, if you wish, for a solid upbringing, and perhaps some wise old parish priest for guidance and inspiration. But you, and only you, decided early on what kind of man you would grow into, what moral compass you would adopt and follow.

You made wise choices, my friend.

And that man you moulded became one of the most beloved figures in our country's history. I'll bet even you have difficulty explaining how that all came about.

In those games at Maple Leaf Gardens, where you played seven times a season, Leaf fans never showed much respect for politicians who showed up for ceremonial faceoffs; they were quick to condemn a bombastic owner, quick to snipe at an over-the-hill coach, quick to vent their anger on game officials who screwed up. But Jean Beliveau? When you came to town, Jean, 15,000 heads bobbed up and down in unanimous approval. This man has our respect, those bobbing heads signalled.

And they were thinking: *This man is what my son should be, my grandson. He's a superb player, a brilliant and courageous captain. But he's so much more than that. A hero and role model to millions of kids, a kind and considerate man, a modest and humble man, a gentle man [two words] and a gentleman [one word]. Montreal was so fortunate to claim such an individual.*

I remember fantasizing once—perhaps it was while watching one of those Miss Universe contests—that if there was ever a Mr. Universe event, where a hundred entrants from a hundred countries competed for "Best Man in the Universe" honours, Canadians would say, "We're sending Jean Beliveau. He'll win easily."

When Ted Lindsay and I worked NBC games together, years ago, I asked him once about you. He said, "Jean Beliveau is the classiest hockey player I have ever met." And Ted Lindsay has met them all. Ted seldom flattered a foe, but he flattened a few.

Jean, I have known you for what—over 60 years now? And we are almost exactly the same age—born a few days apart, in August 1931. I remember clearly how we first met. Your crack junior team, the Quebec Citadelles, came to Ottawa to play my team, the Inkerman Rockets, in an

Eastern Canada junior playoff game. Winner of the series would go on to meet the Barrie Flyers for the Memorial Cup.

It was my bad luck to come down with a silly kid's disease—measles—just as the series got underway, and I was confined to bed for a week. I agonized over missing the first game. You paced the Citadelles to an easy win in the brand new Quebec Colisée. Yes, the House That Jean Built.

Game two, in Ottawa. There was a frenzy for tickets, and your image was everywhere. You were the most heralded junior player of that era by far. Two of your fine teammates, Camille Henry and Marcel Paille—future NHLers—were pushed from the spotlight.

My Inkerman coach, Lloyd Laporte, told me it was my job to cover you. Was I excited! You can't imagine. I skated out on wobbly legs—I'd pleaded with my doctor to free me from my sickbed that morning—and faced off against you. I sized you up as we went head to head. And some of my confidence began to slipslide away, like the perspiration that fell from my chin.

I have often mentioned how intimidated I was before that first puck was dropped. You were big, Jean—bigger, stronger, faster than any centreman I'd clashed with before. And yet, years later, whenever we would meet, I'd think, well, he's not *that* big. Did you shrink a little over the years, Jean?

I spent the next three periods chasing you around the ice. Your stride was so effortless you soon tired me out. And your shot! You blew one past my ear, and I turned to see the puck fly like a bullet past our bare-faced goalie's nose. If it had hit either one of us, it would have been curtains, I'm sure. While I was focussed on you, I neglected to keep an eye on your toughest defenseman, big Gordie Hudson, an Ottawa boy who caught me with my head down and knocked me silly.

When I staggered to my feet, I was angry and humiliated. I said, "Okay, Beliveau, I'm going to knock you on your butt."

I took a run at you across the rink. You were leading a rush and you saw me coming. Reached out. Shoved me aside with one arm. Boom! Down I went again, legs flying in all directions. You brushed me aside like I was a pesky peewee player.

Perhaps it was then, Jean—at that very moment—that I realized I'd never make it to the NHL.

If I can't check Beliveau, I thought, *and there must be a number of players almost as skilled scattered across the country, then I'd better accept the college scholarship I've been offered to St. Lawrence University. I'd better forget about pro hockey.*

Your Citadelles wrapped up the series back in Quebec, and I failed again to stop you from scoring three or four goals. Our little junior team, created by Lloyd Laporte in a town of a hundred people, with no home arena and no league to play in, had never played before such a huge crowd—all of them cheering for you and the Citadelles *en français.*

During the second intermission, we stood around goggle-eyed while they presented you with a brand new car—a Nash Ambassador. That summer, I'd paid $75 for my first car—a '31 Chev. And it had no brakes and bald tires.

In the third period, we realized our season was almost over. So one of our players, during a pileup in the corner of the rink, stole the puck for a souvenir. He tucked it under his jersey and skated to the bench. The game officials looked everywhere for it.

"Où est la rondelle?" they asked. The players shrugged.

Finally, they went to the scorer's bench to seek another puck.

It wasn't much fun playing against you, Jean, but I know I speak for all of the Inkerman Rockets when I say we were so proud to be on the same ice surface with you. One day, we knew, it would be something to tell our grandkids about—and for some of us, our great-grandkids.

Years later, you and I would work together on the Scotiabank Hockey College promotion. Every so often, one of our lucky members would win a trip to an NHL game. One time, I accompanied a young winner to Montreal and a game at the Forum. You met the family and took them to the posh Beaver Club for lunch. The mother of the winner told me later, "That man is such a gentleman. My child will never forget the luncheon today. Mr. Beliveau will always be his hero. And mine too."

You were a hero to millions, Jean. And I know you made every young fan you met feel like he or she was special in some way.

I remember you telling me, "Brian, they are paying me lots of money at Scotiabank, but they don't ask me to do anything. Well, they did ask me to go tuna fishing with some of the bankers, but I expected to do more than that."

One night in Toronto, Jean, the bankers saluted you with a dinner at an exclusive club. I remember Al Eagleson being there, and John Ziegler, and half a dozen bank executives.

One of them got up and spoke glowingly of you, Jean, and then he presented you with a "token of our esteem."

It came in a well-wrapped package.

After the dinner, I took you aside and I asked you what was in the package.

You said, "Brian, you know that I am uncomfortable accepting expensive gifts. But I did not expect this."

You smiled and held up a Scotiabank pen. With the bank's logo emblazoned on it. Must have cost a dollar, two at the most. The bank gave out hundreds of them.

You weren't at all upset at the chintzy gift, Jean. But I was.

The last time I saw you was at a Maple Leaf reunion dinner in March 2007. Hundreds of Leaf fans attended a dinner honouring the '67 Leafs. You and Phil Esposito were the two celebrity guests invited, the two non-Leafs. I flew up from Florida to MC the event. The dinner chairman was upset because Esposito had phoned at the last minute to say he would not be coming. "You've booked me on a flight and they gave me a middle seat," he complained. "I never sit in the middle seat."

"Just ask someone to switch seats with you," the chairman suggested. "You're Phil Esposito. They'll gladly do it for you."

"Hell, no, I won't do that. I'm not coming. You should have booked me in first class, not economy. Screw your dinner."

But you showed up, Jean. And you signed more autographs and posed for more photos than anyone. The dinner went long, but you stayed until the very end. Another example of your remarkable class.

My friend Dennis Hull told me a story about you once that made me laugh. He said, "I was with Chicago when Beliveau led a rush and swept around Pierre Pilote, our best defenseman. I rushed over and gave Jean a whack with my stick—a hard two-hander that should have drawn a penalty. But he shook it off and went in and scored a goal. When he skated past me he said, 'I did not expect that from you, Dennis.'

"Well, I was so upset I chased after him to the Montreal bench. I kept saying, 'I'm sorry, Jean. I'm sorry. I'll never do that again.'

"Then my coach, Billy Reay, called me to the Chicago bench. 'What are you doing? What's going on?'

"I told him, 'I'm apologizing to Beliveau.'

"He growled at me, 'Well, stop that. There's no apologizing in hockey.'

"I said, 'I know. But it's Jean Beliveau.'"

In 1994, you were invited to take an honoured position in Ottawa that would have made you the first hockey man since Lord Stanley himself to serve Canada in such a role. You were asked to be our nation's Governor General.

You were the ideal choice. You would have brought dignity and prestige and your ever-present class to the position. Everybody hoped you would accept. But we all understood when you declined. You put your family ahead of the honour, and nobody can fault you for that. Had you accepted, I say, you would have been the most dedicated and most popular Governor General Canada has ever had.

Jean, I found *enough* words to describe how I feel about you. I hope they were the *right* words.

Rest in peace, my friend.

SPRAGUE CLEGHORN
A Pugnacious Pioneer

I never met Sprague Cleghorn, one of hockey's toughest, meanest warriors, but I wish I had. Cleghorn was struck and killed by a car in Montreal in 1956, a year after I graduated from university and when I was well into my first year in TV broadcasting in Schenectady, New York. Two days later, Sprague's younger brother, Odie, passed away of a heart attack, precipitated, friends said, by the shocking news of Sprague's passing.

I'm grateful Sprague chronicled highlights of his career in hockey before he passed, giving fans and historians a fascinating insight into hockey as it was played long before most of us were born.

In the mid-'60s, while writing King Clancy's biography, I asked the King about Cleghorn. "Sprague was the NHL bad man when I broke in with Ottawa in 1921," Clancy told me. "He played for Montreal and he was fierce. He made no bones about it. He terrified some of us. I remember he kept a big can of talcum powder close by the Montreal bench. He'd skate over there and sprinkle this powder on his hockey gloves. Then he'd run those gloves up and down the shaft of his stick. All this time he's glaring over at our bench. That was his way of telling us he was ready to give one of us the butt end of that stick—right in the belly.

He would slip that butt end into your guts like he was using a carving knife. And he was so slick the referee would never even notice. When he went for the talcum powder, we knew that one of us would probably be going home after the game with cracked or broken ribs."

Years ago, a friend sent me a faded copy of an old article from the 1930s, with no byline, in which Sprague Cleghorn talked to the anonymous journalist about his life in hockey. But there was something missing in his narration. He failed to mention the 1923 playoffs, and how his own manager (the Canadiens' Leo Dandurand) suspended him after he whacked an Ottawa opponent over the head with his stick. Nor did he give details about the time he was charged with spousal assault—laid up with a broken leg, he belted his wife with a crutch. He also neglects to mention the number of "stretcher case" fights he was involved in, once estimated at fifty. Fifty? That's unbelievable, if not impossible. But then, why would he want to reveal any details about any of those embarrassing incidents? I'll fill in some of the gaps in his narrative. But the Cleghorn story is a revealing portrait of a well-travelled hockey star long before the NHL came into existence—a true golden oldie.

One day King Clancy caused me to smile when he recalled a story about Cleghorn: "I got cute with Sprague one night in Ottawa. He was racing in on our goal, and I was on his heels. I called out, 'Sprague, drop the puck.' Without so much as a glance over his shoulder, he dropped the puck on my stick and I wheeled around and led a rush the other way. The crowd roared with laughter while Sprague did a slow burn. He glared at me but said nothing at the time. When the period was over and the players were leaving the ice, I heard a voice from behind me: 'Oh, King.'

"I turned around, and suddenly all the lights in the rink went out. Cleghorn had slugged me. When I finally opened my eyes, I saw a priest standing over me. I thought I must be getting the last rites. When my teammates tried to get at Sprague, he told them, 'Honest, fellows, I was just telling King he has the makings of a great hockey player. And I gave him a friendly pat on the head.' Brian, that's the first pat on the head that required a bucket of water to revive a fellow and brought a priest on the run."

The Cleghorn interview my friend sent me included no mention of where the words first appeared, but the article probably came from the sports pages of a now-defunct newspaper in Montreal or Ottawa.

Otherwise, I would credit it and compliment the writer on his choice of subjects. The old warrior began his life's story by stating:

I'm telling you, hockey is a tough game. All hockey is tough. When you put a half a dozen husky young athletes on razor-sharp skates, hand each one of them a bladed hockey stick and tell them to go out and mix things up with half a dozen other young athletes who are equally husky and similarly equipped, you are starting something that is no pastime for sissies. Hockey under any conditions, controlled by any set of rules a Geneva Peace Conference could devise, would still be a rough-and-tumble proposition, made for men with hair on their chests [notice he makes no mention of women players, hirsute or otherwise], men who know how to take it and how to dish it out.

That is what makes hockey the game it is, the one competitive sport growing amazingly in public favour every year in every country in the world where it has so far been introduced.

Without boasting, I think I can claim to know what I am talking about. I played hockey for 25 seasons. My career as a professional lasted nineteen winters—although some of the wise lads figured I was all washed up ten years before I finally quit—and that is a long time on any man's calendar, a long time to absorb and hand out punishment in competition with the best in the world.

In those nineteen pro seasons, I wore the colours of six different clubs under six different managers. Since I hung up my skates and stick for the last time in 1929, I have managed four other clubs for four different owners.

Sports writers have tagged me "durable" and "the iron man" and others have called me "the bad man" which is okay by me. The writers have to have at least one "bad man" to kick around every hockey season or they couldn't sleep at night.

I have been durable and I have been lucky as well. I have only a half dozen permanent scars on my face. Lots of oldtimers have twice that many.

While I was a rank amateur, a carelessly swung stick in the hands of a chap named Mowatt broke my nose. Joe Hall of Quebec, also known as "Bad Joe," twice split my scalp so thoroughly that club doctors had to do neat hemstitching jobs on my head. Marty Walsh once sliced my left ear in two and left it flapping alongside my jaw. The doctor sewed that one up, too. Jack Laviolette, a good friend, gave me a neighbourly poke in the chest one night with a butt end and broke my ribs. And Ken Randall, then with Toronto, crashed me feet first into the boards, breaking my leg.

No hard feelings. That's what oldtime hockey was like.

I don't remember when I first started to play. Odie and me were given skates for Christmas almost before we could walk. I suppose we began skating on the frozen Montreal sidewalks, batting tin cans around with old umbrella handles before we reached school age.

We were the only sons in a family of five children.

My father, William Cleghorn, was an athlete, a great lacrosse player who once toured Europe with a Canadian lacrosse team. And he was an outstanding curler. He always encouraged us to play competitive games and to play them hard. My mother never went to our games, not even when we were playing on world championship teams. She did see us play in retirement, in an oldtimers' game played for fun. When it was over, she said, "Well, if that was for fun, I'm glad I never saw you play in earnest."

Odie and me have stuck together since we were in diapers. We played on the same school teams and the same amateur teams. We began a professional partnership in Renfrew that lasted for seven seasons, then was resumed in 1921 with the Canadiens and continued on until 1925 when Odie went to Pittsburgh and I joined Art Ross in Boston. Between 1918 and 1921 we were on rival teams in the NHL, Odie with Canadiens and myself with Ottawa.

As a kid, I was long and lanky, Odie was broad and stocky. Anybody who tangled with him knows that he is well able to take care of himself.

From 1906 to 1909, Odie and I played for Westmount Intermediates in the Quebec Amateur Hockey Association. I was a forward then and I am not just being modest when I say that Odie, although two years younger, was the better player.

As a forward, at my best I was just fair and at my worst I was terrible.

Not much exciting happened in those years except when Mowatt broke my nose. I remember that.

In the autumn of 1909 I was working behind the counter of a sporting goods store that Art Ross and Walter Smaill had opened in Montreal. I was 20 years old and had no particular idea of making hockey a career.

Back then, Cornelius Fellowes, a great sportsman and a splendid person, was running a four-club hockey league in New York City. His right-hand-man in hockey was a Montrealer, Ernie Dufresne. I did not know Dufresne from Adam, nor did he know me when he walked into Ross' store one day in October. Dufresne asked to speak to the boss. They went into conference in a little office in the back and a few minutes later Ross called me in and introduced us. Dufresne gave me a careful once-over like a man gives a horse that somebody is trying to sell him. Then he said, "Young man, how'd you like to play hockey in New York?"

Now that was something to hear. I was twenty years old and New York—well, it was New York. I said, "Sure. But I've got to have a job."

"Don't worry. We'll find you a job."

Gosh! I was smart enough even then to know what that meant. I'd have gone to New York gladly—just to work—but to have a job and play hockey and get my name in the papers and live next to Broadway— man, oh man. Then I remembered something.

"I'll go, Mr. Dufresne. I'll be glad to go. But only if Odie can come along with me."

"What's this?" Dufresne said, looking at Ross. "Who the hell is Odie?"

Ross laughed. "Odie's his brother. You can probably use them both."

We got hold of Odie and my father and talked it over. By the end of the day it was settled. We both would go to New York and play for the New York Wanderers. We were to have jobs and we'd be paid $50 per week. We lay awake all night making plans and thinking of all the fun we'd have in New York.

When we landed on Broadway—with eyes wide open and dreaming—it was late autumn of 1909. We were not alone, for Cooper Smeaton, later to become one of the best hockey referees ever to blow a whistle, and a long-time trustee of the Stanley Cup, joined us with the New York Wanderers.

As I have already explained, the Wanderers were owned by Cornelius Fellowes and managed by Ernie Dufresne. It had been agreed in Montreal that we were to get $50 a week each—Odie and myself, that is. I don't know what the other players got. In order to make the thing work, we had to have jobs.

Odie was easily fixed up. They put him in a stock brokerage office, doing sums on a blackboard. That was no good for Sprague Cleghorn. Figures make my head ache.

They offered me a spot in the Spalding retail store and I reported for duty with a light heart. Hadn't I been a salesman for Art Ross?

Unfortunately, Spalding already had all the salesmen they needed—oldtimers who weren't about to let some kid from the sticks in Canada shove his nose into their racket. The store manager took me to a room on the upper floor.

"There you are," said the boss. "Get to work on those footballs."

"What do you want me to do with 'em? Count 'em?"

"No, I don't want you to count them. Blow them up."

I shook my head.

"Not me, mister," I said. "I don't aim to cut my fingers to pieces lacing up a million footballs."

So they threw me out of there. Afterward, they persuaded Cooper Smeaton to go to work on the footballs. For days his hands were so sore he couldn't grip a hockey stick.

Finally they placed me with the New York and New Jersey Telephone Company. I was supposed to be an inspector. What are the duties of an inspector? Don't ask foolish questions. How should I know?

But I reported faithfully on the right day each week and drew a paycheque of $25. The other $25 kept turning up regularly at the rink in the toes of my street shoes and I hadn't a care in the world.

All the clubs of the New York Hockey League—St. Nicholas, Crescents of Brooklyn, Wanderers, the New York Athletic Club and the Hockey Club of New York—played their games at the old St. Nicholas Arena, at Broadway and Sixty-Second Street.

Yep. The playing surface was artificial ice—fifteen years before Tex Rickard lay awake nights worrying about whether or not to put an ice plant in his new Madison Square Garden. The rink, which seated about 4,000, had been made over from a riding academy and there were several queer features about it. The ice floor was built above the old surface with a space between, and the smell of animals persisted, so that sometimes you didn't know whether you were skating or going over the hurdles on a horse.

Sam Austin, publisher of the *Police Gazette*, the famous pink prayer book of the tonsorial parlours in the days when a man still had some rights and a woman would as soon enter a saloon as a barbershop, was the owner. Sam and his buddies were big shots in the sporting and entertainment world of their time, when the theatre was the theatre and Hollywood had never been heard of.

The hockey wasn't anything to write home about. Each of the teams had one or two imports who knew something about the game. The balance was made up of local talent and Canadians who lived and worked in New York. Their notion of hockey was to take a bat at the puck and see what happened. Wanderers finished second in the league, losing in the finals to the New York Athletic Club. And that was that.

But if the hockey wasn't much, we got a lot of fun out of our adventures on Broadway. Odie and I shared a room at Sixty-Fourth Street, and spent all our spare time wandering up and down the Main Stem in company of Mr. Fellowes and his friends.

Cornelius Fellowes was a generous boss, and he took a fatherly interest in us. Through him we met many of the famous actors and actresses of the period. Two of them whom I especially remember were Mademoiselle Daizie, the dancer, and Lillian Lorraine, the musical comedy star.

Daizie, who later became Mrs. Cornelius Fellowes, was a beautiful girl and as bright as they make them. The boss was giving her a heavy rush at the time, and every night when she appeared in New York he sent Odie and myself to the theatre with huge boxes of flowers and candy. When she finished her act, we would march down the aisle and hand her Cornelius Fellowes' gifts. If you think we didn't get a big kick out of that, you're crazy.

One day while I was hanging around the rink with time on my hands, Mr. Fellowes called me over and introduced me to the most stunning woman I had ever met in my life.

He said, "Sprague, this is Miss Lillian Lorraine. She wants to learn how to skate. Do you think you could teach her?"

Could I teach Lillian Lorraine how to skate! I don't know what I stammered but it must have sounded like "yes" because the next thing I knew I was lacing skates onto her pretty feet and then holding her up with my arm around her slim waist. Believe me, I made those lessons last.

We had a swell season, even though there wasn't much good hockey in it and we left New York in the spring of 1910 with many regrets and promises to be back next winter. And yes, I was hoping Miss Lorraine would want more skating lessons.

But it didn't work out that way. We returned to Montreal, I went back to work for Art Ross and played some baseball in the City League. By the time hockey season rolled around again the whole picture was changed.

It all began with the Cobalt mining boom. When the Northern Ontario silver country was opened up in 1905 there followed a hectic period when millionaires were made overnight. By the winter of 1908–09, both Cobalt and Haileybury, just five miles away, were full of rich men looking for excitement, with expense no object.

Author's note: My grandfather, John Henry McFarlane, gravitated to Haileybury from the Ottawa Valley in 1911 to take over as principal of the local school. My father, Leslie McFarlane, began his writing career in Haileybury as a teenager. Later he would gain fame as the original author of the Hardy Boys books, using the *nom de plume* Franklin W. Dixon.

So, toward the end of the 1909 season, the silver country magnates brought the Ottawa and Wanderer hockey clubs up for an exhibition series. When the teams returned to the capital and to Montreal, a full half of the players stayed behind to cash in on the easy dough.

The Temiskaming League was organized with teams in Cobalt, Haileybury and New Liskeard. Later, this grew into the Federal League which took in Renfrew.

The whole mining country was hockey crazy. Tens of thousands of dollars were bet on each game. Often thousands changed hands on a single goal. Spectators fought each other in the rinks during the games and up and down the streets after the games.

During that wild period the best hockey players in the world were performing in this unimportant backwoods league. Some of the boys lived up there, others commuted. It got so that no club could be sure of the services of one of its players until he actually stepped on the ice. On one occasion management of the Montreal Wanderers offered to send up the whole team to play in Cobalt uniforms for a $5,000 guarantee. The offer was refused but it goes to show how things stood.

That couldn't go on and during the summer of 1910 the league passed out of existence to make way for the National Hockey

Association which brought Cobalt, Haileybury, Renfrew, Wanderers, Canadiens, Ottawa and Quebec into the game. The late Emmett Quinn was made president of the new body.

It triggered a big demand for new playing material. Odie and I were offered Cobalt contracts but there had been a smallpox epidemic in the mining town and mother said, "No." This time she made it stick.

Sometime later, George Martel, representing Renfrew, came to Montreal and talked to Art Ross. When he left, he carried with him Odie's signature and mine at the bottom of contracts to play for Renfrew at salaries of $1,200 each. We were honest professionals at last.

The Renfrew Millionaires. You'll never see a team like that again. M.J. O'Brien was a leading citizen of the Creamery Town long before he became a mining man. He made a pot of money in Cobalt but his heart was always in Renfrew. He wanted to put the town on the map, so he threw his bulging bankroll behind the hockey club.

By any rule of sound business, the thing was plain nuts. If you added all the milk cans, the telegraph poles and the travelling salesmen, there might have been 5,000 people in Renfrew.

Total capacity of the rink, seated, standing and hanging by the rafters, couldn't have been more than 3,500. The schedule called for travel to Cobalt and Haileybury, Ottawa, Montreal and Quebec. No, it simply could not be done.

But the O'Briens and their friends did it.

They organized the Renfrew Club in 1908. By the start of the 1910–11 season Renfrew was in the NHA.

One thing about a hockey career, you learn plenty of geography. Until we signed those contracts, neither Odie nor myself had the foggiest notion where Renfrew was.

It might have been in Georgian Bay or in Essex County for all we knew.

Odie reported direct. I wanted to have one last fling at New York and I took the few dimes I had saved over the summer and spent them strutting my stuff among my New York friends. Then it was time to head north.

It was a bitter cold night in December when I dropped off the train at Renfrew. I was wearing a light overcoat. Odie was waiting for me at the station. I shivered and looked around. There was nothing to see but darkness.

"Good gosh, what is this?" I said.

"This is Renfrew," Odie said, chuckling.

"I don't think we're going to like it here," I grumbled. I had just come from New York and my ears were beginning to nip.

"For twelve hundred dollars we gotta like it here," Odie said as we drove away in a borrowed cutter.

"Giddap, horse."

Once we settled down, we liked the place. You couldn't help liking Renfrew.

For one thing, the men behind the club believed in spending money—and how they spent it. The story is that M.J. O'Brien paid $5,000 for Cyclone Taylor's jump from Ottawa. That was more money per game than any pro baseball player received at the time—even the great Ty Cobb.

The Renfrew fans were swell. No club ever bragged of a more loyal following. They came from all over the countryside around to see us play. A twenty mile drive in an open sleigh on a below-zero night meant no more to them than a twenty minute drive in a heated streetcar means to a Toronto or a Montreal fan today. Figure a boy and a girl riding behind a horse for anywhere from 10 to 25 miles in frostbite weather, against that same boy and girl this winter, crabbing because they can't find space for their closed and heated car within two blocks of the rink, and you'll get what I mean when I say that in those days the spectators were tougher too.

Fred [Cyclone] Taylor was Renfrew's idol. Taylor was a big man but lightning fast, an unusual trait with defense players of that era. He was one of the first rushing defensemen and the first I believe to wear padding on his shoulders. These days players go into a game armoured up like a tank. Some clubs are planning to use modified football helmets this season, in addition to all their other equipment. When Odie and I broke in as professionals, you dragged on your long underwear and stockings, climbed into short pants and a sweater, grabbed a pair of light gauntlets and went out there fighting.

Taylor, who was always poking around and figuring things out, picked up a couple of pieces of felt over at Larry Gilmour's livery stable one day, cut them to fit and sewed them to the shoulders of his under-shirt—and that's how padding was born.

The Cyclone never took a drink of hard liquor, but he'd swallow eggnog by the gallon. He didn't believe in dressing up and all winter in Renfrew I never saw him with a shirt and collar on. He'd climb into his underwear and trousers, put on a couple of sweaters and be dressed for anything from church to a card game.

Author's note: I was hoping Sprague would talk about the time Cyclone Taylor scored a goal in Renfrew while skating backwards—if he actually did so. Alas, he fails to mention the feat.

For a while that season, we had a kid with us who was heaven's gift to the smart guys. I've forgotten his name but we can call him Mac. He drifted into town one day from some lumber camp and announced that he was going to play hockey for Renfrew. He knew as much about hockey as I know about Outer Mongolia. But the club carried him around for a few weeks, probably to give the boys something to occupy their minds.

He was the sort of character you read about in stories by Ring Lardner. He had never been in a big hotel or seen a sleeping car. He brought along his own boots and skates. Those boots were white kid and the skates had been bolted—not riveted—to the soles. Maybe they didn't know about rivets where Mac came from. I don't know how he stood on those things, much less skated.

The first long train trip we took after Mac joined the team we suckered him. We told him somebody had to sit up all night and watch the shoes, otherwise they would be stolen. We faked a lottery and Mac was chosen for shoe guard. Then we turned in, leaving Mac on top of the stepladder at one end of the car with our footwear piled up in front of him. He watched, pop-eyed, for train robbers.

Poor old Mac. We pulled the finger bowl trick and the Tabasco sauce trick on him in Ottawa. Naturally, he'd never heard of finger bowls. So, after dinner when they were handed around, with a dinky slice of lemon in each bowl, one of the boys sipped the water, pulled a face and said, "Gosh, this is terrible. Try yours, Mac."

Mac said, "What's it supposed to be?"

"Lemonade."

Mac tasted his and said, "It's mighty weak lemonade."

"It's awful," we told him. "And there isn't enough sugar in it. Call the waiter over and we'll tell him what's what."

Mac called the waiter. We slipped the waiter the wink and he took a terrible bawling out. Mac scolded him harder than the rest of us. The waiter took the finger bowls away, then brought them back, exactly as before.

Mac grabbed his and drained it, smacking his lips.

"Ahh!" he said, "that's more like it."

Then his eyes went wide as he watched the rest of us make a big fuss over rinsing our fingers and wiping them on napkins.

You know the Tabasco sauce trick. The idea is to get hold of a rookie, a greenhorn. You pry the top off a bottle of Tabasco sauce and tell him it's a special brand of tomato ketchup. Mac was particularly fond of tomato ketchup. But I doubt if his tonsils have cooled off yet.

Meanwhile the Cleghorn brothers were finding out about the serious business of hockey. I'll always think gratefully about Renfrew for one thing. It was there I first discovered that I might be a hockey player.

Alf Smith was coaching us and Alf was plenty tough. He believed that the way to learn to play hockey was to get out on the ice and play. We never lacked for exercise. If you played for Smith you had to take it and you had to hand it out. Odie was a sniper, in his day one of the smartest goal scorers in the game, and they watched him every minute.

Remember we were playing the seven man game, two thirty-minute periods, no substitutions except at halftime. A man had to be tough.

In those days, no man figured himself a defense player unless he weighed a ton and was built like the side of a barn. We played the Wanderers one night in Ottawa. This was a game postponed from when the Wanderers equipment got lost en route from Montreal. Postponements because equipment trunks went astray or trains were stalled in snowstorm drifts were common enough back then.

Our team was pretty badly battered up and I was on the spot. The directors knew Odie was a coming star but I looked like a total loss to them.

Just before the game Alf Smith said to me, "You're going to play point tonight." That meant I was going back to the blueline.

"Point!" I said, scared to death. "I never played point in my life."

"You're playing point tonight," he insisted, and walked away.

I don't think Alf had any idea I might be good on the back line. He knew I was no good up front and he needed somebody back there so he took a chance.

Sometimes when a man gets in a tough spot like that, he gives stuff he never knew he had to give. I was frightened and desperate and fighting mad. We beat the Wanderers 5–4 and I still have the clipping from the Montreal *Gazette* that described my play:

Sprague Cleghorn starred for Renfrew throughout. He was shoved in at point when nobody else could be found for the position, and was without doubt the most effective man on the winning team.

You never know what you can do until you have to. Since that date I have always been a defense player.

Yes indeed, the Cleghorn brothers learned a lot that season in Renfrew. One thing we learned was that playing professional was a vastly different proposition from playing amateur or even semi professional hockey. Once you sign a pro contract you stop being your own man right there. You eat what you're told to eat, you go where you're told to go, you do what you're told to do—whether you like it or not. You become property, either an asset or a liability, and you are treated accordingly.

After Alf Smith made me a defenseman, I was feeling pretty cocky. The newspapers were telling the world that I was good, the Renfrew fans patted me on the back—although when I was trying to be a forward they called me nasty names—and the Renfrew directors were complimentary to both Odie and myself. We had made good in our first season as professional hockey players.

Then, after the Renfrew directors examined the balance sheet, things looked different. The club was $5,000 behind on the season and some of the directors had spent as much out of their own pockets to show the boys a good time. It had been good fun while it lasted but there didn't seem to be any sense in throwing away another $5,000 with no earthly chance of getting it back.

Renfrew withdrew from the NHA and went back to the Ottawa Valley League.

Meanwhile, in Toronto, Percy Quinn [Emmett's brother] had ambitions to own a professional team. He gathered some friends around him, obtained a franchise from the NHA, and began to assemble his club.

The Renfrew players were doled out to the other clubs. Nothing was said to the players about this distribution which irked many of us.

Sprague Cleghorn was turned over to Toronto and Odie was given to the Montreal Wanderers.

No, the arrangement didn't please me. Not that I have anything against Toronto. But Montreal is my hometown. I wanted to play there—with my brother.

The National Hockey Association was by no means as tightly controlled as its successor—the National Hockey League. Things could be wangled. I talked to the owner of the Wanderers and he said he'd like to have me on his club. He offered Pud Glass, an older, more experienced player than I was, to Toronto and I went to Wanderers with Odie. We were with Wanderers for the next six seasons.

And what a team that was! We never won a championship although we made the playoffs and we spoiled other clubs' chances often enough. But we sure had fun. I've never seen a club, before or since that time, that was quite as dizzy as that Wanderer outfit.

Nobody knew what we were going to do next. One night we'd beat Ottawa in Ottawa by nine to two. A few nights later, Ottawa would come back and beat us by a similar count or even a larger margin. It was the same with the Canadiens, Quebec and Toronto. We earned a reputation as the wildest in-and-out team in the NHA.

The thing is, we had the players. Both Odie and I were going strong. Art Ross, Ernie Russell, Harry Hyland, Jack Marshall and Gordie Roberts were stars for the Wanderers. Somehow we didn't take the hockey seriously enough. Just a bunch of playboys playing games.

For a lot of this spirit, Sam Lichtenhein, the president, was largely responsible. He would organize parties for the boys, at which champagne would flow from the water taps, buy the players expensive gifts—clothing, jewellery and hats.

When he met one of the boys on the street, it would be, "Come with me. I want to buy you something," and he'd lead him into the nearest men's clothing shop.

His parties were famous. Then, after having had the boys out half the night, he'd scold them the following evening for not giving him their best. He hated to lose and if Wanderers had a bad game he'd storm up and down the dressing room, waving the gold-headed cane he always carried. Some people wisecracked that he took it to bed with him.

That colourful gentleman, Sam Lichtenhein, quit hockey at the start of the 1917–18 season, the year the NHL replaced the NHA. You couldn't blame him. The Montreal Arena burned to the ground and his Wanderers were without a home. He had spent a barrel of money on the club and it never returned him a championship.

Author's note: The Wanderers won their first start in the NHL, 10–9 over Toronto in a game played at the Westmount Arena before it became rubble. Only 700 fans turned out.

I was on the sidelines by then. I was named captain in 1916 and we started out well, stacking up some wins. But one night in Toronto, Ken Randall caught me with a bodycheck along the boards. I crashed feet first into the fence and when they picked me up I had a badly splintered ankle.

The fracture healed slowly but by next winter I was out with the boys for the early practices, testing out the wobbly pin, I figured I was coming back as good as ever. Ho-hum. I was walking down the street one day, slipped on the icy sidewalk and went down heavily. The doctor didn't have to tell me my other leg was broken. Right then, I couldn't imagine it likely that I'd ever play competitive hockey again—not after this second smash.

For the second straight winter, I looked at hockey from the other side of the fence. It so happened that the Cleghorn family was completely out of the hockey picture that season of 1917–18. Odie had joined the Royal Air Force and while they stopped the war when they heard he was in it, he did not get suited up again for hockey until a year later.

Besides myself, plenty of people figured Sprague Cleghorn was through. The wise men of the game went around shaking their heads when they heard I was contemplating a comeback. My old boss was gone, my team was gone so I turned to George Kennedy, owner of the Montreal Canadiens. Kennedy was a playboy but in his sports promotions he was all business.

He told me that no man with two broken legs, however well they might have mended, could ever be worth real money to a hockey team. It sounded reasonable enough, but I was just dumb stubborn enough not to believe it. After several arguments, Kennedy finally made me an offer of $600 for the season—take it or leave it. It is impossible for me to say here exactly what I told Kennedy he could do with his $600.

"I can't afford to carry cripples, Sprague," he told me.

I'll admit I was mad. The salary he offered was the smallest I'd ever agreed to. So I hopped on a train to Ottawa and when I came back I had a contract from Tommy Gorman in my pocket to play for the Senators—and for a lot more money than Kennedy had offered. I was with Ottawa for three seasons and in two of those years the Senators were world champions. I had to break both my legs to get on a championship team for the first time in my long career.

With Ottawa—and I can see this now although it wasn't so apparent at the time—I began to take hockey seriously. Really seriously. My first year in New York had been an adventure. That winter in Renfrew had been a new and amusing experience. Big frog in little puddle stuff. And during my six seasons with Wanderers I had been more or less of a playboy, having a good time, sure my luck would last forever. That jolt on the chin Kennedy handed me changed my whole attitude toward the game. I began to see that hockey was a hard job of work, something to be studied and thought about, demanding sacrifices for the sake of perfect physical condition.

I kept notes on opposing players. Figured out plans to stop them where they were easily stopped. I improved my stickhandling and my puck carrying and I played to stay on the ice. In my three seasons as a Senator I was in a serious jam with a referee only once. That's pretty good for a "bad man."

Meanwhile, Odie signed with Canadiens and for the first time the Cleghorn brothers played on opposing teams. We banged each other around plenty. We'd go into the boards with sticks flying high and using profane language. The fans ate it up. They loved it. But I don't mind confessing it was an act. Isn't it a hockey player's duty to keep the fans amused?

Struggling to maintain public interest in the NHL, President Calder shuffled the deck and in mid-season ordered me to report to Toronto. I only agreed to the move when the Toronto club met my salary demands—$3,000 for the balance of the season. There was a further understanding that, should Ottawa win the league championship, I would be returned to the Senators for the Stanley Cup battles. The whole cockeyed scheme was just another of those desperate measures brought into play when the professional game was fighting for its life against powerful amateur opposition.

When Ottawa beat Toronto in the playoffs, I changed uniforms again and made my first trans-Canada trip with the Senators to the Pacific Coast, where we met Vancouver for the Stanley Cup.

We had to fight Vancouver to the last second before we won the Cup. The five-game series was tied at two-all. We snatched the final verdict by a single goal, netted by Punch Broadbent on a pass from my stick. Ottawa fought it out, four men against six. We did it, but it was too close to be comfortable.

That series was the most successful Stanley Cup series in the game's history up until then. More than 55,000 people saw the games. My share of the playoff cut was $700 and I was pleased with that.

Author's note: Frank Finnigan, an Ottawa star, told his daughter Joan about Cleghorn years later: "I played with and against Sprague and oh, he was tough. He was treacherous. I hit him once and he went down. But if he'd been in a room with me he'd probably have taken me. A big man— I saw him kick Buck Boucher once when Boucher was down on the ice. And there was a scandal when Ottawa went west to play for the Cup in Vancouver. It was said that Sprague had a woman go with him. He sent her ahead on another train. Some of the other players were taking their wives and the wives thought his actions were scandalous, breaking the moral code."

After my Stanley Cup season, once more the big shots who deal the cards were stacked against me. I was in the woods with a gun and some hunter friends when I read in a four-day-old paper that Ottawa had sold me to Hamilton.

And again, my reaction was: "Is that so?"

If I couldn't stay with Ottawa, I wanted to return to my hometown. The situation with Canadiens had changed dramatically. George Kennedy, who had never fully recovered from the effects of the 1919 flu epidemic that had swept through his club the previous year in Seattle, forcing cancellation of the Cup series, passed away. Subsequently, the Canadiens franchise was purchased at auction for the bargain price of

$11,000 by the Dandurand, Letourneau, Cattarinich combination. And those three gentlemen were just as anxious to have me on the Montreal roster as I was to be there. They traded two players to Hamilton and threw in a bundle of cash to acquire my services.

Playing with Canadiens remains one of the pleasantest of all my hockey experiences. Odie and I helped Canadiens win a Stanley Cup in 1924, but my reason for holding especially fond memories of the organization comes, not from achievements on the ice, but from my appreciation of the comradeship and understanding existing between the owners of the club and the players on the payroll.

Through four seasons there was never a whisper of an argument between us. I signed a blank contract at the beginning of each winter. The owners fixed my salary. I never asked for an increase but I always got one if it was coming to me on the record. My hat comes off to those people as the finest sportsmen it was ever my good luck to deal with.

In the 1923–24 season, Canadiens beat Ottawa for the NHL title. Calgary and Vancouver, Western League and Pacific Coast League champs, came East and we turned both of them back to win the Cup.

Author's note: After the final game, when Sprague and his mates were en route to owner Leo Dandurand's house to celebrate the victory, a flat tire delayed their arrival. The Stanley Cup was left on the curb as the tire was changed, and the men drove off without it. When told of the incident, Dandurand ordered Sprague and his pals to go back and retrieve the trophy. It was still on the curb. A new trophy was introduced that season— the Hart Trophy—awarded to the player judged most useful to his team. Ottawa's Frank Nighbor edged Sprague Cleghorn by a single vote.

I didn't see it yet, but I was getting to the end of my rope.

I had been a professional hockey player for fourteen seasons. For twelve of those years I had been a sixty-minute man. Mentally I had all the assurance I had always possessed. Physically, I was beginning to fade.

Your legs show it first and there's no use trying to fight it off because the man who stands behind the bench can see it, even though you swear by all the gods that you're still okay.

The human body can flame for just so long. Then come the ashes.

The manner of my transfer from the Canadiens organization to the Boston Bruins is typical of the methods of Leo Dandurand. He called me into his office in the summer of 1925 and said, "Sprague, I think Art Ross would like to have you in Boston. The Bruins are new to the NHL and he needs an oldtimer to steady that outfit. Make your own deal with him and we'll let you go."

What could be fairer? Ross was my old friend since school days. I made my deal with him for $5,500 and his owner, Mr. Adams, accepted the terms without a murmur.

I spent my final three seasons in the NHL with Boston where I enjoyed playing amidst enthusiastic young players, giving the best that was left in me on the ice, feeling happy and secure because of my old friendship with Art Ross. In the winter of 1926–27 Eddie Shore came to Boston from Edmonton and I claim some credit for making Shore the standout defenseman he became. He had a lot of stuff when he joined us but he still had plenty of things to learn and I taught him those things.

In the winter of 1927–28 an intestinal problem caught up with Art Ross and he could not possibly leave his bed. The active management of the team was turned over to me and under my personal leadership the Bruins won nine games, lost one and tied one. That's not boasting. It's in the record book.

We won the championship of the American Division of the NHL, knocked off Rangers and Chicago in the playoffs only to lose to Ottawa in the finals.

The next season I found myself in Newark as playing manager of a team in the Canadian-American League.

The Newark franchise was owned by a man named J.A. Allan. He owned a team which never played a game on its own ice because there was no ice. Allan's financial backers pulled out before the foundation for the new arena there was ever dug. Home games were played wherever ice was available, in places like Providence, New Haven and Springfield. The club faded out of the picture after one long winter.

After the Newark disaster, I picked up the struggling Providence team around Christmas of 1930. With Sprague Cleghorn handling them, the boys went from the bottom of the standings to the top, finishing the season with a record for points scored.

By 1932–33 I had the Maroons in the NHL. In the playoffs the team was beaten out by one goal and Sprague Cleghorn lost his job. In 1933–34 I coached Verdun in the Senior Group in the Quebec Hockey Association. Verdun made an excellent showing but Cleghorn has to work for a living and he cannot live on air.

So what? Is it all worth it? Parents of ambitious youngsters ask me constantly, "Would you recommend that my boy take on hockey as a career?"

I say, "By all means, if he has the touch. If there is that in a young player today which makes him want to play hockey more than he wants to do anything else in the world, let him go to it.

"Hockey is the finest game on earth. Your boy today has advantages that Sprague and Odie Cleghorn never imagined back in 1910. The game is organized, settled, controlled. And, always providing your boy does not lose his sense of proportion, no occupation in Canada equals professional hockey for a young man, for a few years at least, in financial rewards.

"If he has the hockey instinct and the deep desire, let him play."

Would I do the same thing again, supposing I had the chance?

You bet your life I would.

Postscript: Sprague Cleghorn, despised by many opponents but admired by most of his teammates and his many friends, died from injuries after he was struck by a car in Montreal in the summer of 1956. Two days after the funeral, his brother, Odie, passed away from a heart attack. Sprague was inducted into the Hockey Hall of Fame in 1958. Brother Odie was not quite Hall of Fame material.

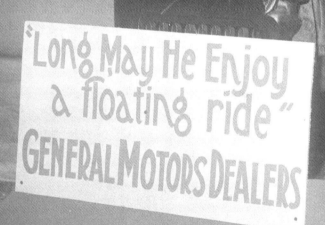

KING CLANCY
Was a Merry Monarch

"If you don't have fun, what's the sense of playing?" That was the motto of Francis Michael "King" Clancy, who for almost three quarters of a century reined as the merry monarch of hockey.

He wore his crown at a jaunty angle and often discarded it in order to play the role of Court Jester. He bounced into the hockey spotlight as a skinny 18-year-old substitute with the famed Ottawa Senators, when the NHL was in its infancy. He signed with the Senators in 1921 for $800, when he had 15 cents in his pocket. It started him off on a Hall of Fame career.

He bubbled and bounced and cackled and sang. The words tumbled out, spiced with a touch of the Ottawa Valley. Here and there a phrase was twisted in some inimitable Irish way that led to a grin or chuckle. His liveliest recollections produced belly laughs, and in a sentimental mood, he could move you to tears with devoted references to his parents, his wife and his family. There was a great joy in his impish Irish heart, a zest for life and love for hockey, "the grandest game that ever was played."

In 1930, Toronto general manager Conn Smythe parted with two players and $35,000 in cash in order to obtain Clancy from Ottawa. "And a bargain at the price," Smythe would later say. "Let's say I paid a fortune for a heart, the gamest heart, the kindest heart in pro hockey. I didn't go shopping for a strong back or sturdy legs. I bought heart, character, courage and devotion."

It was that indefinable something—call it heart if you will, or competitive spirit—that made Clancy so valuable to a hockey team. Obviously it wasn't size or strength, for he was not a big man. Smythe once called him "150 pounds of muscle and conversation." His forte was the fast break, streaking away from his own blueline as though propelled from a springboard, tossing the puck ahead of him, ready to throw a pass to a teammate with uncanny accuracy or fire a wicked shot at a corner of the opposing net.

With a whoop and a holler, Clancy could lift his teammates out of the doldrums. His spirit was infectious. He would fly at opposing players, even magnificent rushers like Eddie Shore, knowing full well he might be knocked senseless in the process. When gloves were dropped and fists flew, Clancy would battle and lose, get up and battle and lose again. Hockey legend credits him with a thousand lost fights, a statistic the Merry Monarch mildly disputes. "Oh, I must have won a fight somewhere along the way," he said. "If nobody recalls me winning one, at least they gotta give me credit for some draws."

Clancy had seen everything in hockey. He played on the frozen rivers and ponds. He watched the great players come back from World War I and join teams in the newly organized NHL in 1917. As a teenage rookie he played with the mighty Senators, and the team's trainer gave him three rock elm sticks. He was told the sticks would last him all season—and they did. His first shot on goal—in Hamilton—went through the side of the net and should not have counted. But it did, and it won the game for Ottawa. In overtime, no less.

He was a witness to the fantastic growth of the NHL. He was in a Maple Leaf uniform on opening night at Maple Leaf Gardens on November 12, 1931, and was on the same ice celebrating a Stanley Cup triumph a few months later. Clancy was a key figure in the rise of the Maple Leaf hockey fortunes. When he was through as an all star player, he tried a stint as coach of the once proud Montreal Maroons at a time when the Maroons were crumbling. He was invited to referee in the league, and he did it with a style that was all his own. If two centremen failed to square off properly on a faceoff, Clancy was known to throw the puck into the corner and bark, "Go chase it!"

While he found officiating to be a lonely profession, good humour and fun were his constant companions. One night at the Gardens, a doctor in the first row kept shouting insults at him. King shouted back: "At least I don't bury my mistakes like you do."

When I acted as master of ceremonies or guest speaker at sports banquets, it was a bonus whenever King Clancy was at the head table. Several times he showed up at the annual Hockey Heritage Dinner in Georgetown, Ontario.

One night—this would be in the early '80s—the honoured guest was my *Hockey Night in Canada* colleague Bob Goldham. Clancy was joined at the head table by hockey luminaries Ted Lindsay, Bill Gadsby, Alex Delvecchio, Leo Reise and Marcel Pronovost, all former Red Wing stars. All but Goldham are Hall of Famers. That Goldham has not been a Hall of Fame inductee is one of hockey's major oversights and mysteries.

In my opening remarks, I poked a little fun at Goldham (a few months later I would be asked to deliver the eulogy at his funeral) and had the audience laughing. Then I got around to Clancy.

Ladies and gentlemen, we're going to bring Hall of Famer King Clancy up to the microphone in a moment. But first I want to tell you some interesting facts about the man, facts you might not have heard before.

For example, King is not the only famous Clancy in the clan. One of King's ancestors, his great-great-great-grandfather, was renowned throughout Ireland as the inventor of the toilet seat. Then about a hundred years later, another Clancy ancestor improved on the idea—by cutting a hole in it.

King has always credited his father for getting him interested in sports at an early age. He says his dad taught him how to swim by taking him down to the Ottawa River and throwing him into 40 feet of water. King says getting back to the shore was the easy part. Getting out of that damn bag—that was the tough part.

Later on, his father taught him how to hunt. He'd take him out in the woods, dress him in a bunny outfit. Give him a three-minute head start.

His father was a generous man. King remembers the time his dad bought him some toys to play with in the bathtub—a toaster and a radio.

His father never taught King the facts of life, so King didn't know anything about sex growing up. Well, he did know one thing. He knew he was going to go blind at any minute.

When he was a teenager, King saw two dogs locked together one day and he asked his father about it. His father said the dogs were merely dancing. No wonder King got thrown out of the junior prom that year.

King won a million dollars in the lottery the other day and vowed he'd never work another day in his life. So he's staying on with the Toronto Maple Leafs.

My wife, Joan, is a big Clancy fan. The other day at breakfast she must have rubbed our old teapot in a peculiar way, because suddenly a genie appeared over the table and said, "Missy, thank you for releasing me from that old teapot. Now I'll grant you any wish you desire." My wife looked down at herself and said, "I think I'd like the two biggest boobs in the world." So we had breakfast with Ballard and Clancy this morning.

I suppose you've heard that Clancy's best pal, Mr. Ballard, has a new woman in his life—the lovely Yolanda. King tells me Yolanda is writing a new book. It's called *I Wish He'd Done to Me What He Did to the Leafs*.

There were a few more cornball barbs directed at King. Then I said, "Mr. Clancy, will you come to the microphone, please."

Clancy shuffled over to join me, and the first words out of his mouth were, "McFarlane, where'd you come up with all this bullshit?" Big laugh from the crowd. "And that's all it is—bullshit."

King grabbed the microphone. "Forget McFarlane, folks. Let me tell you about Bob Goldham. Bob was a great, great player and he was the only player on the Detroit club who never gave me any trouble. When I was a referee, that is. He was a class guy. And as far as I'm concerned, Brian, you shouldn't have made any jokes about him. They might have fit Ted Lindsay over there, or Bill Gadsby. But not Goldham."

"How about Alex Delvecchio?" I asked.

"What?" he cried, glaring at me in mock outrage. "Never Alex. Now there's another class guy. Never swore at a referee in his life." He paused to turn and glance at a grinning Delvecchio. "Geez, Alex, you had words I never heard of before—some real pips. I certainly can't repeat them here. And Brian, somebody here tonight gave me a knock—it might have been you—all because I'm wearing a bandage over my eye. I've had an operation, but I'll soon be 100 per cent. And I'll tell you somethin'. When I was a referee I had a real good eye . . ."

"Just one?" I asked innocently.

"No, no, two good eyes. Listen, how would you like to have the aggregation you've got up here tonight in your hockey lineup? There's Bob Goldham, Leo Reise, Marcel Pronovost, Alex Delvecchio, Bill Gadsby. Johnny Wilson, Harry Watson, Gaye Stewart, and Ivan Irwin. What a team you'd have!"

"You'd beat a lot of teams with that lineup," I suggested.

"You'd beat everybody," King said, then continued:

Now, there's a young man playing in the NHL today. His name is Gretzky, and I think he's the greatest player in the game. Too bad Gordie Howe isn't here. He'd love to hear me say that. Well, I got a few choice words for him too. Maybe some of these fellows here tonight could take care of that young kid Gretzky. You know, Ted Lindsay, for example, he could do it. Ted was one of the greatest players who ever laced on a skate. I mean that, Ted, because you gave me lots of trouble when I refereed, and I gave you lots. When I refereed, all these fellows played—and they were real gentlemen.

I remember Ted Lindsay saying to me one night, "Clancy, you're the blindest son of a bitch I ever saw." And I said, "Ted, you're not seein' the net too well yourself tonight."

Lemme tell you somethin' about Lindsay, Abel and Howe. The Production Line. They were playin' against Chicago one night, and I was in the middle. I don't know why I was there, because Jack Adams, the Detroit manager, had told me once, "Clancy, you'll never referee in the Olympia again." And I said to him, "Thanks very much, Jack. That's good news, because I hate this goddamn place."

On this night, the Wings are leading 1–0. I let everything go until I caught Lindsay giving somebody an elbow in the kisser. I said, "Goodnight, Ted, you're gone," and I waved him to the penalty box. Then, not 10 seconds later, big Howe gave somebody a big wipe, almost knocking this poor fellow's ear off. I said, "Gordie, you're gone too."

Now I went to face the puck off, and Abel is there at centre ice. He growls at me, "Clancy, you don't have the guts to throw three guys off from the same line at the same time." And I said, "Just give me a reason to, Sid." Well, he put his stick down, but he wiggled it around and he wouldn't square away for the faceoff. So I yelled, "Abel, delay of game. You're gone too." You should have heard him cuss me as he went to the box. And all the time I'm sayin' to myself, I hope Chicago scores. That'll really tick the Wings off. And the Hawks did score to tie the game.

Then the Detroit manager, Jack Adams—he was such a nice man, a quiet person who wouldn't say boo—was screaming at me, "You know, Clancy, you just gave Chicago one friggin' point." And I said all inno-cently, "Did I, Jack? That's too damn bad. Here you are leadin' the league by eight points and you're afraid to give somebody one little point. You'll never miss it."

Jack was livid. He said, "We will too." Then he told me, "Listen, Clancy, the next time Toronto comes in here, for chrissake, I hope you're not with them. As a referee, you're a disgrace."

Clancy grinned at his audience. They loved his hockey yarns.

Then he moved along. "But I wanna say somethin' about the fellows we have here tonight, especially the defensemen. Bob Goldham, Marcel Pronovost, Leo Reise, Bill Gadsby—where in the world would you find four top defensemen like that today?"

"Not on the Leafs," I interjected.

"There you go, giving me another shot," said King.

"I'm sorry, King, I couldn't resist."

"That's all right, Brian. Now, about Ted Lindsay. To me, Lindsay was one of the league's greatest. He played like I wish I could have played. He had a neat little trick. Every once in a while, when things got dull, he'd give you a little shot in the jewel box. I don't know if you folks know where the jewel box is . . . but Lindsay did. And Bob Goldham knew, because he would give you a shot there too.

"But listen, I'm here tonight with my friend Walter Bianchi, and Walter's pals from the Mafia. Yes, there are two big guys from the Mafia with us tonight, and Brian, you're going to have a hell of a time getting out of here tonight after some of the things you've said. So be careful when you get out in the parking lot."

I thought King might mention the time his friend Walter won the sweep six—and $250,000—at Greenwood one afternoon a few months earlier. But he didn't. King concluded with some kind words about the dinner committee and the town of Georgetown. Then he sat down to wild applause. It was the last time we shared a microphone.

Driving back to Toronto that night, I thought of the day many years earlier, in the spring of 1965, when I approached Clancy about writing his biography. Back then, he served the Leafs as assistant to general manager and coach George "Punch" Imlach. We met in his office at Maple Leaf Gardens. I said, "King, I'd like your permission to write a book about your life in hockey."

He laughed. "Really? And why would you want to do that? What makes you think anyone would be interested in reading about me and my career?"

"I think a lot of people would be interested," I countered. "My concern is that you've got lots of friends in the media, famous writers like Scott Young and Milt Dunnell. I've never written much of anything. So if you'd prefer to have one of them write a Clancy book, I'll totally understand."

Clancy shrugged. "Nobody else has ever asked me about writing a book. If you want to do it, then go ahead. You have my permission."

I was about to suggest a royalty split of 50/50 on the proposed book, but before I could speak, he made a comment that surprised me.

"Brian," he said, "I'll sit down with you and talk into your tape recorder, and I won't take any money for it. You'll not get rich writing a Clancy book, but I don't want any profits. You keep them."

Wow! Did I luck out.

I used an old Wollensak reel-to-reel tape recorder back then. I tried to set up weekly appointments with King, but often he was unavailable. He was a very popular guy, always in demand for speaking engagements or attending to hockey duties scheduled by Imlach.

There were Leaf games and practices for him to attend, and road trips and junkets to Rochester to scout minor league players.

But over the next three years I was able to pin him down enough times to get his life story on tape. We would meet in a tiny room next to the *Hockey Night in Canada* studios at the Gardens, and wonderful tales of hockey as it was played in the '20s and '30s would spill from his lips.

When I listened to these tapes, every few seconds I'd hear an annoying sound. *Clickety, click, click, click.* It finally dawned on me. Cufflinks! King's cufflinks clicking against the table edge when he spoke.

The book was published in 1968 by McGraw-Hill, one of several publishers I would help put out of business over the years, and while it garnered excellent reviews, sales were only moderately successful—perhaps because the print run was a mere 2,500 copies. But the price was right—$5.95. Last week I paid almost that much for a birthday card.

It remains one of my favourite books.

King was right. I wouldn't get rich writing a book about Clancy. But I was richer for the experience. And I was excited about the contents. He talked about being a rookie substitute on the Ottawa Senators and how, on frigid nights, he and Frank Boucher and Morley Bruce would sit in the Ottawa dressing room, huddled around the wood stove, waiting for a call to get into the game. If an Ottawa player was injured or exhausted, the coach would buzz the dressing room. One buzz was for Clancy, a second buzz was for Boucher and the third buzz for Bruce. Sometimes, for comfort, they'd even untie their skate laces in the dressing room.

Can you imagine? An empty Ottawa bench. A player goes down. The coach buzzes the dressing room for a sub. Three players are huddled around the pot-bellied stove, playing cards. There's some confusion. The wrong player appears. He goes back and Clancy stumbles out. The referee, the fans, the opposing players fume over the delay. They are frostbitten.

The debacle is mentioned in the referee's report to NHL headquarters. President Frank Calder sends an edict to the Senators. From now on, your team's substitute players must remain on the bench, no matter how frigid it may get in the arena.

We talked about the deal that brought him to Toronto. How Conn Smythe won a bundle at the race track, betting a huge amount on a filly named Rare Jewel, who went off at 100 to 1 odds. The horse won, and Smythe used most of his winnings and other cash to purchase Clancy. When he moved to Toronto, Clancy stayed at the Royal York Hotel—for one dollar per night.

In one of our sessions, I talked to Clancy about the time they honoured him with a "night" at Maple Leaf Gardens. He remembered every detail:

Whenever I think back to March 17, 1934, and how the Maple Leafs honoured me with a "night," I'm still amazed at the work they went to just for me. I wasn't a native son, you see. You might even say I was a stranger from another city—Ottawa. Yet they gave me the greatest tribute an individual could ever hope to get. I'm sure I didn't do anything to deserve it. Someone must have said, "Here's an Irishman. Let's give him a 'night.'"

Well, they dressed me up in green from head to toe and they even slapped a big white shamrock on the back of my sweater. There must have been about 11,000 fans jammed into the Gardens to see the pregame festivities and a pretty nasty contest that followed against the New York Rangers, which we won 3–2.

They even brought Conn Smythe [the team owner] to a microphone. He kept trying to introduce me, but he kept getting interrupted by a batch of telegrams announcing my impending arrival. Although the Rangers were very unfriendly once the game started, they were good sports beforehand and joined in the fun. I remember Ranger star Ching Johnson hauling onto the ice a huge float in the shape of a potato, and the crowd was sure I'd step out of it. But they were fooled when some members of the St. Michael's Junior B team popped out instead.

Oh, I was supposed to come out of a lot of floats, but each one revealed a teammate of mine. Ken Doraty came out of a large pipe, and Harold Cotton was hidden inside a gigantic top hat. It's hard to recall everything. But I do recall that trainer Tim Daly appeared from inside a giantsize bottle of ginger ale, and our goalie, George Hainsworth, was hidden inside a big boot. Red Horner appeared from inside a boxing glove, which I guess was a pretty good reference to his fistic ability, and Joe Primeau, always a gentleman, came out of a harp. When a big shamrock showed up, the fans were positive I'd be inside it, but Bill Cook of the Rangers jumped out instead.

When my turn finally came, the lights were all turned out and, dressed in royal robes and wearing a crown, I was ushered in on a big throne pulled by team captain Hap Day. As the float reached the middle of the rink, I got hit in the face with a handful of soot, tossed by Day and Conacher, and when the lights came on I looked like Santa Claus but my face was pitch black! It took me two or three days to get that soot off my kisser.

This was a fantastic "night" to give anybody, and I have wonderful memories of it. There is also a grandfather clock at home that's keeping real good time, which is worth more than any amount of money because of the inscription on it: "From the Toronto Maple Leafs to King Clancy on St. Patrick's Night 1934." And the Knights of Columbus, to which I belong, gave me a wonderful silver service. There was a big bouquet of flowers for my wife, and my father was presented with a case of pipes by the Toronto City Council.

Now what more could a man ask for than to be taken to a city's heart like I was? I think I was the first Maple Leaf player to be given a "night," and the prime movers of this were Mr. Smythe and Mr. Selke. I always look back upon it as one of the greatest things that ever happened to me in sport. You know, when you get into sport like I've been all my life, people think it's just a business. Well, it is a business, but there's more to it than that. If I had it to do all over again and they weren't paying any money at all, I would play for nothing. I loved the game so much and I met so many fine individuals over the years. Sure, I had lots of foes in hockey. I'd knock them down and they'd knock me down, but afterwards they turned out to be my friends and I could call on any of them for help. When you look back over the years, it's the friends that count. After all, how many friends you've made and how well you get along with people is what life is all about.

I remember wearing my green uniform for the first period of that game. It had a big shamrock on it. The late Lester Patrick was coaching the Rangers at that time, and as I was going into the dressing room, he said, "King, you'd better take that uniform off because you're mixing everybody up."

"Mixing everybody up?" I said. "I'm not doing anything out there."

"Well," he added, "that's the reason I want you to take it off. I want you to make a game of it."

Author's note: Can you imagine honouring a hockey superstar in similar fashion today? Imagine asking him to put a crown on his head, to throw on a green jersey and to wear a fake beard. And have someone throw chimney soot in his face before giving him a grandfather's clock. "What the hell is soot?" he'd ask. He'd glance at the clock and ask. "What's that old thing? A clock? You kidding me? I expected a new Mercedes." And today, if he was given one, he'd complain, "Where am I going to park this thing? I already own a Rolls and an SUV. And a stock portfolio that's taller than Chara." He'd make a thank you speech, then tell his rich agent, "You say they want to retire my number? How much will they pay me for that? Why not just get me out of here. I want to play with a Stanley Cup contender. Ask for 20 mill a season."

▮▮▮

*Emile Francis recalls Clancy's
coaching days in Cincinnati*

I played in goal for King when he was coach in Cincinnati. We didn't have a very good team, and my goals-against record wasn't very good either.

I recall King taking me around and introducing me to the goal judge one night before the game. "Gentlemen," he said, "this is Mr. Francis, my goaltender. Take a good look at him, because when he's in the net at your end of the rink, I want you to keep both hands in your pockets. If you think a puck is in the net, there's a good chance it will be gone by the time you get your hands out of your pockets to turn on the light. On the other hand, when you see the opposing team's goalie in front of you, turn on that light if you so much as see the shadow of the puck anywhere near the goal. We can have a grand old argument about it afterwards."

There was another time when we were playing in Springfield against the team coached by King's old rival, Eddie Shore. At the practice the day before the game, King went around to see Shore about turning on some lights in the arena.

"Eddie, throw a few lights on the ice, will you?" said King. "I want to have my boys take some shots at Francis."

Shore, a noted cheapskate, laughed at King, and, pointing to one end of the rink, replied, "Listen, tell your goalie to stand down at that end of the arena. See those glass windows? In about five minutes the sun will be around there, so you'll have plenty of light to practice by."

I guess King mentioned his rebuff to the newspapermen. And he amused everybody the next day when he walked across the ice before the game waving an old railroad lantern he'd found somewhere. He presented it to Shore, in an effort to embarrass him.

■ ■ ■

Even the youngest reader will get a chuckle out of the following Clancy caper. It's a true story, a story of friendship and how two Leaf players conspired to give an old pal—Eddie Convey—a goal. A gift goal!

Here's the way King Clancy told it to me:

He was a great fellow—Eddie Convey. And a real high-class hockey player. He used to lead the American League in scoring almost every year, but he just couldn't score in the NHL. One day he got called up to play with the New York Americans. Geez, we were happy for him. Conacher came to me and he said, "King, our pal Eddie Convey is playing against us tonight at Maple Leaf Gardens. We better let him score a goal. It may keep him in the league." I said, "Charlie, are you crazy? You mean just give him a goal? If we do that, the old man [Leaf owner] Conn Smythe will crucify us."

Charlie said, "We'll fake it so Smythe will never know. If we get two or three goals ahead tonight, what difference does one goal against make? Here's what we'll do. If Convey is coming down the wing, and you are playing opposite him, just let him get by you. Lunge at him but let him slide by. And I'll do the same if he comes down my side."

And I said, "All right, Charlie, I'll do it."

When we shoot into a big lead that night and are winning by 7–2, Conacher skates up to me and says, "It's time to let Eddie score his goal." I nod and say, "Let's do it." So Conacher slides up to Eddie and says, "Eddie, go to the outside of Clancy." On the next rush he goes to the outside of me, I lunge at him and miss, he sails in on goal and takes a hard shot. Our goalie—Lorne Chabot—had been tipped off, and he slides over, giving Convey half the net to shoot at. But Eddie's shot sailed high up into the screen. Conacher comes up to me and shakes his head. He says, "Well, he screwed that up. But I think we should give him one more chance."

I said, "Why not?"

On his next shift, Eddie comes down and we yell at him, "Go through the middle, Eddie! Go through the middle!" He smiles and cuts right through the middle, and skates in on goal. Once again, Chabot slides over, giving Eddie a big opening. He winds up and fires a wicked shot— and hits Lorne Chabot right in the throat! Chabot falls like a rock and he's down on the ice gasping and groaning and clutching his Adam's apple. Conacher moves in to take a look and then he turns to me. "That's it!" he says, "To hell with Convey. No more gift goals for him. Next time he comes your way, King—cut his friggin' legs off!"

Well, that was the end of it. And don't think we didn't catch hell from the old man for that little caper. We didn't fool Smythe for a minute.

Clancy holds one unique hockey record that can never be broken.

He's the only player in NHL history to play every position for his team in a game—and it was a Stanley Cup game. When Clancy's Ottawa Senators met Edmonton for the Cup in a 1923 series, the Ottawa lineup was riddled with injuries. Imagine attempting to win the Cup with only nine players. After playing both defense positions and all three forward positions, Clancy took over in goal when Clint Benedict, the Ottawa goaltender, was penalized.

In that era, goaltenders went to the box to serve their penalties. Benedict handed Clancy his goal stick and told him, "Take care of this place until I get back." Clancy did and was not scored upon.

●

Clancy retired from the Leafs early in the 1936–37 season. On the following day, a hockey scribe wrote: "With the retirement of Clancy, hockey loses one of its most colourful figures and a player who, over a decade, was one of the NHL's most brilliant performers. A lightweight as defensemen go—for King never weighed more than 160 pounds—the King was one of the best defensemen the game has ever known. He ranks near the top in all-time rating of the rearguards of the game. None ever carried a stouter spirit into battle than the lion-hearted Clancy."

Smythe said, "He is the best man we ever had and he finishes his playing career without a blemish."

Big-league hockey without Clancy was akin to big-league baseball without Babe Ruth.

Then came the coaching and the refereeing, and later an association with Punch Imlach that clicked, resulting in four Stanley Cups for the Leafs. Later still, an even closer relationship with Harold Ballard (some say King replaced Ballard's wife in his life after she died) that lasted until Clancy's demise.

On Wednesday, November 5, 1986, King Clancy took ill while watching the game between the St. Louis Blues and the Leafs. The following day, complaining of a severe stomach ache, he was rushed to Wellesley Hospital, a few blocks away from the Gardens.

On Saturday, surgeons removed his gallbladder, but the operation was complicated by his diabetic condition and he went into septic shock. He suffered two heart attacks and died of cardiac arrest on Monday afternoon, November 10, at 2:50 p.m.

King's son Terry, a former Leaf, said his father had been alert though unspeaking in his final hours. "Hey, Dad, it's me, Terry," I said to him. "He had these tubes in his mouth but his eyes lit up and he squeezed my arm. There are four of us—my sisters, Carole and Judith, and my brother, Tom. They say I'm the one who looks most like him." Grieving Leafs owner Harold Ballard arranged for Clancy's open coffin to rest in the directors' lounge at Maple Leaf Gardens on Thursday morning.

On a bitterly cold day, hundreds of friends and fans made their way through the front entrance and along a red carpet to the lounge. Most stopped momentarily to bow their heads, to wipe away a tear, to whisper a brief prayer.

Terry Clancy turned to writer Trent Frayne and said in a whisper, "I never met a finer man in my life. He was a family man. He never hurt a soul. From the lowest to the highest, nobody."

Frayne murmured, "Now there's an epitaph."

I was there that day: first to pay my respects, because I'd loved King— yes, loved him—and then to cover the event for *Hockey Night in Canada*. It was for a weekly Saturday night feature called "Inside Hockey." Our camera was rolling as Clancy's casket was wheeled to the front of the Gardens and lifted into the back of a gleaming hearse.

Ihor, our cameraman, zoomed in on a forlorn Harold Ballard standing next to the hearse, his body protected by a huge fur coat, his expression one of pain and sadness. Ihor held the shot, longer than he normally would have, his camera whirring, and it paid off. He caught the bereaved owner precisely at the moment he issued a final salute to his late pal.

Those few seconds of tape were the most memorable of the four-minute feature which aired on *Hockey Night in Canada*. But almost as remarkable, and captured beautifully on tape within St. Michael's Cathedral, was the tribute voiced by Monsignor Kenneth Robitaille.

In a deep baritone voice filled with emotion, the monsignor said, "Life is good, life is worth living. Life is a gift from God to be used to the utmost. That's the way King Clancy lived."

The monsignor said in his homily that Clancy met each challenge head on. "He fought the good fight, stickhandling on and off the ice. In the game of life, he knew what it was to accept a few bodychecks and unexpected elbows. But Clancy was a success as a person. He was fully alive. This King, this all star, is very precious in our eyes, an inspiration and an encouragement. Persons like King Clancy are not very common, so when we find them, let us not neglect to honour them. This was a man."

Everyone in hockey was there. They came by the hundreds—1,200 inside the church and almost as many, shivering in their heavy coats and gloves, huddling outside. Before and after the service, we sought out former stars like Jean Beliveau, Sid Smith, Lanny McDonald, and former referee Scotty Morrison, for comments about the King.

Clancy's body was taken to Mount Hope Cemetery for burial. En route, the 80-car cavalcade circled the Gardens and then paused for a few seconds on Carlton Street. Outside the main doors, dozens of staff members gathered to wave at the hearse and say "so long."

At the cemetery, Harold Ballard could no longer hold back his grief. As he laid a wreath on the coffin, he pounded his fist on the cover and mumbled an emotional farewell.

Don Cherry called me the following day. He talked about the televised eulogy. "That was one of the most moving tributes I've ever seen," he said. "I was crying like a baby."

Hockey's finest wordsmiths wrote of King's passing with genuine sorrow and deep regret, for he had been a friend to them all, helping to fill their columns on countless occasions with his treasure trove of humorous anecdotes.

Jim Proudfoot wrote in the *Toronto Star*: "Francis Michael (King)

Clancy was the funniest, sunniest individual I ever encountered. His death yesterday was a sad event, to be sure, but anybody remembering him now would have to smile at the thought of him. Your spirits lifted when you saw him coming, charging eagerly forth on the delightful adventure he found life to be."

Milt Dunnell wrote:

The very name—Francis Michael Clancy—painted the picture. There had to be a chunk of Ireland in his saucy face. There had to be a hint of the Ould Sod in his tongue.

Clancy's treasure was happiness and humility and joy in the fellowship of others, whether he met them in marble halls or in the walking ring at Greenwood, where he hoped to pick up a tip on the one horse in the race which he still hadn't bet.

Parents who heard Clancy spinning his yarns of fun and fame in a game which had made him an international celebrity—and then got to meet him—were reassured. If professional sport produced people such as King Clancy, it was good enough for their sons and daughters.

Francis Michael Clancy, wherever you've gone, there will be hilarious stories to tell and longnosed horses to bet. But it is going to be pretty dull around here without you.

DICK IRVIN
Great Player, Great Coach

In 1913, Dick Irvin, an amateur player with the Winnipeg Monarchs, scored nine goals in a senior hockey game. The Monarchs won the game over a strong Toronto team, 9–1. His remarkable scoring outburst earned him a place in Ripley's popular "Believe It or Not" syndicated newspaper column. A year later, his inspired play for the Monarchs brought Winnipeg the Canadian senior championship and the Allan Cup, and prompted one reporter to call him "the craftiest playmaker of the day."

Irvin turned pro with Portland for the 1916–17 season. The following year, he enlisted in the Canadian army. In France, he ran into Al Ritchie, a Regina sportsman. Ritchie convinced him to join the amateur Regina Vics. Dick played centre with the Vics, a fine skater and stickhandler, a dedicated player who neither drank nor smoked.

Dick was promised a job in a meat-packing plant, as a salesman. When Ritchie brought him to the plant, the manager told Irvin he'd changed his mind. The job, he decided, should go to an experienced salesman, not a hockey player. Irvin stood up and said, "That's fine. Forget the job. I'll find a job with your competitor, and I'll sell more meat than any of the salesmen you have on staff." The manager was so impressed with Irvin's confidence that he hired him on the spot, and Irvin was true to his word. He became an outstanding salesman.

In 1921, he joined another Regina team: the Capitals, of the Western Canada Hockey League. In 1925, the Capitals were sold to Portland, and Irvin played there a year before the Western League broke up and the players were absorbed by the National Hockey League.

Curious about Irvin's stats in senior hockey, I was astonished to discover the following. His scoring feats in his first three seasons were phenomenal: he scored 53 goals in a mere 14 games. So his nine-goal game was hardly an aberration. In his career in senior company—and senior hockey was top-quality hockey in his era—Irvin scored 127 goals in 38 games. That's an average of more than three goals per game. If any senior player in history has been so prolific, I'd like to hear about him.

●

In 1925–26, Irvin's Portland Rosebuds (the most unusual nickname for a team until the Mighty Ducks) were sold intact to Chicago interests and became the Black Hawks (now Blackhawks) of the NHL. Irvin played brilliantly for Chicago and, at age 34, as a rookie and team captain, he finished second in the NHL scoring race in 1926–27, a single point behind Bill Cook of the Rangers and four points ahead of Howie Morenz.

Early in his second season as a Black Hawk, Irvin was slammed to the ice by husky Red Dutton of the Montreal Maroons. He suffered a fractured skull and was told that his playing days were all but over. He tried to come back the following season, played a few games and then retired.

When Chicago won a mere seven games in each of the next two seasons, Irvin was called on to coach the team of underachievers. How woeful were they? In 1928–29, the Hawks' leading scorer was Vic Ripley, who tallied a pitiful 13 points. Collectively, Hawk scorers managed 33 goals—for the season!

Irvin was a natural behind the bench. The Hawks improved remarkably and won 21 games in 1929–30. One of Irvin's innovations was to throw three fresh forward lines at the opposition in short shifts. That season, the Hawks won playoff series against Toronto and Rangers before bowing to Montreal in the Stanley Cup finals.

When the Hawks inexplicably dropped Irvin following his impressive coaching debut, Toronto's Conn Smythe snapped him up after the Leafs stumbled through the opening games of the 1931–32 season. Initially, Smythe had some misgivings about Irvin's coaching techniques. Smythe believed his team's forwards should check opposing forwards from the outside, meaning they should get between their opponents and the boards on the backcheck, forcing their opponents into the path of waiting Leaf defensemen. Irvin thought the idea was nonsense. "My players will check from the inside," he told Smythe. "They'll force opposing forwards into the boards. Common sense and experience tells me they'll do less damage there."

"Will you take the Leaf coaching job if I tell you it has to be done my way—checking from the outside?" Smythe asked.

"No, I won't," Irvin responded. "All the coaching decisions will be mine."

"You are a stubborn so-and-so," said Smythe. "Not unlike me. But I'm going to hire you anyway."

Irvin led the Leafs to a Stanley Cup triumph that season—a fitting way to celebrate the team's inaugural season in a new home: Maple Leaf Gardens.

After nine seasons with the Leafs, Irvin resigned, possibly because Smythe could not resist interfering with coaching decisions. Irvin moved on to Montreal, where the Canadiens' fortunes had hit a new low. Seats at the Montreal Forum were half-filled for Habs games, and bankruptcy appeared to be on the horizon. "It can't be any worse than when I started as a player in Chicago," said Irvin. "We'll turn things around." The player who would be most instrumental in the turnabout was a kid named Maurice Richard. It wasn't long before Irvin moulded a winning combination, guiding the Habs to Cup wins in 1944, 1946 and 1953. His 1943–44 team lost only five games out of 50 and established a team-record winning percentage of .830, going 13 games into the season before tasting defeat and later winning 13 consecutive games at home. On November 21, 1943, the Habs rocked Boston 13–4, tallying 35 scoring points in the game. On February 6, 1943, Elmer Lach recorded six assists in a game (8–3 over Boston), and on December 28, 1944, Rocket Richard collected eight points in a game (9–1 over Detroit). All of the preceding became long-standing team records, although the Rocket's eight-point mark was later tied (in 1954) by Bert Olmstead and broken (in 1976) when Darryl Sittler, captain of the Leafs, scored 10.

Incredibly, Irvin's Habs completed the 1943–44 season without losing any of their 25 home encounters, and the following season they lost just two on Forum ice.

In 1946, Irvin's Canadiens defeated Boston in the Stanley Cup finals, four games to one. Elmer Lach led all playoff scorers with 17 points in nine games.

Until April 4, 1950, no coach in Stanley Cup history had voluntarily changed goalies in the Stanley Cup playoffs. Only injury or illness had forced a coach to send a backup goalie into action.

But on that spring day, Irvin, with his team trailing the Rangers three games to none, had a choice between Bill Durnan, his number one stopper, and backup Gerry McNeil. Irvin called both goalies into his office. Durnan told the coach he was suffering from fatigue and a chronic nervous condition. What's more, he had a bruised hand. With tears in his eyes, he suggested that McNeil might be the better bet that night. When McNeil saw the tears roll down Durnan's cheeks, he began crying too, for Durnan had always been his idol.

Irvin made history by deciding to go with McNeil, who played a sensational game. The Habs won 3–2 but were eliminated by New York two days later. Durnan retired that summer.

In the 1953 finals, Irvin called on goalie Jacques Plante to replace Gerry McNeil in the Montreal net. Plante responded with a glittering 1.75 goals-against average in four games as the Habs once again ousted the Bruins, four games to one.

Irvin finished his amazing coaching career back in Chicago in 1955–56, taking over a club that had finished in the NHL basement for seven of the previous nine years. Before he could begin one of his patented rebuilding jobs, he was forced to deal with a personal challenge—a lengthy battle with cancer, one he was unable to win. He died in Montreal in May 1957, one year before he was inducted into the Hockey Hall of Fame.

Irvin missed the playoffs only twice in 27 seasons and passed along his gift for language, his love of the game and his fascination for hockey statistics to his son, Dick Jr., the *Hockey Night in Canada* broadcaster.

During his final coaching season, Irvin told a *Sports Illustrated* reporter he knew exactly how many NHL goals he'd seen—8,705. "My players have scored 4,721 goals and been scored on 3,984 times." He followed up by telling the astonished scribe that his hockey travels had carried him over a million miles—most of them by train. At the time he reigned as hockey's winningest coach. Today, with 690 wins, he ranks third in coaching wins behind Scotty Bowman (1,244) and Al Arbour (781).

One of the highlights of Irvin's annual training camp in Montreal was the scrimmage he supervised on the final day. He would order an inter-squad game, pitting the rookies against the veterans. He'd visit the veterans' dressing room and bark at them, "Fellows, there's an eager bunch of youngsters in the next room dying to take your jobs away. Are you going to let them push you aside?" Then he'd lecture the rookies, "Listen, I've only got room on my club for two or three of you, and today's the day I decide who sticks. A lot depends on who can go out there and knock the Rocket or big Bouchard flat on his arse."

Those sessions were often more entertaining than the regular season matchups. When Montrealers heard what sounded like cannon shots echoing off Mount Royal, they'd nod wisely and tell bystanders, worried perhaps that another war had broken out, "No, it's just Dick Irvin's last-day-of-training-camp game."

Asked about such do-or-die confrontations, Irvin would simply smile and say, "It may sound mean, it may sound brutal, but it seemed to work. Some kids earned their ticket to the NHL by busting their arse in that final day of camp."

●

I enjoyed a lengthy talk about Irvin with former NHL player and coach Johnny Wilson, who was guesting at a hockey memorabilia show in Toronto. Johnny was a hard-working winger who played with Detroit, Toronto, New York and Chicago.

He says, "I hear you gave Dick Irvin Jr. his first job in TV. Is that true?"

I say, "Yes, we were at CFCF-TV in Montreal, a newly licensed station. I was a one-man sports department and I needed an assistant. Dick gave up a better-paying job to come on board. He's had a great career in broadcasting. Over 30 years with *Hockey Night in Canada*."

"Well, I played for his father, Dick Sr., who left the Montreal Canadiens in the '50s to take over as coach in Chicago. He was a fascinating guy.

That's where I played for him—in Chicago. We had our training camp in Welland, Ontario, one year, and Dick had been looking over our team statistics. He wasn't impressed. We had probably the lowest-scoring team in the NHL and the highest goals-against record. So after we lost a couple of games without scoring any goals, he ordered us into the dressing room. And he had a goal net brought in. In a small space with 20 guys gathered around, that net looked enormous. Looked like a soccer net.

"Now he holds up a puck and says, 'You mean to say you fellows can't put a little puck like this into a great big net like that? What's your problem?'

"I guess we all looked a little sheepish."

I interrupt Johnny to relate a story Frank Selke Sr. told me about Dick Irvin the elder. "He was a great scorer when he was a young player," Selke told me. "When he coached the Canadiens in the '40s, there was a spigot—a water tap—on the wall in the Canadiens dressing room. Even though he'd reached middle age, Irvin could shoot a puck across the room and turn on the spigot—years after he retired as a player."

Johnny looks sceptical. "Yeah, well, I'll bet the Rocket could have turned it on too."

"Or knock it right off the wall," I suggest.

(Al Ritchie used to tell a story about how Irvin first developed his shooting prowess. When Ritchie visited the family home in Winnipeg one day, Dick's mother took him up to the attic and showed him where Dick practiced shooting on rainy days. He'd rigged up an old door— sideways—and placed it against one wall. He used to shoot at the door knob. She showed him the pock-marked [puck-marked?] wall. His mother said Dick used to flood the driveway in the wintertime and spent hours skating up and down, stopping and starting and stickhandling in the narrow area. In the summer months, he shot off a board imbedded in the ground and rattled pucks off the garage door.)

"Here's another Dick Irvin story," Johnny says. "One time he sits us down in a room and he says, 'I'm going to give you boys a test. Let's find out how much you really know about hockey.'

"He handed us some pencils and some paper and he placed us about three feet apart so nobody could cheat by looking over somebody's shoulder.

"Then he says, 'How big is the puck?'

"Most of us didn't know what the hell to write down.

"He says, 'What's the maximum length of a hockey stick?'

"Nobody does much writing, so he carries on.

"He says, 'How wide is the net?'

"So he asks a few more questions, and he collects the papers and stares at the results.

"Then he shakes his head and starts to laugh. He says, 'You guys shouldn't be playing hockey. You should be back in school. You don't know anything about the game.'"

I have a couple of Dick Irvin stories for Johnny. Perhaps Dick Jr. told them to me years ago. "One day Dick was coaching the Canadiens and he placed a board in the middle of the net. He wanted his players to shoot for holes in the upper and lower corners of the board. After the practice, Murph Chamberlain's wife, who'd been watching the workout, approached him. 'Mr. Irvin, wasn't Murph wonderful today. He hit that board every time.'"

Johnny chuckles. "What's the other story?"

"Irvin's team won a game at the Forum one night, but he wasn't happy about all the mistakes his players made. In the room, he blistered the Habs for their shoddy performance. Just then Tommy Gorman, the team's manager, bounced into the room and went from man to man. 'Great game tonight, Rocket. Sensational goaltending, Jacques.' Around the room he scurried, pounding backs, praising each and every Hab.

"Irvin never finished his speech. He was too busy laughing—along with all of his players."

"You won't find many modern-day coaches dressing down their players," Johnny says. "Scotty Bowman, maybe, when he coached. And Mike Keenan when he was in the league. Dick Irvin was one of the best at making sure his players didn't ever get swollen heads."

●

Irvin's pre-game speeches seldom reached the ear of the public, but one he delivered on November 5, 1941, was relayed to a reporter at the Montreal *Gazette*.

The Canadiens had not been going well, and they were about to step on the ice at the Boston Garden against the powerful Bruins—no mean assignment. So Irvin reckoned it was an opportune time for strong measures. When his men were nearly ready for action, the silver-haired Dick took the floor, stuck his thumbs in the armholes of his vest and called for silence. He told Canadiens what he thought was wrong with them both collectively and individually.

"I have never seen a team quite like this one, a team so expert at doing things backwards, exactly the opposite of the way things should be done. As a result, I am seriously thinking of switching the right wingers to left wing and vice versa. I may move the centremen back to defense and let the defensemen lug the puck carelessly up the ice. Since that's the way everybody seems to want to play, maybe we'll do better that way."

Then he got personal, starting with his goaltender—Bert Gardiner:

I must confess, Mr. Gardiner confuses me. Most goalies like to stay in their nets. Bert doesn't. He thinks he should come out of them all the time. But perhaps you can't blame him. He's seen the rest of you miss the opposing net so often he doesn't think a goalkeeper is necessary anymore. So he just comes out to see if the other guys will miss his net as often as you birds miss theirs. But of course they don't. And he watches as all the pucks pile up in our net.

I see Charlie Sands over there. He has a great shot. But he has a new theory on how to score goals. Most of you know that when a goal is scored the red light goes on. Charlie must have a notion that the bulb may be loose and a good jolt from a puck will turn the red light on. That's the only way I can explain why he shoots for the end boards and never hits the net with his high shots.

Then there's little Jack Adams. God has blessed Jack with a great pair of legs for skating. But he saves them—for swimming. Yes, swimming—out in Vancouver.

Some of the players grinned at this, but Irvin wiped the smirks off their faces by turning on the nearest snickerer: "As for you, Mr. Goupille, all I can say of you is that you are a friend of the world. You like to be friends with everybody, particularly players in the NHL. You wouldn't hurt anybody in case they wouldn't like you anymore. And that goes for Jack Portland too. Jack wouldn't go out there tonight and hurt poor little Ditty Clapper or Milty Schmidt or Bobby Bauer—his old pals of Boston days. No, he wouldn't want to rough them up."

Dick paused for breath and then swung his head around.

Aw, there's our young rookie Johnny Quilty. I swear he's about to bring about a revolutionary change in hockey. We'll soon have to put the nets on swivels so that he'll be able to score from behind the net, where he always seems to position himself.

And our other young hero Ken Reardon wouldn't pass the puck to anybody—not even his grandmother. But he might put it on the stick of his brother Terry, who'll be playing for the Bruins tonight.

Ray Getliffe? Where is he? [Getliffe was sitting right in front of him.] Ray does seem to become invisible. Now I remember. He's back in Stratford, selling shoes. That's it. That's where he likes to be—in Stratford, selling shoes to ladies.

Then there's that big, strong muscleman Tony Demers. He's so terribly proud of his power and strength that he won't expend any of it in a hockey game. He likes to strut around his hometown of Chambly trying to convince everyone that he is so much stronger and tougher than Jean Pusie.

Elmer Lach, now, another of our young players. He's different. He wants to show how tough he is by using his stick on some other fellow's ears instead of using it on the hockey puck.

Joe Benoit is a fancy Dan out there, and he looks good. But somehow I think he would be just as glad when the game is over so he can go home and read a good book.

Poor old Murph Chamberlain. They call him Hardrock because he was a miner once. And a pretty good driller, I understand. I'd like to see him drill some holes in opposing defensemen once in awhile.

And Toe Blake, the man with the one-track hockey mind. Back in 1926 or thereabouts, he must have scored a goal by dumping the puck between the defensemen and racing around them to pick it up and go in on goal. He's still doing it but he hasn't scored a goal that way that I can recall. There are other ways of going in on a goaltender, but you can't make Blake believe that. [Irwin would coach Blake until he left to take over as coach of the Chicago Black Hawks in 1955–56. Blake succeeded Irwin as coach of the Habs and promptly led Montreal to five consecutive Stanley Cups from 1957 to 1960. Blake won 500 games behind the Montreal bench.]

Then Irvin came to an abrupt halt.

The only man he omitted from that searing denunciation was Tony Graboski, because he was convinced Graboski had been playing his heart out and doing his best.

It was quite a classic and probing talk Irvin gave his boys. They laughed about it afterwards, but that night his words stung. His tongue-lashing prompted them to go out and lay a beating on the Boston Bruins.

●

Dick Irvin was always quick to defend other members of the NHL coaching fraternity. In 1950, Chicago coach Charlie Conacher socked Lew Walter, a Detroit writer, and faced a hefty fine for his actions.

When told of the incident, Irvin said, "If Conacher is fined, I think all the other NHL coaches should chip in and pay the fine." Irvin's suggestion surprised veteran reporter Elmer Ferguson, who wrote: "I know Dick and he's a frugal guy. Why, he wouldn't pay 10 cents to see the Battle of the Marne complete with the original cast."

That same season, Amby Moran, 56, a Winnipeg-born defenseman who had been the terror of several leagues from 1912 to 1928, complained that "there are too many men on a team nowadays. In my day, a goalie and eight players were enough. We played three-minute shifts. Some of us played the full 60 minutes without relief. We were tough. And the best team I ever played on was the Regina Caps of the Western League—with Dick Irvin as our star player. That was in 1921–22."

Hall of Famer Newsy Lalonde recalls a memorable confrontation between Dick Irvin and tough guy Cully Wilson, a terror in the Western League. "It was in Regina one night and Wilson cross-checked Irvin's lower teeth right into his tongue. The blood flowed and Wilson was handed a major penalty. But that wasn't enough punishment, in Irvin's opinion. So he ladled out a bit more of his own. He manoeuvred his way close to the penalty box and poleaxed the unsuspecting Wilson, who toppled over unconscious. Cully collected enough stitches that night to weave an Indian blanket."

Before Irvin passed away, he reminisced with hockey writer Bill Roche:

Hockey has taken me into many splendid places down through the years. First-rate modern rinks, fine trains to travel on and even airplanes.

It's even taken me back into the boondocks as well. When I coached the Canadiens in the forties, one year we took a couple of trips into the backwoods of Quebec and were amazed at the reception we received. What a gold mine we stumbled upon. One man plunked down $3,000 and paid our rail fares for an exhibition game in his hometown. We split into two clubs and were stunned when 3-4,000 fans showed up to watch us play. And they paid big money for tickets. So the promoter made a killing. A few nights later we went so far into the woods I don't think anybody we met knew where we stood in the NHL standings. And we snared $5,000 for a couple of easy games. Once again, the promoter cleaned up by jamming the joint at fabulous prices.

But I don't think I've ever gotten the same kick from any one of hundreds of hockey excursions as I had from a trip that took me to an indoor rink—the first time I'd been in one.

I lived in Winnipeg back then. Kids in our neighbourhood had a pickup kind of team.

We did all our playing on outdoor ice. And there was plenty of that in Winnipeg in those days. With ruts and bumps—lots of them. One day we arranged a game with another bunch of kids living in a small town about 14 miles east. The big attraction for us was that the little community had an indoor rink. That, to me, was remarkable. I had never played in one of those wonderful things. The question was how to get there. Just hop a train and go, you might say. But boys of 15 or so, as I was at that time, didn't just travel around on trains. It was the horse and buggy age.

It was my dad who came up with the answer. He bundled 10 or 12 of us onto a sleigh and hitched up a team of horses and away we went in below zero weather. How excited we all were. I'll never forget the rush I felt when I entered the indoor rink. There were no rink boards or goalie nets. Two poplar poles stood where the goal posts should be, and they extended from the ice all the way up to the roof. A lantern was hung on one of the poles over the goalie's head. Oil lamps were scattered here and there, providing a dim light, a glow that spattered dim shadows across the ice, a strange sight to try to visualize. The indoor ice was smooth and clean, much different than the bumpy, rutted ice we were used to playing on. It was wonderful to skate on that ice, a kind of fairyland for us.

The outcome of the game I don't recall, but the ice I'll always remember.

Then came the return trip to Winnipeg. Teenagers today who travel in heated cars, or perhaps by train, can only visualize our plight. A near blizzard had sprung up while the game was being played, and the road back was filled with drifting snow.

We rode out of town, unshowered but undaunted, huddled down in the bottom of the open sleigh, gasping as the ever-increasing blizzard hurled snow and sleet into our faces. We had gone only a couple of miles when Dad stopped the horses. He said the drifts were getting too deep for the horses to pull through. "You monkeys had better get off the sleigh and walk," he said. "You'll keep a lot warmer that way, anyhow."

Walking that dozen or so miles back to Winnipeg—and the thrill of playing in an indoor rink for the first time—is a cherished memory that I will always carry with me.

Here's another Dick Irvin story:

Away back in the early 1900s, the Winnipeg Vics were playing against the Montreal Wanderers for the Stanley Cup. I was a kid standing outside the office of the *Winnipeg Tribune* getting a sketchy account of the game by telegraph messages flashed on a lantern slide screen. There was no radio in those days. The Winnipeg club's defense consisted of only two men—two brothers as it turned out. They had Magnus Flett playing coverpoint and Rod Flett playing point. They were supposed to stay on the job in their own end of the rink. A defenseman carrying the puck? A defenseman scoring a goal? It simply wasn't done. However, I recall the great commotion, the stunning bewilderment in the crowd that night when word was flashed via telegraph that Rod Flett, by a long backhand flip shot up through the rafters, had scored a goal for the Vics. His goal was the talk of Winnipeg for some time after.

●

Throughout his career, Dick Irvin had an interesting hobby—he raised pigeons.

In 1934, the newspaper in his hometown of Regina reported the following:

Expert raiser and breeder of prize exhibition poultry as well as coach of the Toronto Maple Leafs, Dick Irvin, the silver-thatched hockey veteran from Regina, has entered 21 birds in the poultry show to be held in conjunction with the Royal Winter Fair in Toronto. At last year's show, Irvin carried off two firsts in the cockerel and white Wyandotte classes. Included in his entries this year, Irvin has 13 Wyandottes and 8 white leghorns. Irvin has also entered 32 racing homers in the pigeon division. Irvin maintains his poultry farm and pigeon lofts in Regina, where he makes his home between hockey seasons. What isn't mentioned is whether or not he trained those birds to fly inside or outside.

●

Dick Irvin Jr. told me an amusing story one day relating to his father's coaching renown. A Chicago sportswriter, assigned to write an article about the Hall of Fame player and coach, phoned Irvin in Montreal. "Mr. Irvin," said the caller. "Can you tell me what it was like to coach the Chicago team back in the '20s?"

Dick laughed and responded. "I can't tell you. And the man who could, if he were still around, would be 110 years old now."

EDDIE SHACK
and Friends

"This getting old sucks. The only thing golden about the golden years is your piss." —Eddie Shack

We are dining in a private room at Smith & Wollensky in Manhattan, a fine restaurant just a block away from our hotel—the Waldorf Astoria. It is June 21, 2009, the eve of the Canadian Association of New York's annual hockey banquet, and a select group of head-table guests have been invited to a reception by Paul Levesque, a transplanted Montrealer who has chaired the hockey dinner for 31 years. I've been his MC for the same length of time. We are the only two people who have been to every dinner. One year, we had the player guests add up their Stanley Cup rings, and the total was 47. Henri Richard—with a record 11—was there that night.

In the room this night are Red and Andra Kelly, Eddie and Norma Shack, Senator Frank and Marie Mahovlich, Dennis and Janet Hull. And—well, look who just walked in—singer Michael Burgess. He joins us at our table. Michael has flown in from Toronto. He'll be our anthem singer tomorrow at the Waldorf. Everybody loves Michael Burgess. Why? Because he plays the game. He's a hockey guy.

Red Kelly is sitting next to me. He raises a hand and shows me a huge Stanley Cup ring, delivered to his door in Toronto a few days earlier. It is mammoth, it sparkles. It is heavy. Very heavy. I try it on and can barely hold up my finger.

Red says, "It came in a big box and I had no idea what was inside. I opened the box and peeled back layer after layer of paper and padding. I finally discovered a small box deep inside, and when I opened it, there was this magnificent ring. The Ilitch family, owners of the Red Wings, did some research and discovered that many of us who had been on Stanley Cup teams in Detroit never received rings. So they had a bunch made up and sent them to us. What a surprise! They each must weigh a pound.

"We had a young goalie join us back then to fill in for Terry Sawchuk for three games. Terry was hurt, and this kid Dave Gatherum came in and played over 120 minutes—two full games—before giving up a goal. He set an NHL record for the longest shutout streak by a rookie goaltender." Gatherum played in three games altogether, allowed just three goals in 180 minutes and tallied a goals-against average of 1.00. Despite this fine start, he was sent packing when Sawchuk returned, and that was the end of his NHL career.

Kelly says, "Dave got a ring even though he didn't see any playoff action. The Ilitch family didn't forget anybody."

"I remember the name Gatherum," I say.

"Well, maybe he should have played more," Red says. "Because Sawchuk went cold in the first round. We played Boston and they knocked us off. Terry couldn't stop anything, for some reason. We were out at the blueline trying to force the Bruins to shoot [from there] because Terry was so shaky."

"What's that ring on your other hand?" I ask. It is a puny little thing, but I don't tell Red that.

"That's my Leaf Stanley Cup ring," he replies. "We won four Stanley Cups in Toronto in the '60s, and each year they called in the rings to add another diamond—a tiny one."

I can barely see the diamonds in the Leaf ring. But then, my vision is failing because of my diabetes.

I've always thought it takes an enormous amount of effort and a lot of luck to capture a Stanley Cup ring. But Red tells me a story that proves it's not always so:

I was flying to New York on business after my hockey days were over, and during the flight, I feel a tap on my shoulder. I look up and there's John Bassett, who at that time was one-third owner of the Leafs. Bassett was partners with Stafford Smythe and Harold Ballard.

He says, "Red, I've got a limousine driver meeting me at the airport. Want a ride into the city?"

I said, "That would be great, Mr. Bassett." Turns out he was going to see his granddaughter Carling Bassett play in a big tennis match in New York. She was Canada's top player back then.

So this big limo driver—looked like an NFL lineman—drives us both into Manhattan. The driver lets Mr. Bassett out at his hotel and then drives me to mine. While he's helping me with my bags, he says, "Hey, man, what's that ring on your finger?"

I hold it up. "It's a hockey ring—for winning the Stanley Cup. Nice, eh?"

He laughs. "Yeah, it's nice. I've got one just like it."

I was shocked. "You're kidding, right? How would you get a ring exactly like this one?"

"Mr. Bassett gave me one. I admired his one day and he said, 'You like my ring? I'll get you one. And he did.'"

I tipped the guy and he drove off. *By hang,* I thought, *all the sweat and effort that goes into winning a Stanley Cup ring, one so exclusive you'll treasure it forever. And here's a limo driver in Manhattan wearing one without ever having to skate or take a single hit to get one. In fact, he probably* can't *skate. He's probably never* seen *a hockey game.*

Each year at the pre-dinner reception, Paul Levesque expects me to move around the room and interview many of the guests. I zero in on Eddie Shack. He jumps up, and before I can ask him a question he's already talking.

"Folks, I played my junior hockey in Guelph, and coming to New York I noticed that some guys on the streets were stealing the front end of a car while other guys were stealing the back end. And nobody stepped in. Nobody cared. Nobody came to help anybody else.

"Now here I am in New York City, and my coach is Phil Watson. At that time I was better than Bobby Hull. I was better than Frank Mahovlich." Someone chuckles at the Mahovlich table. "Now, don't look at me like that, Frank. I scored more goals than you and I was better than you." There is more laughter. "And I could kick the shit out of you any old time.

"Now I get a goddamn coach like Phil Watson. And he's going to tell me what to do. Now, I was an individual who could not read or write. And I was not ashamed of it. And I proved to them that you don't need an education to play hockey. It was push, glide and shoot the puck and keep your head up. And I was better than you in junior, Frank. I was better than Bobby Hull. And they shit on me here. That hurt me, Frank, that hurt me. It hurt me big. When Phil Watson died, they gave him a minute's silence. And when it came up to half a minute, I said, 'That's enough for that son of a bitch.'

"That's the kind of a guy I was. And I never got any thanks. Never any thanks. But I had a lot of fun and I got a lovely wife Norma."

The room applauded, but Shack continued: "Now wait a minute. Put the brakes on. Years ago, Brian, you wrote a song about me—'Clear the Track, Here Comes Shack.' It's because [hockey writer] Paul Rimstead saw me knock two guys down on one shift and he wrote about it. Then you came along like a little bird dog, and you said I can make some money on this Shackie guy, right? Now, don't bullshit me. And Ballard said, 'McFarlane, how much are you paying Shack?'"

"Hold on, Eddie," I interrupt. "I never went to Ballard. I went to *you* and asked you if I could write a song about you. You said to me, 'I don't give a shit what you do.' So I wrote the song, and it went to number one for a few weeks, and you came back and said, 'Hey, where's my money?' And I said, 'Eddie, you don't get any money, because you gave me permission to write about you.' What ticked you off was that Johnny Bower had a song out—'Honky the Christmas Goose'—and he was getting three cents a record."

"Well, anyway," Shack says, "I thank you very much for that. The song was unbelievable."

I can't believe it. Shack is thanking me for writing that damn song about him. For 30 years, at sports banquets and golf tournaments, he's been telling everyone what a cheap son of a bitch I am for not sharing royalties with him. In fact, there were very few royalties, for some reason.

(Later, I checked with the company that handles music royalties three or four years ago, and someone there agreed that some royalties should have flowed my way but never did. "But that was so long ago," I was told. "Tell you what, would you take $1,000 and be happy with that?" I said, "Sure.

Send me a cheque." And they did. I didn't plan to tell Eddie. But then, at Dennis Hull's corn roast two months later, I met up with Eddie again. I pulled him aside and told him about the $1,000 cheque. He cackled and bellowed and pumped my hand. "That's great. Good for you.")

Eddie turns to Red Kelly and shouts. "Red, I was traded for you and you refused to come to New York. How come?"

Red shouts back, "My mother-in-law lived in New York, Eddie."

Everybody laughs.

"How's the song go, Eddie?" calls out Dennis Hull.

"I'll sing a bit of it," Eddie promises. "Even if Michael Burgess is in the room. Yah, baby! But first, let me say I've had so much fun in my life as a hockey player. I'm so happy that I got out of the butcher shop in Sudbury and I played a bit of hockey and I met a nice woman like Norma. I met her in training camp in Peterborough, and she was from Keene, not far away. And in Keene, they say *g'dee, g'dee*, and I'm saying, 'What the fuck is *g'dee, g'dee?*'" Shack turns to Norma and says, "You can say *g'dee, g'dee* better than anyone."

"G'dee, g'dee," Norma says.

Shack guffaws. "Oh, my God, isn't she a lucky person," he says.

"Sing the song, Eddie," Dennis shouts.

Shack nods at me, and suddenly we're a duet, singing to Michael Burgess and a roomful of hockey people.

Clear the track, here comes Shack
He knocks 'em down and he gives 'em a whack
He can score goals, he's found the knack
Eddie, Eddie Shack
He started the year in the minors and almost gave up the game . . .

"Wait!" shouts Eddie. "I did start the year in the minors. They sent me down for misbehaving. Can you imagine? I was so embarrassed, eh?"

I tell the audience: "Of all the guys I've met in the NHL, there was no greater entertainer than Eddie Shack. And while we've had our differences over the years, and while I once called him some awful names right to his face, we've both mellowed and now we get along rather well."

I move along to Dennis Hull. "Dennis, you've entertained people all over North America with your humour. Every year you make a special effort to come to this dinner, and we really appreciate it. What have you been up to lately?"

"Well, I don't know if anybody noticed, but I was the host of the Winnipeg Comedy Fest."

"No, we didn't notice," I say.

"I guess you didn't notice that," Dennis chuckles. "Did you notice, Michael?"

Michael Burgess shakes his head. "I didn't notice, Dennis."

"Yeah, well, I came home after the Comedy Fest and I said to Janet, 'How was I?' And she said, 'You looked a little bulky on TV.' So I said, 'You know, the camera puts 10 pounds on you.' And she said, 'How many cameras did they have on you?'"

"I see Bobby is back in the spotlight again," I say.

"Yes, Bobby is doing well. He opened a little business—a combination taxidermist and veterinarian shop. On his business card, it says, 'Either way you get your dog back.'

"Yes, Bobby and Stan Mikita and Tony Esposito, the three greatest players in Chicago history, are now ambassadors for the Blackhawks. And I can see the Hawks being the Pittsburgh Penguins of next year. And Jonathan Toews will shake hands with his opponents after they win the Cup." (This is a reference to Sydney Crosby failing to shake hands with the Detroit players in '09.)

I move to another table and ask Frank Mahovlich to stand up and tell us what it meant to be a member of the Montreal Canadiens. He says, "I'll tell you, it was quite a treat. I was disappointed to leave Detroit. When I got a phone call from Sam Pollock, I said to him, 'Sam, I don't know. I think I may give up this game.' And he said, 'No, no, no. Everything is gonna be all right. When we get back to Montreal we'll have a meeting. Just go to Minnesota—that's where our next game is.' So I went, and we tied the North Stars that night, 3–3, and I scored a goal. When we got back to Montreal, two or three executives with the Habs met the plane, and I was impressed. That had never happened to me before. So we had a meeting and everything went well. I had a ride in Pollock's car, and it was a Lincoln Town Car. Whenever Sam went to the playoffs or a road game, he would never fly. Can you imagine? He travelled thousands of miles in that Lincoln Town Car.

"In Montreal, Beliveau was a class guy. Then Guy Lafleur came along, and he was a class guy too. And Henri Richard. We had so many great guys. I can't believe it when I look at the photos of the guys I played with there. There are 12 or 13 of us who are in the Hockey Hall of Fame. How many teams can say that?"

Frank is about to sit down when Michael Burgess calls out, "Frank, tell them about your first game in the NHL."

"Okay. I was with St. Mike's at the time, and Eddie Shack's team in Guelph beat us out. So the Leafs gave me a three-game trial. I was 19 years old, and Howie Meeker was the Leaf coach. My first game was against Montreal. It was 1957, and Montreal had those great teams that won five straight Stanley Cups.

"In the dressing room, Meeker says to me, 'Frank, you'll be checking Rocket Richard tonight.' I'm 19, the Rocket is 38, and he's got a terrible reputation. Early in the game, Doug Harvey passes the puck up to Maurice and I don't know what to do, but I know what my job is. I'm not the smartest guy in the world at that time. So I reach out and put both of my arms around the Rocket. Have I got a grip on him? There's no way he's going to get away, even though it's like I'm wrestling a bear. Well, he turns around and his nose is right next to my nose and his eyes are wild, they're glaring! And he snarls, 'Let go, kid!' What did I do? I said, 'Yes sir, Mr. Richard.' And I let him go."

We walk back to the hotel with the Shacks and the Kellys. We stop for a light, and Eddie says, "This getting old sucks. The only thing golden about the golden years is your piss."

I have to admit, there's some truth in that statement.

The dinner the following night goes well. Attendees are there to honour the 100th anniversary of the Montreal Canadiens. Bob Gainey and Montreal's new coach, Jacques Martin, fly in from Montreal with Rejean Houle, Yvan Cournoyer and Stephane Richer. Glen Sather, Peter Mahovlich and Bryan Trottier show up, which gives us a nice head-table presence. Paul Levesque tried to get a player from the Penguins to fly in, but they are all still giddy after their Cup victory.

When I interview Shack at the head table, he reneges on his predinner promise not to use any foul language. He tells the audience about the one-minute silence held for the departed Phil Watson, and how "half a minute is enough for that little prick."

This doesn't surprise me. When Eddie joined our NHL Oldtimers many years ago, we played a fundraising game in Belleville against a group of firemen. The mayor hosted a post-game reception that included wives of the local players. Eddie was asked to say a few words. He opened with, "I know how you guys put out fires around here—with your cocks." The mayor was livid. He approached some of us afterward and said, "Don't ever bring him back to Belleville."

Eddie talks about playing in Los Angeles and how he despised general manager Larry Regan. "Regan called me a dummy, and I hated him for that. I called him Pig Eyes and tried to punch him out one day. And I hated that little prick, Jack Kent Cooke, the team owner."

Later, in the hotel bar, after Norma says good night and goes up to bed, Eddie joins the Kellys and the McFarlanes at a table. He overhears Andra talking about being courted by Red and how his family didn't want him marrying that "hoochie coochie figure skater."

Shack bursts out laughing. "Yeah, Andra, you were a hoochie coochie, all right. You probably had nice buns back then. Did you fool around a lot back then?" His comment surprises everybody, because Andra is such a lady.

●

Here's some advice. When you know you're going to be with Eddie, always bring an extra sock. I recall a sports banquet I MC'd in Niagara Falls. This would be in '89—I remember the year because Red Storey, our keynote speaker, was 72 years old that day. I introduced Shack, and he got a lot of laughs with his routine. Then he said:

I played for the Leafs and Red Kelly. If you ever go to Red's house and a fly walks up the wall—well, to Red, that's real excitement. When I played for Red, the crowd would get excited. I'd be on the bench and a cheer would go up. "We want Shack! We want Shack!" So what the hell am I going to do? I'd jump up and wave my arms and get the crowd going. I'd shout, "We want Shack! We want Shack!" And the crowd would roar back: "We want Shack." So Leonard would look down at me, and he'd shout, "Hey, Eddie, if they want you so bad, why don't you go up there and sit with them?"

Most of my hockey was played in Toronto. I never played very much. I sat on the end of the bench and tried to get Frank going. Or Davey Keon. If Punch did put me out there, he'd call out the line change: "Harris and Shack and whoever the Christ wants to go with them." All of the younger players who sat on the bench might be saying, "Play me or trade me." I used to say, "I'll sit here, just pay me." Some guys thought I sat there because I had an injury. I didn't have an injury. But I had a sore ass from sittin' there so often.

One night I happened to get on the ice, and it was against Montreal at the Gardens. A playoff game, eh? Now, I was a bit of a shit disturber, and I always picked on the littlest guy. So there I am up against Henri Richard. Now, Henri was always doing some damage to our club, so I said, "I guess I'll see what I can do to him." I grabbed the little frog . . . sorry . . . I grabbed little Henri, and now who comes nosing around but John Ferguson. I always called Fergie Shithead.

What's he gonna do? I loved that third-man-in rule, right? Fergie can't get involved. What's he gonna do? Get thrown out of the game? Now I'm tryin' to get my arms loose to give Henri a little shot, but I can't get the little bastard—er, sorry, the little bugger—to let go. I gotta do something, so—*boom*—I coco-bonked him, my thick head against his. Geez, the blood started rolling down his face, and the worst language is coming out of his mouth.

Henri's got a big cut over the eye, probably good for five or six stitches, and Fergie is fuming. He snarls at me, "Come on and get me. Come on, Shackie." I say, "Give me a break, eh?"

Now we're on our way to the penalty box, and Henri was steaming. I said to him, "Henri, don't get so upset. It's not your fault that God favoured your brother and gave him all the hockey talent and left none for you."

So that game is over, and the next game is back in Montreal. Playing at the Forum, now that's a whole different story, I'll tell you that. I only hope the return game is close. If we're up or down by a few goals, it'll be, "Shack and Harris and whoever the Christ wants to go with them." Before the game, I can't eat my steak, I can't sleep, I'm thinkin' about the awful things that might happen, and now it's time to go to the rink. Time to face the music, eh? And face Shithead.

Soon as I skate out on the ice for the warm-up, who comes skating by me at centre ice? Shithead. "I'm gonna get you tonight," he snarls at me.

I'll tell you this, I don't like looking at my own blood, but I figure I might be tonight. Now, up in the stands there's that guy with the horn, and he's shouting "Shack the nose, Shack the nose." Holy Jesus!

Now, after the warm-up we head to the dressing room, and who was standing there? "Two minutes for looking so good"—Maurice Richard. Hasn't been to a game in 10 years. Now he comes because he wants to see me get it. He stands up and yells, "Hey Shack! Thank God you didn't hit my brudder with your nose. You would have split him in two."

Eddie looks out over the audience. He's got them in the palm of his hand, and he knows it. He laughs and continues:

It was always hell playing for Punch Imlach. Absolute hell. Especially for a guy like me. If I misbehaved, I was sent to the minors for a couple of weeks. The lines were Keon, Armstrong and Duff. Then it was Kelly, Mahovlich and Nevin. After that it was Olmstead, Stewart and somebody else. That left me and Billy Harris on the bench. Every once in a while, as I've told you, Imlach would yell down the bench, "Shack and Harris and whoever the hell wants to go out with them." That didn't do a hell of a lot for my confidence. But I scored 26 goals for the Leafs one season, and he couldn't squawk about that. And I scored 20 or more goals with five other clubs after the Leafs dumped me. How many guys have done that? But I'll never forget those Leaf teams I played on. And the Stanley Cups we won. I loved playing in Toronto.

When I was with the Leafs, we were always up for our games with Montreal. Well, most of us were up. Frank Mahovlich always looked like he was on another planet for some of those games. And I would yell across the room, "Jesus Christ, wake up, Frank! Get up for this one!" Imlach loved me for that.

When I was with the Leafs, my wife, Norma, and I had a dog named Fou Fou. A little bitty thing. I had the dog in the dressing room one day, and the guys all made a big fuss over her. Then Harold Ballard marched in and saw what was happening. He barked at me, "Shack, get that damn dog out of here." I said, "Harold, I brought her in because she'll bring us luck." He said, "'Bullshit. Get her out. It's not luck she'll be leaving all over the new carpet I just paid for."

A lot of hockey men have stories about Shack.

Former Sabre Mike Byers recalls playing on a line with Eddie in Buffalo. "We were waiting for the faceoff in the other team's zone, and just before the official dropped the puck, Shack yells, 'Hold on a minute.' We all look over at him, and he's taking his hockey stick, turning it around and cocking it like a rifle. Then he put the stick back in its original position and nodded, indicating he was ready for the faceoff.

"Wouldn't you know, when the puck was dropped, it came right back to Shack and he snapped it into the net for a goal. Later I heard him tell reporters he'd stopped the game because his 'gun' was out of bullets. I'll say this: he picked a great time to reload."

Red Kelly tells me about the time Shackie took a goal away from him. "We played on the same line for a time in Toronto, and I set him up for a lot of goals. But one day he comes to my house and says he's got something on his mind. Can we talk? I remember he had his little dog Fou Fou with him. So I invite him in and we sit. After a few seconds he bounces out of his chair and gets down on his knees in front of me. His hands are together like he's in prayer. He says, 'Red, I've got a confession to make. Remember that game when you shot from the blueline and I was in front of the net? The red light went on and they awarded the goal to me. Well, I didn't score that goal, but I took it. And that's always troubled me.'

"I said, 'Eddie, that was years ago.'

"He says, 'I know, but I took a goal away from you, and I've always felt guilty about it. I wanted to get it off my chest.'

"Then he lies down on the carpet and falls asleep. Fou Fou naps too, with all four feet pointed in the air.

"I get a blanket to put over them. Then I get a cushion to put under Eddie's head. But when I go to put it there, Fou Fou growls at me and shows me her sharp little teeth. So I said to heck with the cushion."

I wrote an article about Eddie Shack many years ago. It was a column about his frightening stick duel with Larry Zeidel. I dig it out of my files and discover that the incident took place during the first year of NHL expansion. It occurred at Maple Leaf Gardens, even though the opposing teams were the Bruins and the Flyers. Early in the season, the roof blew off of the Spectrum in Philadelphia, and the Flyers were forced to play several games in neutral arenas.

Shack and Zeidel had clashed before, a decade earlier, on October 1, 1959. Shack was a rambunctious Ranger prospect playing for Springfield. He was speared by Hershey defenseman Zeidel. Shack swung his stick and decorated Zeidel's scalp with a dozen stitches. Both players were ejected from the game.

Recalling that first encounter, Shack says, "The guy speared me once, and I told him if he did it again I'd conk him good. He speared me again, so I whacked him over the head with my stick. We got tossed from the game, and now I'm showered and dressed and watching the rest of the game from rinkside. Who comes up from behind me but Zeidel, and he's yappin' at me, and then he cold-cocks me. So we have a hell of a fight until the cops break it up and haul us off to jail. He's in one cell, I'm in another, and I yelled at him, 'What the fuck is wrong with you? You nuts?' He just glares at me."

That season, Eddie was embarking on a career that would take him from the Rangers to the Leafs and then, in the summer of 1967, to the Boston Bruins. Zeidel was a career minor leaguer whose modest skills had never earned him a big-league berth.

But when the NHL expanded in 1967 to 12 teams, Zeidel prepared a glossy resume of his career highlights and distributed it to the six new clubs. His strategy worked. The Flyers invited him to training camp and signed him to a contract.

It meant he'd get another crack at his old enemy—Eddie Shack.

On March 7, 1968, Shack was looking forward to that night's game against the Flyers because it would be played at Maple Leaf Gardens, his old stomping grounds. He'd been part of four Stanley Cup–winning teams there. "I've got 18 goals [in the season so far], and I'm aiming for 20," he told reporters.

He never expected he'd become involved in an incident that would trigger headlines like "Sickening Night at the Gardens."

Sickening it was.

The Flyers' Zeidel, one of the few Jewish players ever to perform in the NHL, was playing his usual aggressive game. But he appeared to be distracted by taunts coming from the Boston bench. He would later claim the Bruins were shouting obscenities and anti-Semitic remarks at him. One Bruin allegedly shouted, "We'll see you in a gas chamber, Jew-boy."

Then came the rekindling of an old feud when he and Shack collided.

"I saw him coming," Shack would explain, "so I let him have a shot like this—with my stick." He showed reporters how he had gripped his stick and slashed Zeidel. "Then Zeidel comes back at me with his stick, and he hit me pretty good, twice."

Witnesses were stunned by the ferocity of the stick swinging that followed. Blood gushed from a gash to Zeidel's head. Shack landed four solid swipes, but he too was bloodied. Shack told reporters, "I could have hurt the guy more, but I broke my stick—right over his head."

Finally, the linesmen waded into the flying lumber and broke it up.

Both players were penalized, fined and suspended.

Later, the Bruins were questioned about the anti-Semitic taunts they were accused of uttering. Zeidel made it clear that Shack was not among the taunters. The Bruins denied all allegations.

Linesman Matt Pavelich stated he heard no such comments, but he described the bloody duel as "one of the most vicious stick attacks I have ever seen." Fred Stanfield, a newcomer to the Bruins in 1967, told Ross Brewitt, Shack's biographer, "Man, they whacked each other with their sticks. It was the scariest battle I've ever seen."

Zeidel had been in at least three previous noteworthy stick-swinging incidents besides his 1959 fight with Shack. In 1953, playing with Edmonton in the Western League, he and Jack Evans were suspended after a stick-swinging duel. In 1958, with Hershey of the AHL, he cut Cleveland's Bob Bailey with his stick for 19 stitches. And in 1963, he was suspended for four games for "unwarranted stick swinging" against Willie O'Ree of L.A. (O'Ree, who was blind in one eye, had gained fame in 1957 as the first black player in the NHL, with Boston). Zeidel had also been punished by the Western League for spitting at referee Willie Papp. Guys named Willie learned to steer clear of him.

●

Fred Stanfield revealed another little known fact about Eddie Shack's time in Boston. "In training camp, Shack was our first choice for team captain. He was the senior guy, right? And the only guy who'd been on a Cup–winner. It was Phil Esposito who said, 'You be our captain, Eddie.' And Eddie said, 'Nope. A captain has to be able to read.' He turned down the C. So we didn't have a captain that season. Just a lot of A's."

Shack and coach Harry Sinden didn't hit it off in Boston. The Bruins were a rising force in the NHL, and Sinden became irritated by Shack's on-ice antics. "Just play your game, Shackie. We don't need entertainers." When Shack yapped about his role and said, "Why don't you trade me?" the Bruins did—to Los Angeles.

Years later, Shack would tell Brewitt, "But the real reason I was traded was because I made fun of the owner's hats. I used to sell Biltmore hats all around the league. Remember the beauties Punch Imlach wore? They came through me. But Weston Adams, a millionaire and a cheap son of a bitch, wouldn't buy any from me. He used to wear the oldest, crappiest, horseshit hats in the world. And I let him know it."

If Eddie had kept his trap shut, he might have been on the Boston Stanley Cup–winners in 1970 and 1972.

●

Shack's son Jimmy is a delightful person, a successful artist who's been living in New York for many years. Bobby Baun, I'm told, has bought a few of his paintings—or, as Shack would put it, "Baun has a lot of his shit." Jimmy says, "I've been in New York all this time, and not once have I been asked about the Shack name. Not a soul has asked if I'm related to the hockey player. Why would they make a connection? I never talk hockey. I have no interest in the game."

●

Some positive things should be noted about Eddie Shack and the stance he took during the long battle between the NHLPA and the NHL pension fund.

Eddie was among the first to join a select group of retired players willing to put time, money and effort into what surely would be a long, drawn-out struggle in the courts to win millions of dollars for retired players in NHL-mismanaged pension funds. Shack and others—Carl Brewer (the instigator), Leo Reise, Andy Bathgate, Allan Stanley, Keith McCreary, Gordie Howe, Bobby Hull and Bobby Orr—firmly believed that over $40 million rightfully belonged to the retired players (even though Alan Eagleson, the head of the NHLPA, had earlier insisted the money belonged to the NHL—an astonishing concession).

Ross Brewitt writes:

When the opportunity to do something for his fellow man presented itself, Eddie accepted the challenge, took the gamble to make things better, stood up in the interest of making things right. Shack refuses to call it a philanthropic, or benevolent, act; he simply doesn't have the vocabulary to attach a handle to the subject, nor does he care. But one facet of his personality is a dogged streak of fairness, a frontier justice way of making things right . . .

There are those who maintain he's rude, crude, unthinking and unfeeling, that he's inflexible and insensitive. At various times, super-ficially at least, all those terms can have a ring of truth. But only a few things can get a self-righteous rise out of Ed Shack. Phil Watson is one; the NHL pension surplus is another. Watson was a nemesis, a personal, unforgiven foul-up that time hasn't painted over, while the pension surplus became a burning passion that took four years out of the lives of both Ed and Norma Shack.

The Shacks pitched in fundraisers for the group. They helped arrange two golf tournaments and raised thousands of dollars to help pay expenses, mainly legal fees. At one golf tournament, Shack happened to run into NHL president John Ziegler in the men's locker room. Ziegler's pension was a reported $250,000, while the late Jean Beliveau's was around $12,000. Shack showered abuse on Ziegler, who was pinned in a corner, unable to avoid the tongue-lashing.

Brewitt tells of Shack going to Montreal with the hope of receiving a commitment from the Canadiens Alumni for $5,000. But Shack's passion for the cause impressed Jean Beliveau. He stood and said, "Eddie, we're going to make it $25,000."

Carl Brewer and his partner Susan Foster have been applauded as the

pair who diligently pursued the NHL for the pension surplus monies—
and rightly so. But Ed and Norma Shack, according to many witnesses,
deserve equal acclaim. It's difficult to believe that some players berated
them for tackling a league that has "treated us well for all of our careers."

Well done, Eddie. I'm impressed. I apologize for calling you all those
nasty names in a fit of temper in Vancouver many seasons back.

BOB JOHNSON
Revered in Pittsburgh

Has it really been almost 25 years since we lost Bob Johnson, the coach who coined the phrase "it's a great day for hockey"?

November 26, 1991, was a horrible day for hockey. Especially in Pittsburgh, where Badger Bob (a nickname pinned to him for his three NCAA titles as coach at Wisconsin) passed away after a lengthy battle with cancer.

Badger Bob, after 14 months on the job, had become hugely popular in the City of Steel. He guided the Pittsburgh Penguins to their first Stanley Cup in the spring of 1991.

On his first day of work, he plastered a sign on his office door: "Never teach a pig to sing. It wastes your time and it annoys the pig."

Craig Patrick, GM of the Penguins in 1989, lured Johnson away from a desk job at USA Hockey in Colorado Springs. He remembered Johnson as the highly respected coach who took the Calgary Flames to the 1986 Stanley Cup final.

Patrick, Johnson and Scotty Bowman, who was director of player recruitment and development, formed a Hall of Fame triumvirate at the top of a heretofore moribund franchise that had failed to make the NHL playoffs in seven of the eight previous seasons.

Veteran sports columnist Chuck Finder of the *Pittsburgh Post-Gazette* talked with people who knew Johnson. Joey Mullen, a winger and later an assistant coach, was one of the first to comment: "In the beginning, they were kind of looking at him: Is this guy for real? At times, I would have to say, 'Hey. Just give him a chance. He's got a strange way of doing things. But he gets his points across. He's a good coach. And he'll keep things fun.'"

Barry Smith, a former Penguins assistant: "He was so amazingly optimistic, with a positive outlook on things. Always the brighter side. It couldn't help but wear off on you."

Troy Loney, a winger for the Penguins at the time: "It's such a dramatic change from the other coaches in those days—how many positive guys were there? It got to a point in that season where we asked him to show us what we were doing badly, because he was only showing us the good stuff. And we were getting whacked pretty good early on."

Bob Errey, a winger then and a broadcaster now: "He'd come in after a loss and he'd say, 'Bobby, you got a station wagon? You don't? Well, get yourself a station wagon, get yourself a couple of kids'—like you could just go out somewhere and get a couple of kids—'and drive them somewhere.' He thought getting into that family stuff was important. It would ground you, get you away from hockey."

Loney: "Yeah, he'd say, 'You need to get away from the game. You need to take your wife to a John Wayne movie.' There were no John Wayne movies then. Or, 'You need to take your dog for a walk. Don't have a dog? Then knock on your neighbour's door and take his dog for a walk.'"

Pierre McGuire, advance scout then, TV commentator today: "His practices were awesome. They were so perfect. They really made players better."

Errey: "Like, he'd say to Randy Gilhen, 'Gilly, Gilly, I got to get another step out of you. You can do it, kid.' And he'd work with Randy one-on-one at centre ice—just like he was a Mighty Mite."

Smith: "He really loved to go out there for practice. He had his practice skates and his game-day skates. He was a big kid. Just loved to be on the pond. Loved to be around the guys."

Errey: "Every day was a great day for hockey for him. He lived and breathed hockey. He really did."

One-fourth of the team was remodelled mid-year. In December, Bowman and Patrick found Larry Murphy and Peter Taglianetti in Minnesota. In March came Ron Francis, Ulf Samuelsson and Grant Jennings. They meshed, almost immediately, with Mario Lemieux, Jaromir Jagr, Paul Coffey, Mark Recchi, Kevin Stevens and the rest. The Penguins went 9–3–2 down the stretch, and 8–4 through the first two rounds of the playoffs. When they lost the first two games of the conference finals to Boston, Johnson backed off, letting leaders emerge in the dressing room—where Stevens promptly stepped up and guaranteed a Penguin victory.

McGuire: "I remember being in his office with Scotty and the rest of the coaches, and Bob said, 'We'll turn this over to the players.' Kevin had a huge voice and Bob knew to trust certain players on the team."

Mullen: "If anything, there was a lot of talent here. We needed his direction—which he gave us."

Loney: "That team, there were a lot of different personalities there. A lot of different ways that team could have went. He just provided an environment where we all could come together, where we could learn to win. I never found that team to be real close off the ice. But on the ice, I've never been around a group like that. Unbelievably tight. And I think he was the guy, the glue that brought it all together."

The Penguins swept the next four games from Boston to reach the Stanley Cup final. They fell behind, two games to one, to the Minnesota North Stars. Johnson was affronted after reading in his hometown newspaper how Minneapolis's city fathers were prematurely planning a Stanley Cup parade. His Penguins won the next three games, 5–3, 6–3 and 8–0. Johnson entered the dressing room at the end of the second period of the final game, his team leading 6–0. "In 20 minutes," he said, "we're going to be world champions. Don't screw it up."

Mullen: "My favourite memory? Winning the Cup. I had won one in Calgary (two years earlier, without Johnson) and he's the guy who brought me to Calgary. I still felt he was the influential part of that Calgary team. He had moved on, but we pretty much kept everything he was doing."

Son Mark Johnson: "He always talked about climbing mountains.

I don't think when he started that season that he understood it could be one of the biggest mountains he would climb. I don't think even he thought it could be done in a year."

The career coach, as he called himself, also tried the international level, where he earned a fourth-place finish with the U.S. squad at the Olympics in 1976, four years before Herb Brooks's miracle at Lake Placid. Johnson was working with the U.S. team for the 1991 Canada Cup when signs of something wrong began to surface.

On August 29 of that year, Johnson was having dinner at a local restaurant with his wife, Martha, when she decided that her husband required immediate medical attention. He was taken to Mercy hospital in Pittsburgh with stroke-like symptoms. Emergency surgery was performed to remove a tumour, but another, inoperable tumour remained. Brain cancer.

A few days earlier, sportswriter E.M. Swift of *Sports Illustrated* had met with Badger Bob at the Chicago Stadium. Swift wrote:

I hadn't seen Bob Johnson for two years when I walked into the Team USA dressing room in Chicago . . . and, as was his kibitzing nature, he met me in full conversational stride. "Princeton hockey!" he shouted . . . I had played for the Princeton Tigers from 1970 to '73 [and tied a record for most consecutive losses—11—twice in one season], and Johnson . . . knew the lore of all U.S. college hockey teams, their records and their rivalries.

Johnson could tease me about Ivy League hockey because no man had ever done more than he had to support and promote the college game. Hockey was a subject he could discuss endlessly. Unlike many of the great coaches you hear about—Bear Bryant, John Wooden, Paul Brown—Johnson loved to talk. . . .

I never saw Johnson again. . . . On Nov. 26, he died at his home in Colorado Springs at age 60. . . . The entire hockey world mourns him, but it is American hockey in particular that feels his loss. Johnson was American hockey. He succeeded at all levels of it. He began his coaching career in 1956 at Warroad [Minn.] High, moved on to Colorado College and then, in 1966, went to Wisconsin and began putting together what soon became the most successful college hockey program the country has ever had. Under Johnson, the Badgers were 367–175–23 and won three NCAA titles, in 1973, '77 and '81. Wisconsin hockey became an institution through one man's leadership. . . . In '82, he was lured to the NHL by Calgary. College coaches had never fared very well in the pros, but Johnson broke that barrier by amassing a 193–155–52 record over his five seasons with the Flames and taking them to the Stanley Cup finals in '86. That year, in what remains the finest job of NHL coaching I've seen, he steered Calgary past the Edmonton Oilers in a seven-game Smythe Division final; it was the only time between '84 and '88 that Wayne Gretzky's prepotent Oilers were beaten in the playoffs.

Smith: "We were always optimistic that he'd be back on the bench again. That whole second year, it was Bob Johnson's team. It was never Scotty Bowman's team or my team. It was Bob Johnson's team."

Loney: "Oh, for him to get cancer was just awful. It was just devastating. As we found out more what was going on with him, I was so thankful that we won the year before. To have been there and not win and then have him pass away, it would have been very, very difficult to handle."

On November 27, the Civic Arena was the site of a tribute to the career coach. His mantra, "a great day for hockey," was painted onto the ice. Badger patches were stitched onto uniforms, battery-powered candles were borne aloft and hymns were played. The Penguins scored four of the night's final five goals to defeat the New Jersey Devils. Six days later, coaches, players, wives and front office folks flew to Colorado Springs for a memorial service (the Penguins would go on to Edmonton to play the following day). Badger meant so much to so many, memorial services were held in four places altogether: Colorado Springs, Minneapolis, Wisconsin and Pittsburgh.

Loney: "I remember standing at the gravesite. We had just gotten our Stanley Cup rings. Bourquey [Phil Bourque], I think, was the first one to walk up to the casket, and he banged his ring on the coffin. Then we all did. That was really memorable to me. He meant a lot to all of us."

Maguire: "Bob was an educator. Bob taught us all. Taught us about hockey. Taught us about life."

Patrick: "I knew him, and I didn't realize how special he was."

He meant so much to Pittsburgh in so little time, his flame might burn longest there. Until Badger, the Arena knew no banners, no hockey in May, no puck fervour.

Mark Johnson: "That's the thing. It's amazing what all transpired in the year that he was there. Obviously, it's one memory that my mom, my brothers and my sisters won't forget for many, many years, if ever. Just from the impact it had on the city of Pittsburgh and, more important, the impact it had on him. Whether it was one year or 10 years, it put a smile on your face when you saw how he affected people there. Pittsburgh got to know him real quick."

Badger Bob was inducted into the Hockey Hall of Fame in 1992.

MIKE ROBITAILLE

*The Man Who Sued His
Own Team—and Won*

In Vancouver in 1988, I meet with former Canuck defenseman Mike Robitaille, then a commentator on Buffalo Sabres games. I've seen Mike play for four different teams—the New York Rangers, Detroit, Buffalo and Vancouver. When I was with NBC in the '70s, I met him in Buffalo and mentioned I was in a hurry to get to the airport. He jumped up and said, "I'll drive you there." And he did. How many NHL players would do that? So I had him pegged as one of the good guys in hockey. But I learned he had his detractors too.

During our Vancouver meeting, Mike tells me an amazing story about the injuries that ended his career, the inexcusable medical treatment he received from Vancouver team doctors, the cold shoulder he got from teammates and the litigation he brought against the Vancouver Canucks.

Mike went from a 17-year-old shining star in junior hockey to an NHL has-been at 27, unable to earn a paycheque, fishing for pennies in a sandbox.

He speaks out because he wants young players in the game today to be on guard, to know that professional hockey is not all milk and honey.

Looking back to 1976–77, my final season in hockey—which I try not to do anymore, because those were dark days, full of anxiety and depression—I find it difficult to relate the full story, but basically it came down to this: the Canucks were charged with gross negligence, and I was awarded the highest punitive damages ever given in B.C.

Nothing at the trial came out in the Canucks' favour. It's history now, and the people that were there in Vancouver are all gone now. It was a long battle, a lonely battle. It was my wife, Isabel, and me and my lawyer against them. That was it.

The Vancouver players were in a difficult position, perhaps jeopardizing their careers if they supported me as character witnesses.

The whole thing started in New York during the 1976–77 season. I hit Nick Fotiu of the Rangers—a big, strong guy—and I went down. My spinal cord, I was told later, became slightly pinched in the spinal canal. I didn't have any feelings in my arms or legs for a few seconds, which was scary, but the feelings came back very quickly, I'd say after about half a minute. By then they had carried me into the Vancouver dressing room. They told me, "There's nothing wrong, Mike. You'll be fine." The New York doctor patted me down like he was searching for a gun.

They said I was fine even though I'd been complaining about a sore neck and radiating pain down my arm even before the game started. They ignored me. They said it was all psychosomatic, that it was in my head. The Canucks were in the middle of a heavy schedule, and I was needed. I was on the ice a lot, and it was important that I played. So I played in that game against the Rangers, and after the Fotiu check I knew something was seriously wrong.

The trainers and doctors said they'd get somebody to look at me before the next game. But nobody ever looked at me. I was complaining to everyone who would listen to me. Every time I swallowed I had this radiating pain go down my neck and down my back and my shoulder blade, and it would stop at my elbow. But they shrugged. They ignored it.

I went out and played another game. We were back home by then, and I still hadn't had a real checkup. It was nothing but a probe here and there and a few rah-rah words.

They took my medical issues into their own hands, and it turned out they were totally wrong. We played Minnesota and I hit someone coming across the blueline and I went down hard. I had this shocking pain go through my chest and legs, and it lasted for about a minute and a half. Then the team doctor decided he'd better check me out.

They took me into the dressing room. They didn't let me lay down. They propped me up in my stall like they were hanging somebody on a coat hook. My arms and legs were just gone. In fact, when they were getting me off the ice, a camera followed the action. They had it focussed on my legs, and one leg was jerking involuntarily. It was almost comical, because my leg was flying all over the place. The doctor was supposed to come in and check me out after the game. He came in and looked at me. He gave me a disgusted look, talked to the trainer while I just sat there, feeling nauseous. My legs were sensitive to touch and I felt rotten. Finally, he turned on his heel and walked away.

It was said that I was letting the team down, that I was letting my family down, and if I didn't play I'd be sent to the minors.

General manager Phil Maloney was quoted in the Vancouver papers; "I don't know what's wrong with him. But he better start playing. I'll have a talk with him."

Eventually, we wound up in court, and something very interesting came out at the trial. They tried to knock down my character. Their attorney asked me at one point, "How's your eyesight?" I said it was fine. He asked me if I could read a sign outside the window. So I read the sign. He said, "Are you sure you have good eyesight? Are you sure it was this doctor who saw you in the dressing room?" I said I was positive. No doubt about it.

Well, the team doctor takes the stand and hands over this document stating he wasn't even at the game on the night in question. He claimed he was at a meeting with seven or eight other people and the meeting was not over until 10:30. Now we're in trouble, right? Some people called me a lying little prick. But I knew he was there. So at the end of the day the little clerk in the courtroom called us over and he said, "Something's not right here. I'm looking at the bottom of this document and it looks like it's been tampered with." So they had the big X-ray machine there that was used to show X-rays of my spine. They put the document in this machine and it showed that he'd clumsily used whiteout to cover up the original time with another. Well, that's when the judge threw his pencil in the air in disgust. It was just one of the many things they were caught doing.

As for the physical problems I had, the spinal cord was pinched on three different occasions. If they had checked me out early, they would have found out then that I had a critically narrow spinal canal, which I have to this day. If I just jerk my head I get this shocking sensation that goes right through me. It's enough to make me nauseous and want to go home.

As for monetary damages, when you lose the appeal, as the Canucks did, it means the costs are almost doubled. So it amounted to something like $600,000. But I have to be careful the rest of my life. I'm supposed to wear a neck collar, and when I drive, any whiplash or anything like that could put me in a lot of trouble.

When I was in the hospital in Vancouver, I took some neurological tests, and one of the tests was to run a feather down your finger. I couldn't take the feather being run over my hands.

All the time I was in hospital, only one teammate came and visited me. Dennis Kearns. He brought me a jug of Crown Royal. Not a single person from the Canucks front office came around. Not one of them even mentioned there was anything wrong with me. I felt totally ostracized. I had more get-well cards from the owners of the Buffalo Sabres than from anybody else. The media was told I might be having a nervous breakdown, so leave Mike alone.

I'm gonna tell you, I've got a lot of things to say about Alan Eagleson, the biggest disappointment in my whole life. I can understand the Vancouver players not coming around, not wanting to put their jobs in jeopardy or anything. But when I needed character witnesses, Jim Schoenfeld came out, Jerry Korab offered to come out, and Syl Apps and Ab DeMarco. They wanted to say, "Hey, Mike Robitaille played hard, he hit hard, he tried the best he could." I was 27 years old then, and I figured I had four or five years more to play.

But let's go back to that night in the dressing room. That wasn't my last game with Vancouver. They insisted it was all in my head. It took maybe a half hour to regain use of my legs that night, and I guess they figured I was all right. Now here's where you might want to put some of the blame on Robitaille. You might say, "Well, if he's stupid enough to come back after that, well . . ." But you have to realize I did everything but beg for help. I couldn't grab the doctor by the throat, put him in a hammerlock, throw him to the floor and say, "Now please check me out."

So I played the next game, and I came out of the penalty box and had a breakaway. At that point I could hardly swallow and my arm was acting up, but I figured I could be smart like Tim Horton and play rocking-chair hockey. Be coy and use all the tricks. But how can I do that when I'm on a breakaway? The crowd is screaming, and I'm excited because I've had about eight goals in my whole career and now I've got a chance to score another. But the crowd was screaming "Look out!" because Dennis Owchar was making a big U-turn in front of me and I couldn't see him. He came up and smacked me dead-on and I went down. My face was bloody and I thought I was going to die. I felt a tremendous surge of electrical energy go through me and I thought I was finished. Just *whoosh* and everything went dead. I remember looking up and my teammates were there. Patty Dunn, the trainer, was there. But nobody seemed to be doing anything. So I saw Don Awrey of the Penguins standing there and I pleaded, "Please help me, Donny. Help me. Do something for me." Imagine pleading with an opposing player for help.

I guess I was like a fish because my arms were flailing, and finally they went for a stretcher. Somebody picked me up by the ass of the pants and they started dragging me off the ice. God knows how much more damage they did to me at that point. Patty Dunn is yelling to Chris Oddleifson, "Don't drag his skates. Hold them straight."

When I got near the boards I started going down again. All of a sudden I go loose. They yank me back up, and now they get the stretcher. But they leave it on the other side of the boards. I've got Dunn on one side, Oddleifson on the other, and they try to negotiate me through the gate, which is very narrow. They try to put me down and I scream. They yank me back up. They try another way, then another. Finally, they lay half of me on the stretcher and wheelbarrow me off. By then my spinal cord is red hot. I've lost use of my arms and legs. They're just dragging me along.

By this time Isabel, my wife, comes down. She was pregnant at the time. She'd been in the restroom and missed the collision on the ice. She walked up and waited while Dr. Piper was checking my arms and legs, picking them up and dropping them down. I was a smoker then, and I couldn't even hold a cigarette. He came out and gave her this prescription: "Take him home and give him a good shot of Courvoisier.

He'll be fine in the morning." I never played hockey again, and I didn't walk properly for almost a year.

You know, there was an old doctor there—Dr. Brewster. He was a team doctor for teams out there for years. He was with the team the first year, but they let him go. Perhaps he was giving the players too much care. I guess they felt he should have been urging them to play even when they were injured.

Well, old Dr. Brewster came in the room that night and checked me out. We were all alone in there. And when the trainer came in, he told him, "Get this man to the hospital. He's got major problems. Get him in an ambulance right now."

But nobody listened. I guess they were told not to listen to Dr. Brewster any more.

Later, the poor trainer took the brunt of the blame for my condition while the official team doctor came down with amnesia. Later, he would deny he said anything to Isabel about Courvoisier. In fact, he denied he was even at the game that night. People saw him there, talked to him there.

From there, I went into a rehab facility and into the sandbox. The team doctor had convinced other doctors that it was psychosomatic. He actually tapped me a little bit with his hammer and didn't think it was serious. Finally, the head neurological doctor came in and made three or four tests with me and told the other doctors, "Get your ass back in there and check him out again. There's some serious damage there."

The sandbox, by the way, is just that, a sandbox. I was 27 years old, strong and virile and ready to play another four or five years. Think of it. Now I'm in this sandbox. They're putting these pennies in the sand. I could run my hand underneath and try to get these pennies in my hand. What a demoralizing thing it is. I'd sit there and cry. Then they'd throw a beach ball at me. This little guy would toss a beach ball at my face. And it kept bouncing off my face because I couldn't get my hands up.

So I finally got my legs together. Not good, still sloppy as hell, but I came back. If I didn't come back, they said they'd suspend me.

They tried to peddle me off to Joe Crozier in the WHA. Joe was delighted. He was all excited about getting me, and he called me. So I told him, "Hold on, Joe. I can't even play." And I told him the story.

Joe said, "Why that son of a bitch Maloney. That's the second time he's done that."

I finally go down to the rink about a month and a half later, but the big freeze is on. Nobody is to talk to Mike, and I'm getting the silent treatment. Players are looking the other way.

If there was anybody I admired in hockey at that time, it was assistant coach Larry Popein. He was a traditionalist. He was my first coach in pro hockey. We won the championship together. He went catapulting up to pro hockey and so did I. We became separated and suddenly we're back in Vancouver, together again. And I used to stick up for him all the time. The other players hated his guts. I'd say, "Guys, that's his way. Leave him alone. He's from the old school and that's the way it's going to be. You better learn to live with it."

So I called him. Can you imagine how desperately I needed someone to talk to, for a little bit of attention? Other than Isabel, I didn't have any family to come and see me in the hospital. So I really needed a kind word from Popein. But nothing.

He wouldn't say much of anything. Finally I said, "Larry, where can I get my cheques? They haven't mailed them to my wife. Nobody's called my wife to tell her to come and pick them up. So what's happening?"

And he said, "We just have cheques for guys who want to play this game." That's how it came out.

I said, "Oh, geez, Larry, don't be like the rest. If there's one person I need, it's you. Don't be like the rest."

He said, "That's the way it's gotta be. If you want your cheques, see Phil Maloney."

So I chased Maloney around and he calls me in and says, "You're a fucking con artist. You're letting the fans down and letting your team-mates down. You're letting your coach down."

But the Canucks had a new coach. Orland Kurtenbach had just taken over as coach and didn't know what was going on. I'd played with Kurt on the old New York Ranger team and I had a lot of admiration for him. He was almost a surrogate father to me. I was in awe of him.

Kurt calls me in and says, "Mike, can you give it a try on the ice?"

I said, "Kurt, I can't. My legs will not respond. I take a stride and I fall down. Phil watches me and he thinks I'm trying to fool him."

He said, "Lookit, you're going to have to play in pain sometime. For me, can you just give it a try?"

I felt sorry for Kurt. He was stuck in a situation where he didn't know what was going on. He was getting the same stuff the Canucks were feeding my teammates, all this shit. It was all around the NHL about me, and he was getting the same stuff.

So I went out and I tried it. I put my equipment on and it was one of the saddest moments of my life, totally demoralizing. They lined us up across the ice and we're going down on sprints. I want to skate but I can't skate. I try and I fall down. I get back up and do it again and I fall down. When I fall down the third time he says, "Okay, that's enough." That was the last time I was on skates. Finally, they sent me to see a doctor outside of the hockey club. The frustration and the anger was so great by that time, I didn't know who to turn to, who to talk to. I couldn't go to the club. Poor Isabel was pregnant and she lost the last baby. It's touch and go whether she's going to have this one. So I go to see the other doctor, Dr. Hunt. This is about three, five months later.

One employee of the hockey club—Greg Douglas, in public relations—had enough empathy for me to call and say, "Mike, get a lawyer. I've liked you and I don't want to see anything happen to you or your wife. And be careful."

So I see Dr. Hunt. He checks me out. He hits my leg, and boom, it just exploded.

He says, "Well, you're not skating now, are you?"

I say, "Yeah, I am. I have to or they're going to suspend me. What I do is put my equipment on and skate a bit, fall down three or four times. This means I can say I was there and tried and they can't suspend me."

He said, "I can't stress the importance of not getting hurt. No more skating. I don't know if you realize it or not, but I don't think you'll ever play hockey again. Your spine is red hot, and if you fall the wrong way you could be in a wheelchair forever."

It never dawned on me I'd never play again. *It never dawned on me.* I thought I'd get over this and I'd be back to playing again.

I'd been called a con artist so often, I almost felt relieved. At that point, when he told me my career might be over, I wanted to grab a piece of paper—the doctor's report—and throw it in Maloney's face and say, "Here, look at this. Am I still a con artist?"

So we decided to take the Canucks to court. My friend Bruce McColl, a fine lawyer, made it happen. And in a court of law, their people got caught lying left and right. It was pitiful. In court, their testimony was incredible. Lies and more lies. And between sessions, I found myself reflecting on my career.

●

I think I've lived an interesting life when you consider I came out of Midland, Ontario, from a family of 11. I left to play junior hockey in Kitchener at age 14. I was scared and lonely—like Bobby Orr must have been, playing in Oshawa at that age. And how I lived with a kid 17 years old, sleeping in a double bed with a guy who'd been convicted of car theft twice. We were living in behind a furnace, we didn't even have a room. I hadn't even had my first piece of ass, and he's banging these teenage girls every night.

I've been around long enough and I know all the horror stories. It's not my nature to go around beating my chest and spread what I'm telling you. It's the worst story I've ever heard in my life. And it happened to me. And we're talking about five per cent of what's happened. There's lots I haven't even brought up yet. But it's all in the court records. It's unbelievable.

Another thing. You leave home at 14 or 15. You have some people around you saying, "Michael, you're nothing but a big, fat pogie. You're leaving home and you're going to fail. Nobody ever makes it in hockey. One in a million, maybe."

Well, I wanted to be that one.

We had some great minor teams in Midland and some great players. I played with Bobby Clayton, who was a better player than I was. He could have made the NHL, but he decided to become a lawyer.

Reverend [Len] Self, who started minor hockey in Midland, was an icon. I played for a lot of coaches in professional hockey for 10 years, but the greatest coach I ever had was Garnet Armstrong in Midland. He taught me more about the game than anyone else.

In Midland, my idol was a senior player. Ron Hurst had played with the Leafs and he was a star in senior hockey. He took some interest in me. Gave me a stick and a puck and some tape. Little things to him, but huge to me. I reconnected with him recently and we're going to meet soon.

I lived hockey. When I wasn't at the arena, I'd play on the road at lunchtime. After school I'd play on an outdoor rink down on Manly Street. I'd go home for supper wearing my skates, and my mother would put a piece of cardboard underneath the kitchen table. Then I'd go right back out and play until one of my parents came for me.

I grew up playing minor hockey against Bobby Orr. He and I would have our own personal battles when Parry Sound played Midland. And there I was, years later, in the NHL, playing against him.

The only way I knew how to get attention and love, which is so important at that age, is to play great hockey. The better I played, the more attention and love I got. Which is exactly what happened. When I was 18 and 19 years old and was voted the best defenseman in the OHL, which is really like being the best junior defenseman in Canada, then it was great. They were around me, hugging me and kissing me and saying, "You're our Michael."

●

All too soon, after my career-ending injury, the pro life was over.

When you're injured like I was, it's tough getting back on your feet, emotionally as well as physically. Valium? Team doctors gave me so much Valium it was incredible. It was by the handful and the vialful. I was getting these tremendous anxiety attacks while I was playing. You know, tremendous pains in my chest, or a panic attack. It really scared me. The only way I could control them was through the Valium. You'd think once in seven years, at least one doctor would have enough sense to say, "Obviously, there's something wrong here. Go talk to a therapist. He'll explain to you that nobody dies from an anxiety attack. The worse that'll happen is you'll pass out."

But I needed that assurance. I was in the dark all the time. I'd say, "Shit, I'm having one of these attacks and I can't get out of this plane. I can't get home."

Agoraphobia. Another big problem I had to deal with. Not so much before my injuries but after. And it's a prevalent problem with a lot of people right now. I went into the hospital and it was like in one of those movies, the guy kicking the walls and all that. I did all that getting off the Valium. And I got off it. It took about a year and a half before I didn't have that aching desire for it. It's gone away now. I take it as needed, for a long plane trip or maybe before I go on TV or something like that. I just take a small amount.

Here's where I'm sitting right now. The money I got from the suit, I've invested so I can live off that. Not great, but I can live a nice life. My two kids are well taken care of. Physically I'm not able to get up at seven o'clock and work all day. My right leg will shake and my hands will close up. I can't take a lot of stress.

So the radio and TV business, which came my way back in Buffalo, is tailor-made for me. There aren't too many doors open to me right now. This is one, and that's why I'm working so damn hard at it. I look forward to getting up in the morning and setting out to accomplish something. It's important to bring home a cheque. It's tough for a man not to be able to bring home a paycheque. I want to relate to the players.

●

I'll say more now about Alan Eagleson. I never heard from the man for two and a half or three years while I was in that awful situation. I left phone messages and he wouldn't return them. He was listening to guys on the team who were feeding him the same garbage they were getting from management. There are no words to describe the kind of man Al Eagleson was. He was a horrible, calculating human being back then. Eagleson's arrogance was beyond belief. I can still see him sitting there, a wry, smug look on his face. He was so high-handed—this guy who was supposed to be working for you.

Finally, he flies all the way out to Vancouver and he says, "I can give you half an hour." He says, "If it was anyone else but Mike Robitaille, we would support him."

My lawyer says the most useless union he has ever seen would have given me more support than the NHL Players' Association.

Eagleson gets on the phone and calls Joe Blow, and the guys get all excited. The guys start tap dancing. "Oh boy, Al's calling me on the phoone. Al's callin' me on the phone. Al's takin' us out to dinner. Oh, he's comin' in to town."

He could have made a few calls for me, but he didn't. He says, "Call Chris Oddleifson. He's the Vancouver player rep." I called Chris and a woman answers the phone and says he's not home, but she'll give him the message. He never called back.

I got a lot of stuff like that, from a lot of guys. Maybe they just didn't like me. I was kind of a loner anyway. I never really hung around with the guys, and that may be it. That's all right. But give me an answer.

I got along quite well with Oddleifson. He was a pretty intelligent guy and I enjoyed his company, compared to some of the rest. Their whole life was drinking, screwing and skating. And then they take their head out of the ground when they're 30 years old and there's nobody there. You pay for your own dinners and stand in line for the show like everybody else. It's very real all of a sudden.

After much talking with my attorney and Eagleson, they started working a bit together. He was some help. I guess he was so embarrassed, he had to do something. He showed up in Vancouver and he gave us 45 minutes. He said, "Then I'll have to go." Forty-five minutes and it's the biggest issue of my life. This is what I pay the son of a bitch my dues for. This is what I want him for.

Maybe it goes back many years, when Walt Tkaczuk and I turned pro together. Neither one of us went to him. He wanted us to. But there was just something about him. My agent when I signed my last contract was one of my closest friends. His name is Ken Kauffman, brother of Bobby Kauffman, who used to play for the Buffalo Braves. A tremendous family. There was really nothing he could do.

Bruce McColl took everything over for me, and he just ran with the ball. He really did a job. This whole thing wouldn't have happened if it wasn't for my wife and Bruce McColl.

Now here's something. What do you think my wife went through? It was like, I'll pick you up today, you pick me up tomorrow. Now I've got this agoraphobia, I can't even deal with it. I guess it was one of the reactions to this whole ordeal. Brian, I couldn't get out of my room. I was 28 years old and it's not right. I used to sit in my room and cry all day. I tried to walk down to the mailbox, and I couldn't. I'd take four or five steps and I'd have to go back to the house and hug Isabel. This went on and on, and finally I was able to overcome it. It was the toughest thing in my life, not being able to walk again but getting over this damn agoraphobia. It was unbelievable what my wife went through. She never wavered, except for the times when she just had to let off steam.

When I look back on that time when I got hurt, I remember not being able to swallow. It turned out that I had a broken neck. And what some team spokesmen were saying to the media, like: If he doesn't play, we're going to get rid of him. He's letting everybody down. We're really disappointed in him. We don't know what the problem is. That sort of thing. But they knew what the problem was.

I started out with no education to speak of, and yet I won the best defenseman award in Canada for junior hockey, made the all star team, turned pro and helped win two championships in one year, the Central League title and the American League title.

When I joined the Rangers, they compared me to Brad Park, but I broke my ankle in training camp. What a disappointment.

The following season, when I was a rookie in New York, I didn't play one night, and a young kid came up to me and asked for my autograph. Well, remember how as kids we collected all those hockey cards, the Bee Hives, and all the corn syrup our mothers bought so we could get cards, and how we idolized the players pictured on those cards. This kid in New York hands me a card with my photo on it. My photo! It was one of the biggest thrills I'd ever had in my life. I'm 19 years old and I had my own hockey card. It never dawned on me I'd have a card. I stared at it while the kid waited. I signed it for him and then I turned it over. And on the back, there was a little caricature of me skating down the ice—with a microphone in my hand. And the blurb read, "Someday Mike would like to be a hockey broadcaster." I think of that first card I ever saw and I think of the 33 years I spent in broadcasting and I shake my head. Holy shit!

In 1971, I was traded to the Detroit Red Wings as part of a five-player deal and later I was acquired by the Buffalo Sabres.

In Buffalo I was a regular and I met Tim Horton, the greatest guy I ever met in hockey. I never admired anyone as much as him, and when he died in a car accident [in February 1974] I was devastated.

By 1974–75, I was in my fourth year with the club. I'd settled in and was feeling good. The Sabres were young and talented, destined for success. Then, shortly after the beginning of the season, general manager Punch Imlach dealt me and Gerry Meehan to Vancouver for Bryan McSheffrey and Jocelyn Guevremont.

Personally, it was one of the unhappiest times of my life. When I was in Vancouver I missed Buffalo.

It was in January 1977 when I began feeling like somebody was banging away at my shoulder and elbow with a ball-peen hammer. X-rays revealed I'd suffered a hairline fracture of the neck, and spinal cord contusion.

But I kept on playing.

I remember taking that ferocious hit from Ranger Nick Fotiu in New York and then during a home game on February 19, there was the blind side hit by Owchar. And that was it. Career over and not yet 30.

But the Canucks didn't think I was finished. When I didn't feel well enough to report to Vancouver's training camp the following autumn, the club threatened me with a breach-of-contract suit. That's when we decided to countersue. The case went all the way to the British Columbia Supreme Court and was finally decided in our favour.

I spent nine years in the NHL, 33 years in broadcasting, and the only black mark I can think of was the situation in Vancouver. I don't talk about it much—well, I'm talking to you about it—but I don't dwell on it anymore. I choose not to carry that hurt around with me. I'm not going to let it ruin my life. Isabel and I have taken that little segment and put it away somewhere.

Still, I think it's really, really important—and I must emphasize this—to have the younger players coming along understand that bad stuff like this can happen.

●

After Vancouver, I came back to Buffalo and tried to settle down, tried to find some work. Tried to reinvent myself. And we waited for the court case to be settled. Would we win or lose? We had nothing left.

The money in the bank—about $130,000 after almost 10 years in the league—was gone. I took a job as a bartender and found myself serving drinks to some of the Sabres, guys I once played with. Talk about demoralizing, try that. They'd leave generous tips on the bar for me, and I'd have a big lump in my throat. The kids would sit at the kitchen table the next morning and count the tips. We were looking for coupons, and the kids were drinking powdered milk.

Then came the call. We'd won the case and the judge had been furious with the Canucks, who made it clear they'd appeal. "Not on Robitaille's dime," he told them. "I'm awarding him"—I think it was $470,000.

I could have hugged him. As for the appeal, the Canucks lost again. In fact, that judge added about $70,000 to the settlement. We were able to pay all our bills and start all over.

Isabel opened a real estate business, which is still thriving. I don't get involved much in that business, because she doesn't like or need any "coaching."

I was in Buffalo and gone from the game when Ted Darling asked me if I'd come on the first intermission of a telecast with him one day. I said sure and I prepared myself thoroughly, thinking of what he'd ask and how I'd reply. Well, he was impressed and asked me to come back in the second intermission, which I did. Not long after, I got a call. Would I consider doing colour commentary on the broadcasts? I said, "Well, sure," and I was almost jumping out of my skin. I wound up doing TV and radio with Rick Jeanneret and Darling for the next 15 years. Both are media Hall of Famers.

Maybe I was too much a nonconformist, maybe I was a little too harsh when things went wrong on the ice, maybe, like you with Ballard, I didn't give them enough home cooking. I guess I antagonized some of the owners. Anyway, I was fired.

Then John Rigas came along and bought the team. And he said, "What's going on? I love this guy Robitaille. Go get him. My wife and I love him. Get him back."

Rigas owned a local radio and TV station [Empire Sports], and we started a show called *Hockey Hotline*. Boom! We had great ratings, and sometimes we had better ratings than the team telecasts. That gig lasted a lot of years. At first I think the players disliked me, but as they grew older they liked my work. Things change when you grow up.

Every year, Mr. Rigas would tell me, "Michael, just keep on doing what you're doing, because you're doing it well. But promise me this: If you tell something with real bite to it, something really controversial, make sure you're correct. Check and check again. If you're not right, then I'm not going to be happy." The Rigas attitude and approach was incredible.

Let's leave Mike for a moment and explore the John Rigas story. He was a World War II vet and CEO of Adelphia, the fifth-largest cable company in the U.S.

On March 27, 2002, a single question brought down his billion-dollar business empire.

No one saw it coming: not the executives at Adelphia, not the independent auditors, not the corporate lawyers, not even the man who asked the question.

At the windup of Adelphia's quarterly conference call with investors, a man named Oren Cohen asked, "What about this $2.3 billion in off-balance-sheet debt I see listed here in a footnote?"

John Rigas and his three sons owned private companies managed by the public one—an extremely complicated arrangement. Major banks had offered billions in loans that either side could draw upon. The footnote revealed that the Rigas family had taken out $2.3 billion in loans that Adelphia could be responsible for paying. Cohen wanted to know what assets the Rigas family had to back that up. What assurance could the Rigases give that Adelphia would not have to bail them out?

Cohen was familiar with the intermingling of public and private businesses, but he had no idea his question was such a bombshell, one that would lead to devastating results.

Adelphia's chief financial officer—a man named Brown—and John's middle son, Tim Rigas, stammered out a response. They said they'd get back to Cohen.

Then there was silence from the Rigas group for weeks, but there were rumours and suspicions. The company's stock began to plunge. By May, the Rigases had resigned.

In June, independent directors of the board were accusing them of fraud and preparing to take the company into bankruptcy.

In July, John Rigas, 77 years old at the time, was charged with conspiracy and fraud. Two years later, he and Tim were convicted in federal court in Manhattan.

Did any major bankers testify at the trial? No.

Was evidence introduced indicating that the bankers were fully—or almost fully—aware of what had been going on? Yes.

No auditors testified. No company lawyers. Strange.

The star witness was Brown, Adelphia's former director of finance, who admitted to orchestrating much of the alleged fraud. More than a decade later, he remains free. Even stranger.

John and Tim Rigas, now serving 17- and 12-year sentences, respectively, at Allenwood minimum security penitentiary, have never admitted any wrongdoing.

My letter to John Rigas asking him to comment on Mike Robitaille went unanswered.

The Rigas attorney, Larry McMichael, continues to fight in federal court for their release. He calls what happened "overzealous prosecution." McMichael points at the sentence of defrocked Philadelphia priest Edward Avery: "He gets two and a half years in jail for raping a 10-year-old," McMichael said, "while John Rigas is sitting in jail for what amounts to a life sentence because he got bad advice from accountants and lawyers. The Bush administration found a great opportunity to prove they were tough on crime by treating the Rigas father and son like war criminals."

Auditors, lawyers and independent board members—all of whom said the 2002 Adelphia audit was "the best ever" before Oren Cohen spoke up at the conference call—suddenly decided to back off, their tongues firmly tied.

"When the government makes it impossible for people to defend themselves, convictions become a self-fulfilling prophesy," said McMichael.

After the trial, all but two of the family's private cable systems were surrendered to the government and sold. The remaining two served about 4,000 people in three small towns in the northern tier.

In the past decade, two other Rigas sons, James and Michael, have built a new company with 35,000 subscribers in 12 states.

Some of the company's profits go to the lawyers.

Even if John and Tim Rigas were guilty of fraud, haven't they served enough time? Shouldn't their sentences be commuted? Their prison terms were harsh, considering that few corporate executives have received jail time for fraud charges (Harold Ballard served a year, Bruce McNall five years), and none of the executives at Bank of America or JPMorgan have faced criminal charges from the bank frauds that sent the U.S. economy into a tailspin in 2008.

And why hasn't Brown, the Adelphia financial officer, the man who admitted he orchestrated much of the chicanery, never served a day?

Just asking.

Back to Mike.

Honest to God, Mr. Rigas was unbelievable. First, he paid me more than I was worth. Paid me like all hockey broadcasters would like to be paid. And every year, he'd tell me, "Michael, you're doing great. And if those little brats down in the dressing room get upset about what you say, I'll have Darcy [Regier] straighten them out."

Yeah, he was every broadcaster's dream.

So *Hockey Hotline* lasted a lot of years, and then I went back to doing Sabres games for another 10 years, and 33 years later, it was time to say goodbye. Actually, I stayed on a couple of years more than I intended because it was so enjoyable.

During my final game, the team held a "night" for me, and it was a surprise. I thought it meant they were going to have me on during an intermission and look back, and I'd have a minute or two at the end of the game to say my goodbyes. But it turned out to be more than that.

My family and friends—there must have 50 to 60 people came in from out of town for my last game—well, I never expected that. When I got to the game, they brought me down to centre ice and they said some very nice things about me. It was a humbling experience. They gave me a beautiful watch—a Rolex. And there was a big party after the game. All the guys and gals I'd worked with, the cameramen, everybody showed up. And it makes me so grateful for what I've had. I can't believe what I have. And that I got it—and how I got it, with so little education. And so many hurdles to overcome. As for the Rolex, I turned it in for the women's model because I felt Isabel deserved it more than I did.

As for my injuries in Vancouver, I was kind of a walking time bomb for about 40 years. The docs all told me that a slip on the ice, a stranger triggers a fight in a bar—and it could be all over for me.

Wouldn't you know? In Buffalo, there was a car accident.

I'm driving to a game against Boston, and I stop at a light. And there in my rear-view mirror is a guy zipping along, and he's coming fast. And I'm saying, "Is this guy going to stop?" And he didn't stop. He ploughed right into me while he's got the phone up to his ear and a cigarette in the other hand. And when he hit me, all those old feelings came back. My nose was itchy and I went to scratch it and I couldn't move my arm. The pain shot across my chest. Well, they got me out of the car—through the window. In the hospital the next day, a doctor showed me the X-rays and he said, "You don't have a drop of spinal fluid in your neck. We should operate. Why haven't you had this done years ago?"

And I said, "Doc, I have a phobia, a real fear of going under."

Well, he took care of that, and I was operated on and in intensive care for six days. The surgeon did a lot of delicate work on my spine and inserted titanium rods and screws and I got wonderful care. It took me about two and a half years to fully recover.

So that's it.

Give me a final word or two and I'll say this. My wife Isabel has been incredible. We've been together since junior hockey—45 years now— and on Saturday mornings we spend a lot of time talking things over. We've thrown all the bad things into the back seat. And last Saturday, after 45 years as a team, I told her, "Isabel, I think I'm falling in love with you all over again."

ACE BAILEY
The Career-Ending Hit
That Almost Killed Him

At some time during my travels along the hockey highway, probably during the early 1980s, I became a friend of Irvine "Ace" Bailey, one of the few Toronto players to win the NHL scoring title, a feat he accomplished in 1928–29. In 44 games that season, he tallied 22 goals and 10 assists for a league-leading 32 points. Puny numbers by today's standards. But look at Ottawa's Cy Denneny. In 1923–24, he led all NHL scorers with a mere 23 points—22 goals and a single assist. How about Joe Malone? In the NHL's first season, 1917–18, he won the scoring crown with 44 goals and no assists—the only season helpers were totally ignored.

Bailey was the first Leaf to lead the NHL in scoring, although Babe Dye won two titles when the Toronto team was known as St. Pats. The last Leaf player to win it was Gord Drillon who tallied 52 points in 1938.

Ace Bailey was 87 years old and proud of his sound memory when I went to visit him one day in 1990. He lived close by, in a seniors' home and was obviously quite popular with many of the white-haired widows who resided there—and their grandsons. In the cafeteria, they flocked around him, so much so that we retreated to a place where we could talk without interruption. But not before he signed a couple of photos of himself posing in a 1930s Leaf uniform—one of them for me.

"The photos are all I have left," he says. "I'm always amazed when someone asks for one."

"I kept 164 scrapbooks. I donated them to the Hockey Hall of Fame. My obituary is in one of them. It appeared in all the papers—not in the '30s, when I was near death from a hockey injury, but in the early '60s. Somebody made a big mistake. You see, it was another Ace Bailey who died. But the newspapers and the radio said it was me who passed away. When I showed up at Maple Leaf Gardens that night, some people almost fainted in shock."

●

Maple Leaf Gardens was barely two years old when the classy Leaf forward suffered a tragic injury in the Boston Garden—a black day in the history of the NHL.

On December 12, 1933, a savage check delivered in anger—and from behind—by Bruin tough guy Eddie Shore ended Bailey's career and left him near death with a fractured skull. It remains one of hockey's greatest tragedies.

On that December night in Boston, the largest crowd of the new season howled for blood as they watched the Bruins and the Leafs pound each other from the opening whistle. Before long, there were two violent incidents, spaced seconds apart, leaving pools of blood on the ice. Many spectators turned away, sickened at the sight.

In the second period, Eddie Shore made one of his patented rushes and was tripped up by King Clancy inside the Toronto blueline. Clancy grabbed the puck from Shore and made a dash of his own toward the Boston zone. Meanwhile, Shore jumped to his feet, fire in his eye, and targeted the nearest Leaf for a return check. The innocent opponent was 30-year-old Ace Bailey, who had turned his back to Shore.

Frank Selke, Toronto's assistant general manager, was sitting in the front row of the press box. He wrote in his memoirs, "Shore arose and slowly started back for his end of the playing arena. He was behind [Red] Horner and Bailey. Whether he mistook Bailey for Clancy, or whether he was annoyed by everything in general, nobody will ever know. He struck

Bailey across the kidneys with his right shoulder and with such force that it upended Bailey in a backward somersault, while the powerful Shore kept right on going."

Bailey's head hit the ice with terrific force, fracturing his skull in two places. An awesome hush fell over the arena. Everyone realized immediately that Bailey, his body quivering, was very badly hurt. Clancy would say, "I had many battles with Shore, but I never thought he was a vicious player. He wasn't out there to maim anybody. But that night he hit Bailey as hard as he could. It was a shocking thing to see."

While doctors, trainers and players hovered over the inert Bailey, Toronto's Red Horner, a muscular, fearless defenseman, skated past his unconscious teammate, then made a beeline for Shore. Horner shook Shore by the shoulders, then poleaxed him with a right to the jaw. Shore collapsed to the ice, out cold. Blood flowed freely from a deep cut to his head and spread across the ice.

Bailey says, "I was told it took three men on each side of a stretcher to get me off the ice that night. And when we reached the exit at the end of the rink, a crowd had gathered, blocking our path. Leaf owner Conn Smythe worked feverishly to help get me through, but a fan blocked his path. The fan was half cut—he'd been drinking—and Smythe went right at him and—*smack!*—he socked him on the jaw. The crowd jumped back and we got through. But the police moved in and grabbed Smythe. They hauled him off to jail, and I think he spent most of the night there. In the morning a sympathetic judge let him go."

In the visiting team's dressing room, Bailey began convulsing. His head was packed in ice and then, barely conscious, he was rushed to a Boston hospital. "There was a doctor there—Dr. Munro—and he saved my life. He drilled two holes in my skull to relieve the pressure and to remove blood clots that had formed. They tell me he spent two or three hours working on me, getting those clots out. They came out in pieces, so it wasn't easy. When he was finished they gave him a good shot of brandy."

Two delicate brain operations in the next 10 days were necessary to assure that Bailey survived.

"Eddie Shore came around to see me," Ace recalls. "But the nurse on duty refused to let him in the door. She was afraid that it might get nasty, we might have words, I guess. But I think he came to apologize."

Even when the crisis passed, doctors were concerned about permanent damage to the brain that might result from such a severe concussion. The Leaf forward never played hockey again, but he made a satisfactory recovery and lived to the age of 88—a year after I talked with him.

Back in Toronto on the night of the incident, Bailey's father, having listened to Foster Hewitt's call of the game on the radio, grabbed a revolver and hopped a train to Boston. He fully intended to shoot Eddie Shore—if he could find him. But Smythe and Selke intercepted the elder Bailey. "It was in the hotel lobby," Ace says, "and my dad was packing a big .45. With enough bullets in it to kill Eddie Shore. Smythe found some security men and they all went up to Smythe's room for a drink. Smythe slipped some pills into my dad's glass and he fell asleep. They relieved him of his gun, the security men took him to the Canadian border and turned him over to the Ontario Provincial Police. By the time he woke up, he was back in Canada."

Shore's head wound required several stitches. He left for Bermuda a few days later, after learning that he'd been suspended for 16 games.

"I was all for suing somebody," Ace says, "but they talked me out of it. They told me a couple of benefit games were planned for me and that I'd get more money from them than from any lawsuit."

The Bruins announced that all the profits from a Boston–Montreal Maroons game on December 19 would go into a fund for Bailey. But a modest turnout at the gate produced little more than $7,800. Two months later in Toronto, a game between the Bruins and the Leafs brought the stricken star another $20,000.

"With the money we bought some land and built a house on it," Ace tells me. "You could do that for $7,800 in those days. And the rest of it went into a trust account, and we got a cheque from that every month for years."

During the pre-game ceremonies at the benefit game in Toronto, Bailey received a standing ovation. After the crowd quieted, Eddie Shore skated up to Bailey and offered his hand. Bailey smiled and took it. His firm handshake convinced the crowd he held no grudge against his adversary. Shore was forgiven. Ace recalls Shore saying, "It's good to shake your hand, Ace," and adding something jokingly, like, "'If I grab your hand you can't punch the shit out of me.' He said something like that. No, I never held a grudge."

The Toronto fans roared at this display of sportsmanship. "We gave Shore a dark blue Maple Leaf jacket. He probably never wore it. Anyway, I appreciated the ovation. Before the game, we had dinner down at the King Eddie Hotel, and I remember the Coca Cola being a little stiff."

He chuckles at the thought. And he grins when I ask him to talk about his hockey beginnings.

I used to play street hockey up north in Bracebridge with wooden pucks made out of oak. My father made them for me. When I was a teenager, I moved to Mimico to play lacrosse. I was really good at both sports. I played junior hockey for the Marlboros when the team was managed by Frank Selke. I had many offers to play senior hockey but chose to play in Peterborough.

Later, in Toronto, I joined St. Pats, the NHL team before they became the Leafs. We played in the Mutual Street Arena. Conn Smythe and some others bought the team and renamed it the Leafs. They paid $225,000 for the franchise. Today the Leafs would cost you many, many millions.

We wore the green-and-whites until we wore the blue-and-whites, in '34. Then Smythe took a big gamble. He got King Clancy from Ottawa . . . a smallish defenseman. Weighed about 140 pounds, but what a competitor.

I remember Billy Taylor as a little kid. He skated between periods at Leaf games, and the crowd loved him. He had lots of talent and later became a big star in junior hockey with the Oshawa Generals. After he made the NHL, he and Don Gallinger got themselves in serious trouble by gambling on games. That was during the '40s, and NHL president Campbell investigated and banned them both from hockey for life. For life, mind you. That was a huge story. Players often gambled on games in that era but after Taylor and Gallinger were banned they thought twice about it. Smythe was always a canny operator. I remember when Hap Day and I signed with the Leafs, the contracts stated the club would provide the player with a complete uniform—after the player put down a $30 deposit, said deposit to be returned to the player at the end of the season. Can you imagine a manager in today's hockey asking a top draft choice to kick in 30 bucks before he was issued a uniform? They'd think you were nuts. Getting that deposit back was important. It didn't give us much chance to sneak off with a game jersey at the end of the year.

Myself and the other Leafs felt very pleased and proud on opening night at the Gardens in 1931. We wondered if Smythe would ever find enough fans to fill the place. Well, he did, and it's been filled every night since then. That's amazing.

After my hockey career ended, Smythe got me a job coaching at the University of Toronto. Some of my players there went on to become doctors, lawyers, and one is on the Supreme Court of Canada. We won three university championships. After that I worked for a brewery and we moved to Welland, then on to Niagara Falls. When I moved back to Toronto, I worked as a penalty timekeeper for 47 years at the Gardens—most of them for Harold Ballard. And not even a thank you on the day he cut me out. Never spoke to him again.

My favourite players have always included Hap Day, the Leaf captain the eight years I was there. He was our leader along with Clancy.

We'd play the Montreal Maroons on Tuesdays at the Forum and stay over for a Thursday game with the Canadiens. There was always a big party Wednesday night. Hap Day would be there, but he never took a drink, since his father killed himself drinking. Clancy promised his mother he wouldn't ever take a drink and he didn't. But he often looked and acted like he was into the sauce.

Howie Morenz was the best of the Canadiens. A wonderful player. And fast! You couldn't skate with him unless you picked him up in his end. My, he was smart. Like me, a serious injury ended his career far too soon. He broke his leg, and not long after he died in hospital. I would have died too if it hadn't been for Dr. Munro. The Habs had Georges Vezina in goal. They called him the Chicoutimi Cucumber because he was so cool between the posts. A hard man to beat.

We played jokes on each other. I remember our goalie pulled a prank on us, and when he came out of the shower, he found his shoes nailed to the floor. And you had to watch Charlie Conacher. He liked to snip your tie off, just below the knot. Charlie was strong. He once dangled a teammate out of a hotel window in New York for some reason, holding him by the ankles. The player was terrified, so Charlie hauled him back in. Smythe wasn't too pleased when he heard about some of our antics, so we stopped.

I remember negotiating my own contract with Smythe for $8,500 when the limit on salaries was $9,000. I remember the organist in the

Chicago Stadium playing "Three Blind Mice" whenever referee Bill Chadwick came on the ice. One night Chadwick jumped the boards. He wanted to crucify the organist, but he couldn't climb up to the organ loft. Not with his skates on. I was talking to Milt Schmidt up in Nobleton, and he asked me to name the best bodychecker in hockey. I said "Black Jack" Stewart, he wasn't so bad. When I told Milt I remembered the time he bodychecked Leaf captain Syl Apps into the goalpost and broke his leg, he said, "You s.o.b., don't ever remind me of that."

Somewhere along the way they retired my jersey, number 6. It was the first NHL number ever to be retired. When Ron Ellis was an up-and-coming star with the Leafs, I asked them to let him wear number 6, and they did.

They put me in the Hall of Fame in 1975—that's over 40 years after my final game, but it was still a big honour. You know, I never thought of myself as a big star. I only had three 20-plus goal seasons in eight years of play. Gretzky scored 92 goals one year—almost as many as I did in my entire career. I finished with 111. And one season he had 212 points. I collected 193 points over eight seasons.

Sometimes it was hectic when I worked all those Leafs games in the penalty box. I recall that Tiger Williams and Eddie Shack were always talking and causing a disturbance. Dave Schultz of the Flyers was the only player to take a swing at me. I told him how many minutes he got, and he let one go. But I moved fast and he didn't hurt me. I remember the police sergeant took him to the dressing room. I was told Schultz gave him some lip and the sergeant beat the hell out of him, but that's hard to believe. Schultz came out of the dressing room a changed man. He said to me, "Ace, anytime you come to Philadelphia, I'll have a pair of tickets for you."

I timed penalties at the Gardens for 47 years. It may be a record, I don't know. And I worked next to a wonderful little man—Joe Lamantia. Everybody called him "Banana" Joe because he worked in the fruit-and-vegetable business. The ref would blow his whistle and I'd say, "What for, Joe?" And he'd tell me what the penalty was for and I'd write it down.

Joe and I could write a book about certain players. While serving their time, they'd spit and spew nose droppings all over the floor of the box. Two of the worst offenders were the Leafs' Borje Salming and Wilf Paiement. Whenever those two left the box, we hoped someone would come along with a mop and clean up the floor.

I like this young fellow Gretzky, he doesn't have a swelled head. I met his father and mother. Good parents. For one big dinner, Wayne sent a telegram saying he couldn't make it, the club won't allow it. But he sent 18 autographed hockey sticks for the Big Brothers banquet. That was thoughtful of him.

I like his dad, Walter. He built the rink in the backyard. Wayne spent hours and hours on it. Well, you have to practice a lot—even if you're all alone—if you hope to be any good. When I was a kid, we had the Muskoka River running right through Bracebridge. All we had to do was clear the snow off it. I fell through the thin ice once, but a fellow by the name of Francis Murphy came along and saved my life.

My biggest thrill was in '32, when we won the Stanley Cup. Smythe gave us rings worth about $300 each. Now they are worth about $7,000. That was the first time they gave rings to the winning players.

One day I got a letter signed by Harold Ballard saying my services were no longer required. I accosted him and caught him in a lie. He said, "I didn't sign any letter to you."

I said, "Look! That's your signature on the letter."

And he denied it. "I didn't sign that. Somebody else must have."

I said, "That's bull, Harold. I know your signature."

He said, "All right, then, I lied to you. But you're not coming back."

I was hot. That's when I told him, "Harold, take this job and shove it up your keester—as far as it will go."

I was hurt too, because I never got so much as a thank you note for all those years I put in.

"But you got paid?" I queried.

"No," Bailey answered. "No pay. I didn't want pay. I got two free tickets to each game. But I never got to sit in my seats. Never."

Ace Bailey died on a spring day in 1992. He was 88, the oldest living Leaf. The white-haired widows in the seniors' home were among hundreds who mourned his passing.

PATSY GUZZO
and the Laughingstock Olympic Team

Patsy Guzzo was reluctant to leave Ottawa for the Winter Olympics that gloomy January day in 1948. His wife had suffered a miscarriage, and no one meant more to Patsy than Mary. But his mother-in-law told him, "You go to Switzerland. You win a gold medal. I'll look after Mary. This will be the chance of a lifetime for you."

Patsy wasn't so sure. He was afraid his team—the RCAF Flyers— would make fools of themselves during the games in St. Moritz. During training camp, the team had looked dreadful. One critic had called them "the laughingstock Olympic team."

The Flyers were the brainchild of Air Force squadron leader Dr. Sandy Watson, who was granted permission to form a team of RCAF regulars and challenge for the Olympic title. The games were the first since the end of World War II, and permission to assemble the Flyers was granted at the very last minute. It came after the Montreal Royals, Allan Cup champs in 1947, with future NHL stars like Doug Harvey on the roster, declined the Olympic invitation.

Initially, Canadians counted on the Flyers to avenge the embarrassment of a 2–1 loss to Great Britain in 1936, the first time a team wearing Canadian colours had lost an Olympic hockey title. Here's how that happened. Wily promoter Bunny Ahearne, described by journalist Jim Coleman as "a double-dealing, self-serving little rascal from the opening faceoff to the final buzzer," set it up. Ahearne, a Brit, contacted 10 top amateur players born in Britain but immigrants to Canada, and lured them back to England specifically to seek Olympic gold. Representing good old England, of course. And he pulled it off when Britain edged Canada 2–1 in the first of two games behind the spectacular goaltending of Canadian Jimmy Foster. Ahearne then cancelled the second meeting between the clubs, stating it was "unnecessary." When Canada lodged a protest, Ahearne smugly called for a vote. He'd already lined up several nations to support him, and his ploy was upheld. Utilizing players who hadn't lived in England since childhood, Great Britain won its first ever gold, even though its team's Olympic record was 5–2. Canada's was 7–1. Go figure.

Now, 12 years later, the Flyers had a chance to erase memories of that stinging defeat in '36. But after their lacklustre start, prognosticators said they'd be lucky to win any kind of medal in '48.

About 90 players tried out for the team, but few of any quality. Only a handful were considered Olympic material. The club played an exhibition game against a mediocre team from McGill and lost 7–0. Future Calder Trophy winner Jack Gelineau, who moved on to play for the Boston Bruins, was McGill's goaltender. Patsy said, "I hated to read the papers the next day. We were called so many unflattering names." Dozens of self-appointed experts predicted a humiliating defeat for the Flyers in Switzerland. The Flyers played a second game—against Bill Cowley's army team—and lost 6–2. It was a disaster. Critics laced into them again.

Luckily, the Flyers were bolstered by some fresh, more experienced players. George Mara and Wally Halder were brought in from Toronto, and Andre Laperriere from Montreal.

Then there was a goaltending crisis. Dick Ball, a University of Toronto netminder, failed his physical and was hastily replaced by Murray Dowey, a handsome 19-year-old practice goalie with the Toronto Maple Leafs. Nobody knew much about Dowey, but Halder told his mates, "Don't worry about him. He'll be fine."

But would he? The team met Dowey for the first time on the train to New York, where they boarded the *Queen Elizabeth* for the ocean crossing.

Patsy was assigned to "A Deck" and soon found himself conversing with a number of Hollywood celebrities: Paulette Goddard and her new husband, Burgess Meredith; Johnny Weissmuller, the silver screen's Tarzan of the Apes; and Henry Ford of the Ford Motor Company were aboard. So was the U.S. Olympic hockey team.

The voyage was rough, and many of the passengers were seasick. Patsy wrote in his diary: "The vastness of the Atlantic staggers the imagination."

In London, the Flyers were booked into the Crofton Hotel. The lobby was so cold the receptionist wore a fur coat and gloves. There was no heat in the rooms. The Americans stayed there as well, and Patsy thought they were a little too full of themselves. "They held a practice the next morning and we resented their cocky attitude. They grinned at us as we took the ice but after a few minutes watching our fast-paced workout they became very sober and left in haste. We opened their eyes."

During a team meeting, Sandy Watson stressed the importance of winning the Olympic title. "It's one of the greatest opportunities a hockey player could ever expect," he told his men. "Win the Olympic title and your names will be remembered forever."

By then, Bunny Ahearne had risen to the position of secretary of the International Hockey Federation. He was singularly unimpressed with the Flyers. "Because of the adverse publicity you received in Ottawa," he told them, "plans to have you play games in Sweden have been cancelled. Nobody there wants to see you perform." That riled the Flyers. "We were very indignant," Patsy wrote in his diary.

The Flyers tied a top British team 5–5, and Ahearne did an about-face. "I'm thinking you may be invited to Sweden after all," he told them.

Two players, Andy Gilpin and Irving Taylor, saw no ice time in the game and complained bitterly. "If we're not going to play, then send us home," they told coach Frank Boucher (not to be confused with Hockey Hall of Famer Frank Boucher).

The players toured London. Outside Buckingham Palace, Irving Taylor impishly asked a bobby to place a call to the King. "Tell him there are some Canadian hockey players outside and they'd like to meet him."

The bobby didn't even blink.

At Piccadilly Circus, Patsy was amazed to see women approaching men, offering the oldest commodity on earth. He wrote: "I pitied these unfortunate souls who found themselves existing under such revolting and degrading circumstances. Despite the great number of males who needed no second invitation, I feel quite sure that there are many pure men in this old world of ours, some because they have not had the opportunity, others deterred more from fear than any moral repugnance. And there are those of us who are innocent because it is a sin against the Ten Commandments."

Before leaving London for Paris, the Flyers played a game against Brighton and won 7–6.

Patsy wrote: "Ahearne told us to be friendly with opposing players and help them to their feet when possible. He said it would have a desirable effect on the crowd, who could easily sway the referees."

In Paris the game was delayed because a huge crowd was en route to the stadium. Fully 16,000 attended the game. "It was the largest crowd I'd ever played before," Patsy wrote. "And the penalty box was called 'PRISON.'"

The French players did everything but chop the Flyers' heads off. The Paris team was the best in Europe, with Canadian stars Ossie Carnegie and Manny McIntyre on the roster. The Flyers won 5–3. A Paris official told Patsy after the match, "Your Olympic title is assured."

The team flew on to Zurich, Switzerland, a city near the German border. They stayed at the Dolder Grand hotel. Indeed, it was grand. Patsy wrote:

The rooms were beyond description. Rugs on the floors, two sinks, double beds with thick comforters. Excellent meals. Everything spotlessly clean.

The rink was on the grounds of the hotel. There was artificial ice but no roof. On one side the boards were only 6" high. On the other side the boards were regulation height. For the game, one of our players, Hubert Brooks, was selected to be a linesman. He sat at the blueline, off the ice. Brooks was a war hero. He was shot down, captured, escaped three times and learned several languages while working with the underground. While a prisoner in a German camp, he learned he had won the Military Cross.

Snow began to fall which turned into rain. We dressed at the hotel and took a bus to the rink. Over 14,000 attended with umbrellas and newspapers for protection. An inch of water covered the ice surface. We won 6–3. With two minutes to play, the Swiss coach removed his goalie but there was no further scoring. The last whistle sounded a good three minutes after the end of regulation time. We were soaked to the skin and hurried back to the hotel where hot baths were waiting— plus a shot of cognac.

There we learned that Barbara Ann Scott, an Ottawa girl, had won the World's figure skating title in Prague. She would be with us in St. Moritz competing for Olympic Gold. And we learned that the gate receipts from the game had been $16,000 but we got nothing.

The Flyers were reluctant to leave Zurich, but there was another game to play—in Basel, a short distance away. Seats for this game were sold out. The arena held 16,000 people. Canadian hockey teams were very popular with the Swiss.

We booked in at the Euler Hotel and peeked in the room occupied by Irving Taylor and Red Gravelle. It looked like a diplomat's suite, complete with expensive paintings and statues. We went for a stroll and two of the players met a couple of females. The rest of us kept walking. The women are not very attractive. They cannot apply makeup properly, their clothes are out of style and their hairdos leave a lot to be desired. But they look healthy. We passed City Hall and someone said it was built 500 years ago. In Ottawa, anything older than a hundred years is considered really ancient.

At the arena, the crowd was immense. Some watched from nearby buildings reaching several stories above the ice surface. I scored the first goal but the ice was sticky and fast skating was impossible. We played poorly and were beaten 8–5.

While we waited around afterward to catch the train to Davos, huge crowds milled around us. People reached out to touch us. I doubt if reigning monarchs received such attention. The Swiss national team that had beaten us was on the train. It was their day to howl and they showered us with cakes, candies and drinks.

We checked in at the Palace Hotel in Davos, which is close to the Italian border. I could now practice my parents' language as most people spoke Italian. We opened the large windows in our rooms to let in the fresh mountain air. The view was almost heart-stopping. To our right we could see five rinks in the very centre of this resort city of 12,000. In the distance, we could see Barbara Ann Scott skating and practicing a few turns, getting ready for the Olympic competition.

The ice was smooth and fast for the game in Davos. I scored two goals and gathered two assists. The score was 10–3. Wally Halder was his usual self and banged in three goals. Perhaps the happiest person on the ice was Murray Dowey. He has proven himself to be a high-class goalie. Ten of our players had been with us for just a handful of games. Now we are coming together.

The Olympic rules are archaic as only eleven players are allowed on each team. Therefore six of us will not be playing. The eyes of almost the whole world will be on us in St. Moritz.

We left by train for St. Moritz the next day and found the U.S. and British teams already aboard so we had no seats. I spent much of the time in the baggage car. We were in for some grief upon our arrival. Nobody had made hotel arrangements for us. We finally got bussed to the Victoria Hotel but half an hour after we checked in we were ordered to pack up and head across the street to the Stahlbad Hotel. At the Stahlbad were the Czechs, Norwegians, Romanians, Yugoslavians, British, Poles and Swedes.

There we learned that the All American Brass Hat Avery Brundage was stirring up trouble. It's hard to believe but the U.S. sent two teams to the games. Brundage wants his team of Simon Pures to play in the Olympics but the International Ice Hockey Federation recognized only the team sent by the U.S. Amateur Hockey Association. What a fiasco! Someone heard Ahearne shouting, "Brundage will not sabotage the hockey games. I'll run my own Olympic Games."

Meetings were numerous because of this situation. It's possible the whole Olympic program might be thrown out. Tomorrow the opening ceremonies will take place. The first game will be at 10 a.m. between the Swiss and the United States. Canada will meet Sweden at 2 p.m.

All teams but ours had transportation arranged to the site of the opening ceremonies. We finally located a bus to take us to the parade ground. We saw all the countries involved standing near their respective flags. We were dressed in air force blue and Barbara Ann was in front of our group. Scores of cameras were grinding. Spectators stood in precarious positions on cliffs and ledges to get better shots. We paraded through the streets, then circled the stadium where thousands were seated to witness the proceedings.

When the last country reached the ice rink, an official recited the Olympic oath in French. After breaking off, we rode back to our hotel in horse-drawn cutters. Our driver charged us double the usual fare and when we asked why he said, "Look, my cutter uses two horses." It made us laugh.

That afternoon we played Sweden, reported to be the toughest team in Europe. I was one of the eleven chosen to play and I was elated. We won the game 3–1 and we felt nothing could stop us now. Sweden was the dirtiest team I'd ever played against. One player wearing a baseball mask kicked me in the shins and when I turned on him he merely said, "Okay." Wally Halder was struck over the head deliberately and that almost precipitated a riot. I saw Wally go down and I said, "There go our gold medals." But he was tough and recovered for the next shift. Our goalie was given a penalty for throwing the puck in front of him. I backchecked well and no shot was propelled from my wing during the game.

The next day our trainer took our skates to Davos by train to get them sharpened. No sharpening machine existed in St. Moritz. We took in some of the other games and were impressed by the Czechs, coached by Mike Buckna of Trail, B.C. Zobrodsky, their big centreman, was by far the most outstanding Czech player and we knew we were in for a battle.

"On Sunday I went to 8:30 mass at St. Karl's and noticed for the first time that females did not have to wear hats or other headdresses.

In company with the British team, we travelled by bus to the Palace rink. We shutout the Brits 3–0 in a snowstorm. Dowey was sensational in nets. And I got three penalties, all undeserved. The referees were slap-happy about giving penalties and the fans severely criticized them.

At 2:30 on Monday we played the Poles at the Suvretta Rink and trounced them 15–0. The next day we had little difficulty beating Italy 21–1. I got three goals and two assists for my best production to date.

I had a chat with Hubie Brooks after the game and he told me he was getting married on Monday the day after the Olympics. He said we would be getting 200 francs each on Sunday. This was good news because I wanted to buy Mary a watch.

The next day, we were awakened at 6:30 a.m. for our 8 o'clock game against the U.S. The ice was not ready when we arrived at the rink and we waited in our bus for an hour. We trounced the Americans 12–3. It was the worst beating an American team had taken since the Olympic Games began in 1924. On the *Queen Elizabeth* coming over, some of the Americans had bragged that they would beat us by ten goals. However, we did no gloating as their team had much trouble and many uncertainties. I am sure they would be the first to come to our aid if we ever needed help.

In the afternoon we watched Dick Button of the U.S. put on a masterful show in the men's figure skating event. Paulette Goddard, in her ankle-length ermine coat, and Burgess Meredith were among us. I spoke to Meredith and was surprised to discover that he knew more about hockey than I expected. He told me of a party at their hotel and how Joan Crawford and Jennifer Jones had attended. Big-name movie stars.

Friday, February 6, was our big test against the Czechs. Their coach, Mike Buckna, played a "kitty-bar-the-door style" and the game ended in a scoreless tie. We outplayed them and did everything but put the puck in the net. Wally Halder was sick for this game and George Mara needed a replacement so we were not at full strength. The referees were a Brit and a Pole and they were the worst we had ever seen. In the afternoon, we watched Barbara Ann win the Olympic crown in figure skating. She was far ahead before that day and she performed flawlessly on the wet, mushy ice surface. She made us proud. Eva Pawlik of Austria, trying to catch up, fell on her fanny three times and had a very wet bottom at the finish.

It snowed the next morning and our game against Austria was postponed a couple of hours. We beat them 12–0 for our fourth shutout. We had only to win against the Swiss the next day.

Sunday, February 8, 1949, would be a day to remember for many, many years. We were somewhat worried because the weather turned mild and a game had been played before ours on the same ice surface. In the dressing room, George Dudley of the CAHA told us, "Canada and the CAHA are proud of you, win or lose. You fellows left Ottawa under a cloud of uneasiness and distress. You were under heavy criticism from the newspapers and from a lot of self-appointed hockey experts." It was a great, brief talk by a wonderful gentleman. It was very inspiring and we left the dressing room very determined.

The ice was cleaned, the game began and Wally Halder promptly skated through the entire Swiss team to score. Then there was a delay and talk about postponing the game and playing it in Zurich the following day. That would have caused havoc as thousands had booked flights home.

The ice was ordered cleaned every ten minutes. And play resumed. In the second period, I got the thrill of a lifetime in hockey. I took a pass from George Mara in my skates and moved the puck up to my stick, rounding the defense. I deked the Swiss goalkeeper and scored the second goal, a back-breaking goal.

Now we contained the Swiss in their own end without much trouble. But the crowd became noisy and frustrated and we, along with the referees, were pelted with snowballs that came from all directions. Then Reg Schroeter scored an insurance goal to make it 3–0 and the gold medals were ours. What a thrill!

The presentation of medals took place following the game and someone placed a Canadian flag outside our bus for all to see. A man stole the flag and ran off with it, Red Gravelle giving chase but to no avail.

Cheers were in order for George Boucher, father of our coach, Frank, who selected the team weeks earlier. After we bathed at the hotel, there was a reception for us. Hundreds of telegrams began arriving when news of our victory was made known. Great Britain had won the last Olympic title in 1936, a tainted victory, and now we had redeemed Canada's lost glory in 1948. We were a very happy group of hockey players.

I was first to bed that night but got little sleep. I was too excited about the events of the day. I'd been told that I'd played the best hockey of my career. But the whole team had played well.

The next morning we were awakened early to attend Hubert Brooks's wedding to Birthe Grontved in the chapel of St. Morizio's Church. Barbara Ann Scott, our champion figure skater, was the bridesmaid. Sandy Watson was best man. After the ceremony, the players held hockey sticks over the heads of the bride and groom. Photographers were on hand along with Jack Sullivan of Canadian Press. A reception followed at our hotel.

Then we entrained for Arosa and the first game of our post-Olympic tour. Now we could afford to relax. We won the game 18–4. Training rules were no longer in vogue. I visited an old friend, Arnie Charbonneau, at his apartment and gave his wife a pair of nylons. I gave another pair to the wife of Jimmy Sands, a fellow airman serving in England.

We hoped the people back in Canada would learn about the terrific obstacles we were forced to overcome to bring back the Olympic Hockey Championship.

The Flyers toured Switzerland, Czechoslovakia, France, Holland, Sweden, England and Scotland. They played 42 games, winning 31 and losing only five. Six games ended in tie scores. The Flyers scored 263 goals and gave up only 105. They travelled 15,000 miles and for most of the games were without their two top players, George Mara and Wally Halder, who returned to Canada following the Olympics.

The most sobering part of their journey was a visit to Spielberg Castle, Czechoslovakia, once the largest torture chamber and concentration camp in Europe. Patsy wrote:

We proceeded 75 feet underground and were shown the instruments of torture used in medieval days: the stretching of limbs, the dripping of water on heads, the chains that bound the poor souls for weeks. The cells had no beds, no light or air and prisoners were forced to occupy chambers too small to even breathe in.

Another dank chamber had a trench down the centre. Prisoners were forced to sit with their feet dangling. The rats did the rest. We were taken to the women's side where, in one big chamber, the "witches" were given no food or water. They soon died. Adjoining this was the chamber of the unfaithful wives. Five at a time were bricked in and cold water dashed on them until they died. All of the above, of course, took place centuries ago.

When the Germans conquered the Czechs in 1939, they converted Spielberg into a modern gas chamber. There was a guillotine where we were told that 13 heads per minute were lopped off. We entered a room with dozens of photos of Czechs who were murdered by the Germans.

Those who were finally liberated had aged by at least 25 years during the time they were incarcerated. We were told of the coming of the Russians and how they could have saved 3,000 Czech lives but did nothing to help. We were told of an incident in which the Russians were repairing a bridge and a soldier fell into the river below. Some residents offered to pull him out but a Russian commander refused to allow it. "If he can swim, he can save himself,' they were told. 'If not, there are many more to take his place."

At long last, the Flyers reached Southampton and boarded the *Queen Mary*, bracing themselves for another trip across the Atlantic. At last they were headed home. But it was a slow, uncomfortable journey. The ship ran into a storm and slowed to nine knots. Patsy wrote:

An overpowering wave struck the ship. I thought from the sound we had collided with another ship. It was a most unpleasant trip. Everyone got seasick. Birthe Brooks made an appearance. She was a beautiful woman. She looked like Ingrid Bergman. I wished her and Brooksy much happiness.

Finally, we began to enjoy the trip. I was told that getting seasick is good for you, it cleans you out, I would rather have used other means.

At last the big day arrived. We reached New York. We were all on deck and glancing down at the dock when, lo and behold, there was Mary and my four-year-old daughter Rosalee. What a thrill!

Air Commodore Mackell came aboard with Jack Koffman, sports editor of the *Ottawa Citizen,* and Bill Westwick, sports editor of the *Ottawa Journal.*

Author's note: The summer after the Flyers won Olympic glory, I worked as a copy boy at the *Ottawa Journal* and aspired one day to be a sports editor like Bill Westwick.

Dozens of photographers were allowed on board and movies were taken to be shown in theatres later.

We all looked forward to a big reception in Ottawa. There we were hailed like conquering heroes during a motorcade that started at Union Station and ended at the RCAF Beaver Barracks where we were wined and dined in splendid military fashion. What a wonderful ending to the saga of the RCAF Flyers, Olympic and World Champions of 1948. We were sent to do a job and we were successful. What more could Canada ask?

●

In April, 2008, my friend Pat MacAdam, columnist with the *Ottawa Sun*, attended an induction ceremony in Calgary, home of Canada's Sports Hall of Fame. He was fuming that day because an editor had screwed up a paragraph in his column that week. He likened it to a Buffalo TV film editor who was given a number of Fred Astaire/Ginger Rogers films with instructions to shorten them for TV viewing. The man cut out all the dance scenes.

Pat knows more about the Flyers' saga and the career of Barbara Ann Scott than anybody on the planet. He sent me this email after sharing most of the details of their saga with me:

Sixty years after winning gold in the 1948 Winter Olympics in St. Moritz, Switzerland, Ottawa's RCAF Flyers were finally inducted into the Olympic Hall. Canada's Sweetheart, Barbara Ann Scott, the only Canadian to win a gold medal in figure skating singles and a Hall member since 1949, was elevated to the Olympic Order—the Olympics pantheon. Barb is tiny. She weighs 98 pounds—the same as in 1948. When she stood on the huge stage at Calgary's Roundup Centre, her presence filled it and she towered above it as the applause from a six-minute standing ovation rolled over her.

The RCAF Flyers, a hastily assembled, last-minute team, given no chance of winning, stunned the hockey world by winning seven games, tying one, scoring 69 goals and allowing only five. They proved that victory has a thousand fathers and defeat is an orphan. They left Ottawa looked upon as losers and returned home as national heroes for an Andy Warhol 15 minutes—and were promptly forgotten. Meanwhile, Edmonton Mercurys, 1952 gold medallists, vaulted over the Flyers and were inducted into the Olympic Hall.

The Canadian Forces named the Flyers as Canada's greatest military athletes in 2001.

George Mara
and Wally Halder

Mara and Halder had the most prominent post-hockey careers of all the Flyers. I interviewed Mara in 1969. He owned the William Mara wine company in Toronto, was a director at Maple Leaf Gardens and served briefly as president of the Gardens while Harold Ballard was serving a few months of jail time. I recall wishing at the time that his presidency would become a permanent position. He was a founder and chairman of the Olympic Trust of Canada, which raised millions to help deserving Canadian athletes. Before playing for the RCAF Flyers, Mara turned down an offer to play for the Detroit Red Wings. He died in 2006 while undergoing heart surgery.

Wally Halder drew attention in hockey circles after he was named MVP of the Toronto Hockey League in 1947. He turned down a pro offer from the New York Rangers after he demanded a no-trade contract (unheard of at the time) and the Rangers refused to give him one. It was Halder who recommended goaltender Murray Dowey to the Flyers. Pat MacAdam tells me Halder and Mara, en route home from the Olympics, stopped off at a Paris race track, pooled the $400 Sandy Watson had given them, and bet on a longshot. The horse won and they scooped up a ton of money. Pat says the odds were either 100 to 1 or 40 to 1. The winnings became the genesis of the Olympic Trust.

Without Mara, Halder and Dowey, the Flyers would not likely have become Olympic champs. Following the Olympic victory, Halder coached at the University of Toronto and later became the founding president and CEO of the Olympic Trust of Canada. He died of cancer in 1994.

Patsy Guzzo
and Red Gravelle

I never met Patsy Guzzo. He was obviously a decent player, a decent man and a decent writer. His account of chasing after Olympic gold is a treasure. He lived not far from our home in Ottawa during the War years. I knew Red Gravelle from my Ottawa hockey days and met him later in life at a sports banquet in the Trenton/Belleville area. He was hit and killed by a train (he was deaf and didn't hear the train coming) while walking his dog a short time later. He proudly took his Olympic gold medal with him to many sports functions. And he took his skates with him into his grave.

Barbara Ann Scott

In shop class at Glebe Collegiate in 1947, after Barbara Ann won her gold medal at the world championships, I fashioned a miniature yellow papier mâché Buick convertible just like the one the city gifted her. Avery Brundage threatened to declare her a professional if she accepted the real car, forcing her to give it back. When she won Olympic Gold in 1948, over 70,000 turned out in Ottawa to welcome her back from St. Moritz. And she received another car.

She went on to star in the Ice Capades and the Hollywood Ice Revue. She befriended Andra McLaughlin, another professional skater, who eventually replaced her as the star of both shows. Andra became Mrs. Red Kelly. During her career, Barbara Ann collected an amazing number of trophies, medals, gifts and awards. Her memorabilia has been assessed at over a million dollars. Perhaps the City of Ottawa should establish a museum in her name to house the collection.

From time to time we exchanged emails. She had fond memories of the Flyers and was especially proud to be bridesmaid at Hubert Brooks's wedding.

Barbara Ann was named Canada's top female athlete in 1946, '47 and '48, and Canada's top athlete in 1945, '47 and '48 (in 1945, the female-only prize was not awarded). She was named an officer of the Order of Canada in 1991.

Forever known as Canada's Sweetheart, she is the only Canadian female figure skater to win an Olympic gold medal. She died on September 20, 2012, at her home in Florida.

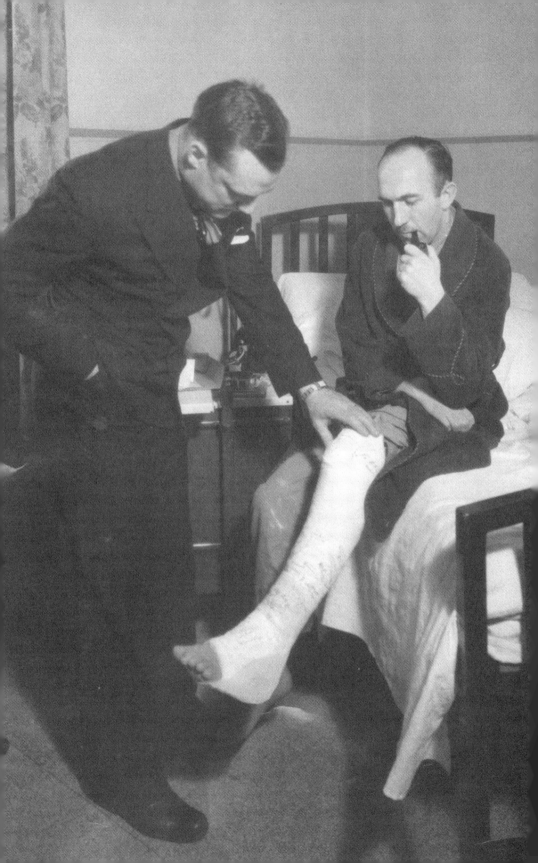

THREE GOLDEN OLDIES
Who Died Too Soon

HOD STUART

On June 24, 1907, the sudden death of a hockey hero was newsworthy enough to make the front pages of newspapers across Canada and even in U.S. cities like Pittsburgh and Houghton, Michigan. The following, from the Montreal *Gazette*, attests to the popularity of one of the game's greatest stars.

Hod Stuart, coverpoint of the Montreal Wanderers, Canadian Hockey Champions and holder of the Stanley Cup, considered to be one of the finest all round athletes in Canada and perhaps the greatest exponents of defense play in Canada's winter sport, met a sudden and shocking death in the Bay of Quinte near Belleville yesterday afternoon.

News of Stuart's death spread rapidly. There are few in Montreal or Ottawa, even among those who take no interest in sporting affairs, who have not heard of Stuart and his prowess. Outside of the general public who knew him only through his athletics, he had a large circle of acquaintances and intimate friends.

Stuart met his death after diving from a platform at a lighthouse about a quarter of a mile from shore.

Stuart with two companions went for a walk down Front Street in Belleville to the end of the Grand Junction Wharf which stretches out into the bay. He decided to take a swim, the weather being fearfully hot. He took to the water, calling to his associates, "I'm swimming to the lighthouse and back."

He swam over and climbed upon the wooden platform which surrounds the lighthouse. The watchers saw him sit down for a few minutes. He rested, then poised for a dive from the platform which is six to eight feet above the water. He was seen to dive and the watchers waited for him to come up and swim toward them. Minutes passed and there was no sign of Hod.

The watchers realized something must be wrong. They ran to the boathouse but it was about a half mile from the dock. It was fully half an hour before the party secured a boat and got to where Hod had gone down. There he was at the bottom with a ghastly wound in his head and his neck broken.

He was unaware that only two or three feet of water surrounded the boathouse with jagged rocks all around.

The body was recovered and taken to Ottawa last night where the funeral will take place.

Hod Stuart was known internationally. He was one of the best and most popular players wherever he appeared. He was especially revered in Pittsburgh where he played on artificial ice. For nearly two years he played coverpoint and captained the local team in the International Hockey League. His work was always on the sensational order and he was the idol of the fans, occupying much the same sphere in the hockey world as Hans Wagner and Napoleon Lajoie did in baseball.

Stuart was 28 years of age and married. He leaves a wife and two young daughters.

Last winter he was the most talked about hockey player in Canada and in the hockey district of the United States. He was an Ottawa boy by birth and played for many years with the Ottawa senior hockey and football teams. He was physically almost a perfect development, over six feet in height and weighing 175 pounds. He was of rather slim build but strong and muscular and possessed of a splendid courage that made him the hero of many a hard fought battle on the gridiron and on the hockey ice.

A huge crowd gathered at his funeral.

Despite a heavy rainstorm, members of every athletic club in Ottawa united in paying a last tribute to the unfortunate young athlete. Mr. James Strachan of Montreal, president of the Wanderers hockey club, with which Stuart played last season, said, "I cannot tell you how greatly shocked I was to hear of the terrible accident and how deeply I regret poor Stuart's death. He was a splendid hockey player and one of the finest fellows in the game. No one who knew him as I did could have anything but good to say of him. In his death Canadian sport suffers a very great loss."

In 1907, Stuart, then a Montreal Wanderer, was involved in what was described as the "worst exhibition of butchery on ice." Ottawa's Alf Smith was seen to dash across the ice and slash Stuart over the head with his stick, laying him out like a corpse. This was after Montreal's Baldy Spittal tried to split Blatchford's skull open with a mighty swing of his stick. Blatchford was carried off, leaving a stream of blood in his wake.

One of the officers of the Ottawa hockey club stated, "I believe Hod Stuart was the greatest coverpoint in the world. He was a hero on the ice and a gentleman off it and his death came as a great shock. His was one of the saddest deaths I have ever heard of and no person sympathizes more deeply with his widow and family members than the Ottawa Hockey Club."

Ernie Johnson of the Montreal Wanderers said, "Hod helped us win the Stanley Cup last season. No one had ever made so many friends in such a short time in Montreal as the deceased. Several of the players were heartbroken at the news of Hod's demise."

The late Hod Stuart, said a friend, as a child was eager to be on skates and gave his parents no peace until he had a pair. He'd played hockey on the Rideau Canal and soon became quite expert. He went to the United States when he got older—to Pittsburgh and Houghton, Michigan. He told his father that he did not wish to play in Canada and pretend to be an amateur while taking money under the table. When Hod left for Pittsburgh he had offers from several Canadian teams to play but he declined them all.

He went from Pittsburgh to Houghton and then the following year went to Calumet [Michigan]. There he organized a team and interested some capitalists who put up a $30,000 rink. The Calumet team won the championship that year. The following year, in 1905, Stuart returned to Pittsburgh.

He was William Stuart, really but so was his father, so they gave him his mother's maiden name Hodgeson. The boys at school soon shortened this to Hod and the name stuck to him ever afterwards.

One thing that made Stuart such a great player was his long reach and wonderful strength of his arm. He always used a much heavier and longer stick than the other players, even in his early hockey days.

Hod was happy to move back to Canada because he found "the referees are very cruel over there. The officials had more to do with running the game than the players." People in Pittsburgh often wondered why Hod seldom lifted the puck in the games there. He said that a lift was no use in the Pittsburgh rink which was fully 50 feet longer than any Canadian rink. He developed a habit of securing the puck and always trying to take it down the ice.

Although Hod Stuart made the biggest salary ever made in hockey he died too young to make sufficient provision for the future of his wife and two little baby girls.

It seems that he did not notice the dangerous character of the spot where he was diving when he met his death, but it seems that he was always fairly reckless in individual sporting matters. He had no fear of drowning and in fact had experienced two narrow escapes of losing his life in deep water.

When he was a youth of about 16, he was playing hockey on a frozen lake on the outskirts of Ottawa, when he broke through the ice. Bruce Stuart, his brother, now with the Wanderers, rescued Hod after lying down on the ice and putting out his hockey stick, which Hod grasped. Then several companions helped Bruce to pull him out. It was thought for a time that life was extinct but he was soon brought around. The water was about 25 feet deep. If not for prompt efforts by Bruce and the other players Hod would have drowned.

A couple of years later Hod had a miraculous escape from drowning when he was working with his father around the erection of the leprosy hospital in New Brunswick.

Author's note: There was a leprosy hospital in Canada? Indeed there was—in the town of Tracadie-Sheila in New Brunswick. It closed in 1964 and is now a museum.

The building was put up close to the ocean and one day Hod saw a flock of wild geese land on the water. He jumped into a canoe to get a shot at them. He paddled along close to shore and fired his shotgun. The canoe upset and he was thrown into the water. A workman in the hospital noticed the upturned canoe. Hod's father and a couple of other men secured a fishing boat and put out after the canoe, which was drifting rapidly out to sea.

It was fully half an hour before they reached the upturned canoe with Hod clinging to it. He had drifted a mile from shore and was rescued none too soon, for the tide was going out and soon would have carried him hopelessly beyond aid. When hauled into the fishing boat, Hod collapsed, completely exhausted. He could not have held on much longer.

Hod Stuart lived in one of hockey's most exciting eras. The *Ottawa Citizen* reported on December 17, 1907:

People are going hockey crazy. Team owners are doing everything possible to obtain players from other teams. There is an epidemic of hockey fever and it is worse than it has ever been. People seem to lose their heads entirely. They are offering ridiculous prices for men, prices which are bound to ruin some of the clubs. They are telling all sorts of stories about their opponents, in many cases without the slightest foundation. They are using all sorts of underhanded means to get players away from other teams, false representation being one of them. They are forgetting everything except the idea of getting a team that can beat the others and the whole thing is so mixed up that even the principle officers of the various clubs are almost unable to make head or tail of the affair.

Billy Nicholson of the Shamrock team says "I get a man and then some other club immediately approaches him and offers him a couple of hundred dollars more, that's the way things are going all the time. Now it looks as if some cases might be taken to court. No doubt the lawyers who make a speciality of hockey issues are awaiting the next event with great interest."

In Toronto in 1907, the year of Hod's death, there was talk of building a new arena and the installation of an artificial ice plant. It would have been the first arena of its kind in Canada. But talk was all it amounted to. It was left to the Patrick brothers—Lester and Frank—to bring artificial ice to Vancouver and Victoria in 1911.

In Montreal in 1907, Hod and his mates would have marvelled at the passion people were showing for skating. On December 3, there was a remarkable scene at the opening of a new arena. For some reason, the electric lights could not be turned on, and management intended to postpone the grand opening. But the anxious skaters—hundreds of them—simply barged through the doors and donned their skates. They skated around in the darkness, which was only relieved by four small torches and two or three bicycle lamps. They were thrilled to be there, they seemed to enjoy themselves immensely, and the crowd grew all the time.

In 1907 in Pittsburgh, where Hod Stuart became a legend, shortstop Honus "Hans" Wagner of the Pirates major league baseball club declined an offer to captain a hockey team. William McCormick of Uniontown, Pennsylvania, offered Wagner $5,000 for four months' work to organize and play on the Uniontown hockey team. The amount equalled that of his baseball salary. The team was to be a member of the Central Pennsylvania Hockey League.

Wagner and other baseball stars—Hans Lobert of the Cincinnati ball club and Patsy Flaherty of Boston were named as potential members—would be the backbone of the team. Wagner finally declined the offer, fearing that it would aggravate the rheumatism that he had suffered the previous year. The Montreal *Gazette* does not state whether Wagner or the other two big-league ball players had ever played hockey before in their lives. The *Gazette* does have this to add to Stuart's obituary:

Hod Stuart was a very adventurous chap and was always doing things in his youth that the majority of other boys would never attempt.

When but seventeen years of age he got the gold fever. Nothing would do but that he must start for the Klondike. His parents tried to persuade him against it but he was determined and started with a companion for the gold country. They crossed the Chilcoot Pass with packs on their backs and on reaching Bennett Lake set to work to build a boat. They felled the trees and whipsawed them and it took them over six weeks before the raft was completed. Within two years they started on a seven hundred mile journey down the Yukon River to Dawson, having to pass through Three Rapids on the way. How they got safely through those unknown, dangerous waters puzzled even the trappers in the far North at that time.

When Hod and his companion reached Dawson there was not a house there with the exception of a couple of trappers' huts in the woods, but nine months later when his father, Mr. William Stuart, arrived there the place had 6,000 inhabitants. Hod and his companion suffered many hardships but they were endowed with hearty constitutions and came through it all right. Hod worked on a claim at Bonanza Creek with the temperature around 40 below all of the winter, but after being there a year and a half his father, who had gone to the Klondike after him, persuaded him to return home.

When they started back, Hod and his father came down the Yukon River in small boats for 2,000 miles to St. Michael's then visited Alaska and returned all the way to Vancouver and San Francisco.

In his travels, it was estimated that Hod had covered 13,000 miles.

Hod Stuart's death prompted hockey officials to promote the first all star game in hockey—with the proceeds going to Hod's widow and children. On January 2, 1908, at the Montreal Arena, 3,500 fans attended the benefit game between the Wanderers and players from the Eastern Canada Amateur Hockey Association. Over $2,000 was raised.

When the Hockey Hall of Fame was created in 1945, even though he had been dead for almost four decades, Hod Stuart was one of the original 12 players inducted. His brother Bruce, also a stellar player, followed him in a few years later.

BABE SIEBERT

Albert "Babe" Siebert was a brawny, hard-hitting, fearless hockey warrior who dazzled fans in the '30s, but whose career was haunted by an unkind fate. He had joined the Montreal Maroons as a rookie forward in 1925–26 and played on a Stanley Cup–winner in his initial season. He thrilled Montrealers as a member of the potent "S Line" alongside Hooley Smith and Nels Stewart—one of the most productive lines in the game.

Everybody knew Siebert, the hockey hero. His feats were legendary. But few knew the tragedy that soon would stalk him, casting its shadow on his life but never able to dim his courage in adversity.

His fans were shocked, and some wept openly, when he was sold to the New York Rangers by the cash-strapped Maroons in 1933. But he claimed another Stanley Cup that season, in New York. Then he was traded to Boston, where he shared ice time with his archrival, Eddie Shore. They had clashed often in the past: fists had flown, and Siebert had once pummelled Shore into submission in an on-ice melee. Shore was never one to forget or forgive the humiliation of a beating, especially from someone who stood only five-foot-nine. They were teammates, but they never spoke to one another.

When Siebert lost a step as a forward, it's likely Shore—a mean-spirited individual—tried to persuade the Bruins management to get rid of the Babe. "Can't you see the man is obviously over the hill?" Shore may have grumbled.

Back came Siebert to Montreal, where he donned a different uniform. The Maroons had folded, and the Canadiens had big plans for Siebert. They wisely placed him on defense. Revitalized, he became one of the dominant rearguards in the league. The Habs also promised him a coaching opportunity with the Habs when he decided to hang up his skates.

Siebert was perhaps the only non-goalie in NHL history to wear number 1. An all star for the next three years, he enjoyed such a superb season in 1936–37 that he was awarded the Hart Trophy as MVP—a rare honour for a defenseman.

His comeback, after he had seemed to have reached the end of the trail in Boston, was an epic feat. But behind the scenes . . .

For years, Siebert's attractive, blonde wife, his childhood sweetheart, was confined to a wheelchair, helplessly paralyzed.

When Babe's team played at the Forum, she pleaded with him to take her to the games. He would carry her to a rinkside seat, from which she would adoringly watch her sturdy husband wallop incoming forwards who tried to penetrate his team's defense, then rocket ahead to the attack.

He would often defend himself with stick and fists, draw penalties and hear the razzing of the crowd.

But afterward . . .

Afterward, he would talk briefly with the sportswriters. One of them—Elmer Ferguson—said, "Babe was anxious to be on the move. I saw him stride cheerily from the dressing room, a picture of strength and power. He moved quickly along the promenade to the seat where his fragile, lovely wife was waiting. Reaching down, he would kiss her, then lightly gather her in his muscular arms, as lightly as a feather, and stride away. Outside the building he would deposit her carefully in a waiting car and then drive her home to the two waiting kiddies. He adored his children and they, in turn, worshipped their gentle giant of a father."

The rest of the world saw Babe the athlete, a player renowned for his unswerving strength on the attack. Only his closest friends knew the battle he was fighting so courageously behind the scenes.

Babe's wife had become a hopeless invalid after their second child was born. It was said she was a victim of polio. The resulting expenses ate up every penny of Siebert's reserve income. Bills for hospitals, doctors and nurses, in addition to everyday living expenses, devoured his income. Siebert was a quiet man in his private life, devoted to his family.

Ferguson wrote, "He lived frugally, worked hard and in the off-season had no idle moments. It took a stout heart like the one Babe possessed not to break under the vast load of responsibility he shouldered."

When his wife required expensive hospital treatment, Babe was left penniless. He could not afford a nurse or housekeeper. He actually did the cooking and the nursing and the washing for his little family. For days he wouldn't leave the house, and then only when women friends of his wife came in voluntarily to assist him.

Babe never lost his courage or his cheerfulness. He did the house-work, a big apron wrapped around his waist. And he looked after the babies. No wonder that, as they grew up, his two kids simply worshipped the ground he walked on.

After three triumphant seasons as a Hab, he accepted the head coaching job with the Canadiens. A natural-born leader, he was expected to become one of the great bench bosses in the NHL.

Instead, he would become the only coach in history to win no games, lose no games and tie no games.

In the off-season, on a warm summer day in August at his cottage near Zurich, Ontario, a village on the shores of Lake Huron, a swimming expedition brought his family to the beach. His children were playing in the water with a large inflated rubber inner tube from a tire.

It floated away, caught by a breeze.

"Get it, Daddy, get it!" the children cried.

Babe swam after the tube and was closing on it some distance from shore, when suddenly he stopped swimming. Perhaps he suffered a cramp, possibly he simply became fatigued. Before his horrified family, he sank below the waves and perished within their sight. One of the NHL's greatest players and a wonderful family man passed when Lake Huron's chilly waters claimed the Babe.

A Memorial Game was played at the Forum in his honour weeks later, and the gate of $15,000 was turned over to the Babe's stricken widow. It would have been a more substantial amount had the attendance at the game not been so sparse, a mere 6,000 fans.

Babe Siebert was inducted into the Hockey Hall of Fame in 1964.

HOWIE MORENZ

From time to time, hockey fans may ask, "Why is there no number 7 on the roster of the Montreal Canadiens?"

When Howie Morenz died in the spring of 1937 at age 34, while recuperating in hospital from a broken leg, his coffin was placed at centre ice at the Montreal Forum, the scene of his greatest triumphs. The date was March 11, 1937.

There has never been a more solemn occasion in the long history of the NHL. The arena was jammed to capacity with his devoted fans. Morenz's flower-banked bier was passed by an endless line of teary-eyed people, young and old. They came to pay their respects to the Mitchell, Ontario, native, a magnificent athlete. There were hundreds of floral arrangements, even floral 7s, his uniform number—a numeral that, in retirement, would never grace the back of any other Canadien.

Canadiens manager Cecil Hart sobbed, "It's just terrible. I can't talk about it. I have known and loved him since I first signed him to a Canadiens contract in 1922."

"No one can ever take his place with us," said Aurel Joliat, his tiny linemate.

"He was the greatest of all time," lamented coach Dick Irvin.

While his body lay in state, thousands shuffled quietly past his resting place to view one final time the player who would later be named "the best player of the half century."

Earlier in the 1936–37 season, on January 28, Montreal's 6–5 victory over Chicago had been overshadowed by an alarming incident in the first period. Morenz darted after a puck and was bodychecked by Earl Seibert (not to be confused with Babe Siebert). Morenz's skate blade caught in a crack in the boards and, imbedded there, his leg twisted around and snapped with a crack that could be heard throughout the arena. He went down, writhing in pain. In an instant his season was over—and almost surely his fabulous career.

Earl Seibert, the six-foot-three Black Hawk defenseman who went on to become a Hall of Fame defenseman, shouldered the blame for the Morenz tragedy. "I was the guy who killed him," he said. "I didn't mean to hurt him—I would never do that—but I pinned him to the boards when his skate got caught, and he fell. I was stunned when I heard he'd died. I simply couldn't believe it. He was the greatest all round player in the game."

Seibert was absolved of all blame and did not receive a penalty on the play.

Some people said Morenz died of a broken heart—because he knew he would never skate again. His son Howie Jr. told me over lunch one day, "Several years after my father died, I met a nurse outside the Montreal Forum one day. She told me the cause of his death was negligence. She was on duty the night he passed away."

In 1990, when Seibert died of cancer, his son Oliver said, "My father never got over that incident with Morenz. For years afterward, the fans in Montreal booed him at the Forum." Seibert, a 10-time all star, didn't deserve the jeers. Only a handful of friends and relatives attended the Seibert funeral.

For 14 years, Morenz was one of the most dynamic figures in the game. He scored 270 career goals and led the Canadiens to three Stanley Cups. He was named league MVP on three occasions and placed among the top 10 scorers in 10 of his 14 seasons. There never was a skater like

Morenz. He broke through rival defenses like a cannonball, and his wicked shots appeared to curve upward in flight. King Clancy told me, "I was on defense for the Ottawa Senators one night when this brash kid came flying down the ice and sifted right between me and my partner. He whistled the puck into our net, and when he skated past me I snarled at him, 'Try that again, kid, and I'll cut your effing legs out from under you.' He laughed and said, 'I'll be right back.' Sure enough, a minute later, he flew past us and scored again. Holy Jesus. I told my defense mate, 'Let's try not to get this guy mad.'"

So highly was Morenz regarded around the NHL that a rival coach once ordered his players not to hit him during a game. In New York one night, Morenz skated out to face the New York Rangers. Ranger coach Lester Patrick admonished his players. "Don't hit Morenz tonight. The little guy is nursing a leg so sore he shouldn't be playing. He only dressed because he knows the New York fans are anxious to see him perform. So get in his way, but go easy on him and his gimpy leg."

Montreal hockey writer D.A.L. MacDonald was impressed with the Morenz modesty. "I got to know him rather well, travelling with Canadiens on their trips around the NHL when he was the great star of hockey. I always wondered, talking to him, if he ever read the newspapers and all the glowing things that were being written about him. He was undoubtedly the most publicized hockey player of his day, idolized by Canadian fandom and admired all around the league particularly in New York. But you would have thought that he was blissfully unaware of it all to talk to him."

Esteemed hockey writer Jim Coleman said Morenz was "Man o' War, Rudolf Nureyev and Dylan Thomas all rolled into one."

He was among the 12 original players inducted into the Hockey Hall of Fame when it opened in 1945.

BOBBY BAUN
Boomer Was a Hardass

One night, years ago, I was working a sports call-in show on CFRB in Toronto when I heard a familiar voice on the line. It was Bobby Baun calling in to make a point. I was really surprised, because pro athletes and former pros almost never call in to a radio station. But I knew Baun was trying to help me out, trying to make the program a little more entertaining, and I appreciated his call.

But that's the kind of man Baun is—always helping others.

For many years, I MC'd his annual golf tournaments, which brought out a raft of hockey celebrities. On what was, I believe, his final tournament, I steered clear of the quips and reviewed the remarkable career of the hard-rock defenseman.

My spiel went something like this . . .

Gentlemen, our friend Bobby Baun has held this remarkable tournament for his friends—and for charity— for many years now. And I'm guessing most of you think you know him well.

But do you? I've done some research into this man's background, and I wonder how many of you know the following fascinating facts about our host, Bobby Baun.

At an early age he had a fascination for cars, and when he was four years old he jumped behind the wheel of his dad's car and took off down the avenue, standing up on the seat to steer, finally crashing it into a house at the bottom of a hill.

At age 10, Don James entered Baun's life, and the pair became lifelong friends. A diving accident cut short Don's career as a promising athlete, but he never said, "Oh God, why me?" He carried on as a quadriplegic and worked for a cable company and eventually bought the company. Married, with three grown children, he does wonderful work for charities, including this one every year. A truly great Canadian.

Bobby Baun says in his youth he was a better football player than he was a hockey player. But once the Toronto Marlies signed him, that was the end of his football career.

Bob Davidson, the famous Leaf scout, saw Baun play as a teenager but was not overly impressed. Davidson decided that Mike Nykoluk, Baun's teammate, was a better bet for the Marlboros. But Nykoluk refused to sign unless the Marlies took his friend Baun. Baun went from the Marlie midgets to the Weston Dukes to the Marlies' Junior A club, just like that.

Baun almost didn't get into Maple Leaf Gardens for his first junior game, because he wasn't wearing a suit. Later, he became tailor Harry Rosen's best customer and enough of a fashion plate to make Don Cherry turn green with envy.

The Marlies offered him $50 a week to play—plus a $100 signing bonus. Baun was gutsy enough to demand $75 a week and a $200 bonus. It was his first experience as a negotiator. He was obviously a skilled one.

The Marlies, coached by former Leaf goalie Turk Broda, went on to win the Memorial Cup in Regina in 1955, and Baun recalls the victory party at team president Stafford Smythe's house after the season. Smythe was a man Baun respected. The Marlies won again the following year—this time on home ice, at the Gardens.

At his first Leaf training camp, Baun was teamed on defense with Tim Horton, who would become his lifelong friend. Horton was recovering from a devastating check delivered by Detroit's Bill Gadsby, one that left him with a broken leg in two places and a fractured jaw and cheekbone. Some said he'd never play again, but he laughed at that prediction. He played for 24 seasons in the NHL. Late in his career, Horton and partner Ron Joyce, a former policeman, went into the donut business. If Horton had survived the high-speed car crash that night in 1974 when he drove his Italian Pantera sports car back to Buffalo after a game in Toronto, he would be a multi-millionaire today.

In 1956, Baun signed his first pro contract with the Leafs, for $8,000 a year plus a $4,000 signing bonus—negotiating a much better salary than most of the other young junior stars. Even in junior hockey, he drove to the Gardens in a Cadillac.

He started his pro career in Rochester of the American League and was called up for his first game as a Leaf on November 19, 1956—at the Forum in Montreal.

Howie Meeker was his first NHL coach. Baun says, "Howie brought in a lot of new ideas that nobody listened to—especially the veterans." When Howie was fired, he allegedly punched Stafford Smythe, one of the team owners, right in the face.

Defenseman Carl Brewer joined the Leafs in 1957 and his play surprised Baun. "I remember when Brewer could hardly skate, and suddenly he came streaking out of nowhere, blowing past everybody. Carl was a wonderfully gifted athlete."

Baun says Bert Olmstead, a veteran winger acquired in a deal with Montreal, was the key to future Leaf success in those days. "Bert really knew hockey—as did Allan Stanley, Tim Horton and, later, Red Kelly. Bert would stand up to coach Punch Imlach. When Punch diagrammed a play on the chalkboard, Bert would get angry. He'd jump up and say, 'Punch, that's not the bleepin' way to do it. I'll show you how it should be done.' And Imlach would stand back and toss Olmstead the chalk."

A young lawyer, Al Eagleson, became involved with the Leafs about that time. His friendship with Baun, Bob Pulford, Brewer and other young Leafs led to the formation of the Blue and White investment group.

Eagleson had earned Pulford's respect during their lacrosse days together, and their friendship remains tight to this day, despite Eagleson's conviction in 1998. Incredibly, even in the face of Eagleson's guilty plea in a Boston courtroom and subsequent jail term, Pulford maintains that Eagleson "never did anything wrong. I was in those meetings. It's all bullshit. Pure bullshit." Eagleson became a player agent representing

Carl Brewer for a time. Later, he landed teenage phenom Bobby Orr. It wasn't long before both Brewer and Orr would learn to distrust and revile the man.

Baun says Pulford, as a young player, was a notorious cheapskate. He and Brian Cullen roomed together. When Cullen found a quarter on the floor one day, Pulford insisted they share the quarter, but Cullen refused. When Cullen fell asleep, Pulford took the quarter and bought a newspaper. When he returned, he told Cullen, "Look, I bought us a paper with the money we found." Baun chuckles whenever he tells the story. "Should I put it in this chapter?" I ask him.

"Sure, why not?" he chuckles.

Baun defies any team to match the two defense pairings Imlach had in the '60s, when the Leafs won four Stanley Cups. Stanley and Horton, Brewer and Baun. "There wasn't a team in the league that could come up with four as good as we were," he says proudly.

He's well aware—as we all are—that there's a fine line between those who get inducted into the Hockey Hall of Fame and those who don't. Stanley and Horton are honoured members; Brewer and Baun are not—not yet, anyway.

After the Leafs won the Cup in 1962, beating Chicago in the finals, Baun and his family posed for photographs with the Cup. Later, when son Brian was placed in the famous trophy, he promptly peed in it, setting a standard that Red Kelly's son matched when the Leafs won again in 1964.

Baun says of the Big M, "When Frank Mahovlich scored 81 goals over two seasons in the early '60s, he met with the Leaf brass and was offered a $1,000 raise—take it or leave it. Frank decided to leave it. Chicago owner Jim Norris, while boozing with his NHL cronies following the all star game which began the season, stepped in and offered a million bucks for the big winger. At first the Leafs jumped at the offer. The Leafs almost accepted the Norris cheque when it arrived at the Gardens the next morning. But sanity returned to the Leaf front office. The Big M was told he'd not be joining Bobby Hull in Chicago. He was given a much-deserved raise—at least we were told he was—and appeared to be happy with it. Norris said bitterly, "The Leafs welshed on the deal."

Baun's pal Kent Douglas was named rookie of the year in '63. Baun says, "Kent was a player with a hair-trigger temper combined with nerves of steel. One night he threw his stick around Gordie Howe's throat and told him not to move. And Gordie didn't move. Most players were intimidated by Howe. Not Kent. Kent had a weakness for the ladies—well, didn't most players back then—and in several battles of wills with Imlach, Kent Douglas probably won more times than he lost."

My presentation went on—too long as usual. I was an eyewitness to a memorable bench-clearing brawl at the Gardens one night against Chicago. And Baun was in the thick of it. It was December 7, 1963—Pearl Harbor Day. It was impossible to keep track of all the one-on-one battles. It was the night Murray Balfour and Carl Brewer got into it. Balfour chased after Brewer—they were bitter enemies—and shoved Brewer through the open gate into the Leaf bench. Balfour was cut in the melee and blamed Leaf trainer Bob Haggert and Punch Imlach for interfering. But those close by say it was Toronto Argonaut football star Dick Shatto, whose son was a Brewer fan, who ran down from his box seat nearby to take a punch at Balfour. Baun was at his belligerent best and attacked Stan Mikita and another Hawk player in the penalty box. It was one of those wild nights that were not uncommon during the Original Six era.

Brewer's life was changed forever by the melee. "I never recovered from it," he told me. "I was never the same player after the Balfour incident. Psychologically, it destroyed me. Balfour ruined my life because our fight shamed me."

An incident from a previous game had triggered the ugly events of that night. Three weeks earlier, in Chicago, the Hawks' Reggie Fleming caught Eddie Shack with an elbow, breaking his nose. Shack claimed that Fleming was a "hit from behind"-type player. "Face to face," Shack told reporters, "Fleming's like a little cat who runs away."

Bill Hewitt and I were in the gondola for the December 7 game. Shack hauled Fleming to the ice, earning a minor penalty. When Shack emerged from the box, Fleming pitchforked him in the stomach and was waved off for spearing.

Bobby Baun went nose to nose with Fleming. They snarled at each other, and a brief ruckus broke out, one that soon involved Stan Mikita. Referee Frank Udvari ordered all three players to leave the ice and go to their respective dressing rooms. As they crossed the ice, another skirmish began. Suddenly, both benches emptied.

As Mikita remembers it, "Balfour took off after Brewer and chased him down like a dog after a rabbit. Around and around the rink they went. And when he caught him, he proceeded to beat the snot out of him."

Brewer didn't see it that way. Sitting across from me at our kitchen table one day, he stated, "I had a bad arm injury at the time and didn't want to damage it further by throwing punches."

The brawl lasted for 20 minutes and resulted in seven major penalties, six misconducts and three game misconducts. A total of 135 minutes in penalties were handed out, which surprisingly did not set an NHL record for penalty minutes in one period. That mark had been set 10 years earlier, in a game between the Leafs and Montreal Canadiens— back then, however, players leaving the bench were given 10-minute misconducts through a rule that was abolished prior to the 1959–60 season. Had the old rule been in place, referee Udvari would have issued 355 minutes in penalties.

Baun's fine of $2,800 was a whopper. But Conn Smythe sent his wife Sallie a note at Christmas with a $2,800 cheque enclosed. "I can't pay Bob's fine," he wrote, "But I can give you a $2,800 Christmas present."

In total, the Black Hawks and Leafs were fined $4,925 for the brawl.

The final score was 3–0 Toronto. George Armstrong, Frank Mahovlich and Eddie Shack scored the Toronto goals. Goalie Don Simmons skated off with his second shutout in two games.

Baun was upset with the 1964 deal that sent friends Dick Duff and Bob Nevin to New York for Andy Bathgate and Don McKenney. "Dick Duff carried the Leafs on his back during the lean years of the '50s, and Nevin was the number one right winger in the league."

Now we come to his crowning moment—the 1964 final playoff series with Detroit. Game six in Detroit—a must-win situation for the Leafs. Baun steps in front of a Gordie Howe blast and feels the pain but plays on. Moments later, he turns from a faceoff and hears something pop in his leg. He goes down and cannot get up. He's carried off on a stretcher. In the dressing room, a doctor freezes his leg and he returns to play some more. The game is tied after 60 minutes. Then, in overtime, he slaps at a puck rolling out to the point. The puck flies toward Red Wing defender Bill Gadsby, bounces off his stick and dribbles into the net behind Terry Sawchuk. The Leafs win the game on Baun's strange overtime goal— which becomes one of the most famous goals in history. Baun's biographer, Anne Logan, ranks it right up there with Paul Henderson's winning goal against the Soviets in '72—a bit of a stretch, perhaps. Two days later, on home ice, the Leafs win the Stanley Cup. Only then does Baun agree to have X-rays taken. They reveal that he'd been playing with a broken bone in his leg—a hairline fracture of the fibula.

In that series, Red Kelly played on a leg that was perhaps just as painful. After the '64 Cup win, both Baun and Kelly were in agony. Kelly went from the hospital to the airport because he was a Member of Parliament and the Liberals needed his vote in the House of Commons the very next day. Baun downed a couple of stiff drinks and a handful of Tylenol.

There was great joy in 1967 when the Leafs won the Cup again—over archrival Montreal. But there was no joy in the Baun household. Baun had been replaced by Larry Hillman on defense, and he felt like an outcast— no longer an integral part of the team. He was the only Leaf missing when the team was honoured with a huge parade up Bay Street to City Hall. Along the parade route, people chanted, "Where's Baun? We want Baun!"

Within weeks there was an expansion draft. The NHL doubled in size—six teams to 12. There was a great exodus of players from the Original Six teams.

Baun was left unprotected by the Leafs and signed on with the California Seals—a team based in Oakland. Baun was happy to move because the money was good. When Seals general manager Frank Selke Jr. offered him $87,500, it was said to be the best contract ever offered to any NHL defenseman.

That season, Baun replaced Bob Pulford as president of the NHL Players' Association. The Seals warned him not to accept the position. Bert Olmstead, his old friend and coach of the Seals, told him he'd be fined $1,000 a day until he resigned from the post. Baun stubbornly refused and racked up a fine of $13,000, which was eventually waived. Later, Norm Ullman replaced him in that position.

In May 1968, Baun was traded to Detroit. Team owner Bruce Norris, known for bizarre antics when he was in a drinking mood, wanted to test the legendary Baun toughness. At their very first meeting, in the posh Beaver Club in Montreal, he started a wrestling match with Baun. It was an incredible sight, with tables and food flying in all directions. Norris was a big man—six-foot-five—but Baun was the winner. He threw Norris on his back, and figured he was through in Detroit before he even started. What an interesting way to meet your new boss. What an idiotic way to greet your new employee.

"I'd rather it had been Emile Francis," Baun would say. "He's only five-foot-six and 150 pounds."

The following year, Carl Brewer joined the Red Wings, and Baun's job was to keep him away from Gordie Howe. For some reason, Howe bristled whenever Brewer was around, which was almost every day. Baun took Gordie to lunch one day and said, "Listen, you old fart. You'd better go ask for a raise. You're the biggest name in hockey, and I'm making twice as much money as you are."

Gordie was shocked. He always thought—he'd always been told—he was the highest-paid Red Wing. Obviously, it was a lie.

Baun said, "They're paying me $125,000. What do you say to that?"

Gordie gulped and said, "You're right. Twice as much. More than twice."

The following day, Gordie met with Norris and demanded a raise—to $125,000. When Norris agreed, he told Gord, "I hope this makes your wife happy." Gordie snapped, "Colleen doesn't score the goals for you, I do. And I wonder how long you've been doing this to me."

Baun says, "I found out later that Carl Brewer had us both beat. He'd signed for $150,000." What Bruce Norris and manager Jack Adams did to Howe was shameful. A disgrace. They were willing to pay two ex-Leafs more than double what they were paying the greatest player in the history of the franchise.

But Gordie—and Colleen—can be faulted too, for not realizing how valuable the big right winger was. And because he—and others, like Rocket Richard—were willing to play for peanuts, the rest of the players in the NHL suffered accordingly.

In 1971, Baun turned in his Detroit uniform. He was picked up on waivers by Punch Imlach, who had taken over the Buffalo Sabres franchise. Not long after, his rights were traded to St. Louis. In St. Louis he was told that coach Scotty Bowman was much like Imlach—cold, arrogant, pompous, egocentric. I said to Baun, "Scotty may have been like that as a coach but he was fun to work with as a broadcaster."

Baun refused to report and soon found himself back in Toronto, playing where he began his career, where he loved to be, winding down a wonderful career. In 1970–71, he helped Leaf goalie Jacques

Plante to a remarkable 1.88 goals-against average and was awarded the Bickell Award as the outstanding Leaf player that season.

Around that time, Harold Ballard and Stafford Smythe were charged and convicted of income tax evasion. Stafford died before being sentenced; Ballard served jail time. Baun says Stafford's funeral was a fiasco, with Ballard trying to pull him out of the coffin. "Come on, Staff, you're missing a hell of a party."

This was the same boorish owner who, at a major banquet in Toronto hosted by Dave Hodge, had to take a leak. Instead of shuffling off to the men's room, he lifted the skirt of the head table and peed all over the hotel's carpet. Stafford, on the other hand, "was not a boor," states Baun. "I was truly saddened by Stafford's sudden death."

During the 1972–73 season, Baun was checked hard by Mickey Redmond and fell on his neck. The injury would end his career. Doctors told him he might be paralyzed if he continued to play—especially with the fearless approach he brought to each game. Leaf general manager Jim Gregory said, "Don't worry, Bob. We're obligated to pay your salary for another two seasons."

Three years later, after a disastrous cattle-farming venture that left him bankrupt, Baun came back to hockey as coach of Johnny Bassett's Toronto Toros, a WHA team—for $80,000 a year, plus a car and life insurance. No NHL coach was making more at the time.

Baun didn't really enjoy coaching, so he quit the Toros and got into selling homes, then cars, then insurance. He worked hard and, not surprisingly, began to prosper again. He was able to lend Tim Horton $10,000 to get into the donut business. Baun was closer to Horton than to any other Leaf player. He was inconsolable when he learned of Horton's death.

Horton was killed after a game Bill Hewitt and I called at Maple Leaf Gardens in 1974. We had named him one of the three stars. Andra Kelly would say to me, "I've never seen Red cry. But the morning he heard Tim was gone, he broke down and shed many tears." Baun would shed many tears that day too.

Ten years later, Baun opened a Tim Horton's store in Pickering [later the chain would drop the apostrophe from its name, in response to Quebec language laws], and it became the most successful franchise in Canada for four straight years. He opened a second location nearby, one that did almost as well.

Tim Horton's had a spectacular growth record. It began when Horton teamed up with Ron Joyce in Hamilton, where they owned one store. Within a few years, it became a multi-million dollar enterprise. Baun wound up with two of the most successful stores in the chain.

Less of a visionary was my good friend Ray Bradley. A former hockey player from South Porcupine, Bradley was working for Molson in Hamilton. On his way to head office each morning, Bradley stopped in at the Tim Horton's for coffee. His boss, former NHLer Gaye Stewart, suggested to Bradley one day that he take a second job—coaching the local Provincial Police hockey club. Bradley said, "Sure. I'm a hockey guy. Why not?" He became the head coach, and one of his two assistants was officer Ron Joyce. They formed a friendship that led to a meeting between them—to discuss business, not hockey. Joyce said, "You're from the north country, Ray. Why don't you move back up there and open the first four Tim Horton's donut shops in Northern Ontario? All choice locations. I can get you in for $25,000 per franchise. You'll make a killing." Ray went home and talked it over with his wife, Doris. "Are you out of your mind?" she said. "Northerners won't go for Tim Horton's—especially the French. Besides, you're moving up the corporate ladder with Molson. You've got a great boss in Gaye Stewart. And finally, I don't want to move back north." The Bradleys passed on the opportunity.

Baun began to hold his celebrity golf tournaments in the late 1980s. After dinner, Baun would always come to the microphone to single out pals in the room. He genuinely loved these individuals, and tears would flow down his cheeks before he was finished.

Baun married Sallie, his childhood sweetheart, and they have weathered the good times and the bad—like all of us. They were apart for a long time, but they came together again. They have five children whom they cherish and 12 grandchildren they dote on. Baun's son Jeff, a former university star, played on our oldtimers' team for several seasons and displayed all the skills of an NHLer. Strange he never became a pro. Bobby's grandson Kyle, a star at Colgate, has pro scouts nodding their approval.

Reflecting on Baun's outstanding career, if one hockey memory stands out, it was that long, looping, apparently harmless shot that changed direction one night in 1964—one goal out of 40 he would score in his career—and found the net to win a game in overtime. It was the night Bobby Baun became a hockey legend.

Sports Illustrated placed his goal at number 17 on the list of all-time great sporting moments of the last century in North America. It's amazing that a lofted shot taken by a crippled player could rank so highly on the list.

While many of us remember that shot and that goal, what we should remember is the courage, the tenacity, the spirit, the backbone and the downright guts it took for Baun to come hobbling out of the visiting team's dressing room and back to the ice in time to take that winning shot.

But then, he was never lacking in guts.

FRANK CARLIN COACH

FRANK CARLIN
Minor League Marvel

It was Scotty Bowman who suggested I meet with Frank Carlin. This was back in the '80s, when Scotty and I worked a lot of games together on *Hockey Night in Canada* in Montreal.

Scotty had been talking about his parents and how they came over from Scotland many years ago and settled in Montreal. They soon learned an old Canadian custom—ordering from the Eaton's catalogue. Scotty's mom bought a chair from the catalogue and had it delivered COD. Scotty's dad was home alone when the big box arrived—labelled "COD."

"What in hell did she order all that cod for?" he grumbled. "We'll never eat all that. Take it back."

Scotty knew I was collecting stories for a book, and he said, "Frank Carlin knows more about hockey than any man you'll ever meet." Up to then, I thought Scotty was the most knowledgeable hockey man I'd ever met.

Frank and I met for lunch at the famous Montreal Amateur Athletic Association. I had never been there before, which was embarrassing. What kind of hockey historian are you, McFarlane? After all, this was the club that won the first Stanley Cup, in 1893.

Frank Carlin's name may not be familiar to you. His expertise covered eras long gone by. He was a veteran hockey manager and coach of the minor league Montreal Royals back in the '40s. It was said he would someday be the boss of the Montreal Canadiens. That never happened, but he was still highly respected for his hockey smarts. He had groomed many young players for the Habs, had guided the Royals to an Allan Cup and had rubbed elbows with most of the greats of the game.

He began by telling me about a hockey excursion overseas back in the 1920s.

Brian, many years ago, I was invited to take a Canadian team to Sweden to show them how to play hockey. It happened because two journalists from the main newspaper in Sweden were sent to the 1924 Olympic Games. The controversy over hockey versus bandy had been ongoing for a few years. Many people argued about the merits of one game over the other. These two journalists were sent to Chamonix, to the Olympic Games, to write on winter sports, but they took in as many hockey games as they could. When they came back to Stockholm, they wrote about how thrilled they were with hockey.

The Toronto Granites were Canada's representatives at the Games—always a good team, with future NHL stars Hooley Smith and Dunc Munro on the roster.

They walloped every team they faced, did they not?

Of course. They started off with a 30–0 win over Czechoslovakia, then whipped Sweden 22–0 and Switzerland 33–0. In the gold medal game, they downed the U.S. 6–1. Harry Watson, their star player, racked up 36 goals in five games.

So the two Swedes saw some good hockey games—well, let me say they saw some *high-scoring* hockey games. They came back home raving about hockey as compared to their bandy. But I guess nobody listened very hard at that time.

What was bandy like?

Bandy was played with a hockey stick about the size of a field hockey stick. I have a bandy stick at home. The Swedes played with a ball—a cord ball—and they played on an outdoor ice surface about the size of a soccer field.

But they played on skates?

Oh, yes, on skates. They were great skaters, but they wore what we called reachers, which are speed skates, because they had to go the long distance. So when they played hockey, they couldn't stop and start like we did, and that was a great disadvantage. The Swedish players were in wonderful condition and could skate like hell. So these two journalists wound up in a bar with other newspapermen, and they started arguing about the merits of hockey over bandy. They had a helluva argument, so the two men who went to the Olympic Games said, "We should get this thing settled once and for all. Let's ask our newspaper to sponsor a team from America, a good amateur team to come over here and show our countrymen what hockey is all about."

The only contact they had in America was Spalding, the sporting goods manufacturer. I guess they bought basketballs and other equipment from them. So they contacted Spalding, and Spalding recommended a team I managed in Montreal. We were strictly an amateur club but a pretty good one. We were all good enough to play in the Montreal Senior League. So we got the invitation.

Now I had to scramble to get enough players to go on this trip, because it meant we'd have to take a couple of months off. So we held a meeting, and nine players said they would go. The Swedes tried to peddle us to other countries, to cut expenses, but they got no takers. But once we got over there and showed them our stuff, suddenly everybody wanted us. When we got to Stockholm, we found out Berlin wanted us, and Vienna, Milan, Davos, and Paris wanted us too. So we travelled everywhere, playing game after game until every country saw us. They accepted us for sure.

Were these artificial ice rinks you played on?

All of them except Sweden. Sweden was natural ice.

Artificial ice was invented before the turn of the last century, Do you know anything about the history of artificial ice? The first arenas to have it in North America, I believe, were in New York, Pittsburgh, Baltimore and Washington. But they had it in Europe before that.

Yes. We played on artificial ice in all these exhibition games. The trouble was, when we got to Sweden it turned quite mild and they had to send us off to a place farther north. Then the temperature dropped, so we were able to return and fulfill our assignments in Stockholm.

Were these games or clinics with the Swedes? You were just teaching them how to play hockey?

No, no. We played against them. They played hockey against us. They could skate, but they couldn't stop and start.

Because they had the long speed skates—the reachers?

Yes. That was a disadvantage to them. We saw them play their own game, bandy. Geez, they could really play. They asked us if we wanted to play against them, and we said nothing doing. They would have left us flat-footed. I have this bandy stick at home and a ball. I offered it to *Hockey Night in Canada*, but the man I talked to wasn't interested.

We enjoyed a wonderful tour of Europe. We arrived in Paris, and some promoters there wanted us to play on a tiny little ice surface located in a nightclub. It was the poorest excuse for a hockey rink I'd ever seen. So I turned down the offer. But we went to see a game played there, and it was hilarious. The rink was so small the teams played three aside. And one of my players was recruited to be referee. The rink was surrounded by brass rails supporting red velvet curtains designed to keep the puck in play. Every time the puck flew through the curtains the referee dove in after it, often landing between some woman's legs. One lady spectator patted him on the head and said, "Oh, you naughty boy." Seems to me he spent most of the night diving through those curtains. He had a wonderful time.

A few days later, in Milan, Italy, I looked down the ice, and my team's net is empty. The other team was pressing, and my goalie—a chap named Beaudry—was over against the boards, chatting up some blonde. Of course, the score didn't really matter anyway. In 15 games over there, we scored 162 goals and gave up only 10.

Scotty Bowman said to be sure and ask Frank if he's got any Jacques Plante stories—about knitting his own toque and that sort of thing. And of course about the Montreal Royals.

Well, Jacques was never ashamed of his knitting. We used to travel first class with the Royals. We would have a private car on the train, and he would sit there knitting. People would come through and stare, but he wouldn't pay any attention to them. He would hold up his work and tell his friends, "Hey, take a look at this."

What was your first recollection of Plante? Where did he come from?

Well, I knew him playing juniors and he was on the train with us one night, juniors and seniors coming back from someplace on the same train. I wanted him for the next year because he was awfully good and I had spoken for him. So he came to me and said he didn't know I had spoken for him but he wanted a chance to play for me. I said that I was already working on it. That was my first contact with him. He was very good—an outstanding goalie.

Yes, he turned out to be one of the best ever.

When he joined the Canadiens, I think Dick [Irvin] was very foolish to fool around with him. I mean, he made him take off his toque, and that was a talking piece. He stopped him from moving around outside his net. I told Dick to let him do what he wanted, because he was very colourful.

I had Doug Harvey playing for me then. And Harvey said Plante saved him from all kinds of trouble in our own end of the rink. Jacques used to go in the corner to get the puck and skate like hell. I used to run a skating race, two or three times a winter, and one time, with all his equipment on, I think Plante came in second. He could skate very, very fast. So I never stopped him. I said, "Go ahead, Jacques." But Dick would say, "I don't like that guy's speediness." I said, "Dick, I think you're wrong." Plante saved Harvey from taking a lot of punishment. He'd get into the corner fast and get the puck out. Saved his teammates from taking a lot of bodychecks.

It's unfortunate Irvin didn't let him play with his knitted toque on—and do the colourful stuff. We need more colour in hockey.

They told me that his knitting started out of necessity. His mother made all the kids—there were eight or nine of them—knit their own socks. He used to knit his own undershirts. So she taught them all how to knit, and they had to do it.

What kind of money would a player on the Royals make in those days?

I can tell you exactly in one case. Kelly Burnett was suspended by Eddie Shore, and I wanted a goal scorer badly, and he was a goal scorer. So I contacted Eddie Shore and I said, "Eddie, Burnett is on your suspended list. You're not using him and I could use him. I'll give you a player for him." So he said, "All right, it's a deal." So Burnett came to Montreal and I said to him, "Kelly, I'm willing to pay you $4,000." He said, "Frank, hand me your pen?" He was our leading scorer for the next three years. What a bargain! But of course, $4,000 then would be equal to what today— eight or 10 times as much?

Oh, easily. Who was the greatest player you ever had?

The best in the world—Doug Harvey. Nobody has ever been as good as he was. Best defenseman in the world.

How long did you have him?

Well, right from juniors.

Tell me about Doug. He had a most colourful career.

He could speed the game up or slow it down. He could do anything he wanted. I had him on the way up, and I had him on the way back down when I went to Quebec as the manager, after I retired from the

Royals. Doug was a terrific guy. We would have a practice at nine in the morning, and he'd stay out on the ice afterwards with all of the defensemen. He'd tell them to stay out, I certainly didn't tell them to. He coached them and taught them all his tricks—and believe me, he had a lot of tricks. He did an awful lot of good. Some may not agree with me that he was the greatest defenseman that ever lived. You have Eddie Shore and all those guys, but I don't think anybody was as good as Doug.

Not even Bobby Orr? Orr was the best I ever saw.

Orr was a different type, very colourful. Doug wasn't that colourful, but he had tremendous ability and a great work ethic. By contrast, I had Phil Watson one year. If the practice was at nine, he would be out of the rink at 10 to 10. Geez, what a difference! He wouldn't even say good morning to me in the morning. No companionship.

Vic Stasiuk was terrific. I had him one year. I would go into his office and I would say, "Vic, have you had your lunch yet?" and he would say, "Oh, geez, I forgot about that." He would work till three o'clock without even taking a lunch break. A terrific worker.

Boom Boom Geoffrion was one of our coaches, and he was terrific. Great person to go out with after the game—you couldn't go out with the players. Here's a funny story about him. We were in Rochester in a motel where they had these twin beds. You put a quarter in a slot by the bed and they give you a massage. Boom Boom, as soon as he hit the sack, fell asleep. It takes me about 10 minutes to drop off, so I waited until he was sound asleep and I dropped a quarter in the slot. Jesus, the bed started vibrating like hell. Five minutes with that bed bouncing around must have felt like an hour to him. He just laid there and oh my, the curse words he used. He used all the sacraments of the Catholic Church and then some. What a character! He was great company. They all were, except for that stinkin' Watson.

I interviewed Watson a couple of times when he coached the Rangers. He gave me some good lines. He told me once that the Rangers were going to go on a tour of Europe with Chicago after the season. He said, "You know, the funny thing is, I was talking to Gump Worsley the other

day and he said, 'Phil, the first puck that hits me in the belly, the bur-
gundy is going to squirt right out of my ears.'"

That sounds like just the sort of thing Worsley would say. I got some good players on the rebound. At one time, 97 of the players who played for me played in the National Hockey League. I have a little book at home with all these names in it.

How close were you to people like Rocket Richard, Jean Beliveau and
Dickie Moore?

Not too close. Dickie played for me but Beliveau played against me. Beliveau played junior and then senior in Quebec.

I was with the old Inkerman Rockets then. We were pretty well beaten
up by Beliveau and the Quebec Citadelles in 1951.

You fellows did a helluva job with the Inkerman Rockets.

It's an interesting little story, how a town of about a hundred people got
a Junior A franchise. How Lloyd Laporte, a one-eyed bookkeeper, put
that team together. In 1951, we ended up playing against Beliveau and the
Citadelles. They beat us out, but we beat out the Ottawa champions, the
Northern Ontario champs and the Maritime champions. It was a pretty
good run, and we made it to the final six in the Memorial Cup race.

I was amazed at how well that little team played.

I'm pleased somebody remembers Inkerman. Well, now, tell me about
early-day hockey in Montreal.

I'll tell you. I have a book at home, and I was reading about the Victorias when they were Stanley Cup–winners here in Montreal. That's at the turn of the century. Hartland MacDougall—his picture is on the wall over there—is mentioned. He played in the Stanley Cup game that was never finished—in 1896. The referee got mad at the players, so he took off his skates and went home. Some officials chased after him, but by the time he came back it was too late. The game was never finished. It was against the Winnipeg Vics, I think.

That would be Charlie Coleman's book, The Trail of the Stanley Cup. *I have those too. Wonderful books. A team from this club—the MAAA— was the first team to win the Stanley Cup. Did you know they almost gave the trophy back? There was some sort of friction between the hockey team and the association. When the hockey team won it, they said to the Cup trustee, Sheriff Sweetland, who brought the trophy down from Ottawa, "We don't want that trophy. Take it back." Apparently the MAAA had to meet with the hockey club and say, "Look, Lord Stanley would be insulted if you refuse to accept it. You'd better take it whether you like it or not." So they said, "Okay."*

It's a wonder they just didn't accept it in the first place.

I think they were upset that someone came and presented it to the MAAA president, instead of presenting it to the manager of the hockey team. It's an interesting little story.

Indeed it is.

You played yourself. What arenas did you play in here in Montreal?

The Victoria rink. And the Forum, of course. I went to Loyola College, which is on Drummond Street, by the LaSalle Hotel. We had no facilities at all. No swimming pool, no gymnasium and no grounds. So anybody that came as a student to Loyola automatically became a member of the MAAA. It was included in my fees. So I have been a member here for 70 years.

The Victoria rink was quite a famous arena wasn't it?

Yes, it was. Very famous. They played the first Stanley Cup game there. It had very low boards. Another arena was in Westmount, where the ice manufacturing plant was, on Westmount Avenue. That burned down in 1917. So the Northeys got a group together and they built the Forum.

The Westmount rink burned down the first year the NHL was in operation.

Yes. They played in the Mount Royal Arena until they built the Forum. We played for the championship of Quebec there.

But you ask me anything you want.

I am interested in all of your memories, Frank. Especially the unusual things that happened in early-day hockey. Like a coach putting two goalies in the net during a Stanley Cup game. I had never heard of that before. Rat Portage did it in a game against Ottawa. And there was a time when Ottawa flooded the ice with two inches of water in the spring so that they would slow the visiting team down.

Tommy Gorman used to do that in Ottawa when we went up there.

Someone wrote that a team put sand on the floor of the visitor's dressing room. The sand would take the edge off the skate blades. Things like that.

When you mention two goaltenders in the same net, it reminded me that I was the first coach to pull a goalkeeper out. I was too young to realize that someday it would be a big thing. I did it in a junior game. The press thought nothing of it, and it was just passed off. We lost the game anyway. This would be in the early '20s. We didn't score. It was a team I handled called St. Gabriel's. I kept trying to get people interested in that strategy, but nobody was interested.

Finally, in the Mount Royal League a year or two later, they decided such a move was perfectly legal. By then I was coach of the Victoria Seniors. We were playing in the Forum one night and we were one goal down, and I took the goalkeeper out and there was a huge uproar. The president of the league started it. He said, "What are you trying to do, make a farce out of hockey? You can't take the goalkeeper out!" I said, "Oh, I can't?" He said, "No, you can't." So I said, "Okay, I'll tell the goalkeeper to play forward." He said, "You can do what you want, but you can't take the goalkeeper out of the game." So I told my goalie, Barky Robinson, to go up to the opponents' blueline with all his equipment on. We gave him a regular stick, and he went up and fell all over the goddamn ice and really made a farce of hockey. I was still too young to realize that someday it might be a good thing. After all, it's even done in international hockey now. The fans know, with a couple of minutes to go, the coach will be taking the goalie out. It's automatic.

Oh, I just remembered. Here's one for your book—if anybody will believe it. We went into Boston once and there didn't appear to be a referee for the game. There were two linesmen but no ref. When I mentioned his absence to the linesmen, they just laughed and said, "He's up there"—pointing skyward. Sure enough, high over the ice, sitting in a gondola, was the referee. Somebody figured he'd have a better overall view of the game if he was high over the ice in a kind of basket. I swear it was the only time I'd ever seen such a thing. So we played in the only game in which the referee was perched 40 or 50 feet above the action. If he called a lousy penalty, the players below had nobody to argue with, except for the linesmen. And they would shrug and say, "Don't tell us about it. He's the guy who made the call." And they'd point skyward again.

In those games in the States, I experimented with taking the goalkeeper out. I did it the first night we played in New York. I took the goalkeeper out with 10 minutes to play, and we were leading 3–1. This character sitting beside me said, "Is this the way you play hockey in Canada? Don't you know you are two goals ahead?" I said, "Yes, I'm just trying something new. It's an experiment." Nothing happened, and we won that night, but when I tried the same thing in Boston, they scored on us. That was the end of that. It made me look bad.

Why would you take him out with 10 minutes to go?

I was just experimenting. Another trick I conceived, when we were in trouble and needed a rest, was the water bottle trick. In those days we used an ordinary glass bottle for the players to drink from, so on my signal the player would drop the bottle on the ice. It would break into a hundred pieces, and the maintenance men would have to come out and clean up the mess. By then my best players would have their breath back.

That is like Jacques Demers or Mike Keenan a few years ago, throwing pennies on the ice to get a delay. Or junior coach Ernie McLean. He threw the other team's water bottle at the referee when his back was turned. The ref saw the logo on the bottle and penalized the wrong team. McLean's team scored with the man advantage, won the game and went all the way to win the Memorial Cup.

Another night, we needed a point to make the playoffs. We had to have that point. It came down to where we had a tie game going and we got a penalty. It was a tough situation. So they broke away, and I quickly put an extra man on the ice to stop the rush, even though the ref gave us a penalty. And I kept putting men out there and taking more penalties. That was better than giving up the tying goal. Finally time ran out, we won the game and the league decided to change the rules. From then on, they'd give the other team a goal if there was interference from the bench.

Frank and I talked on and on, and when I left the MAAA, I had recurring visions of the Swedes on their reacher skates, the naughty boy who slipped through the curtains and dove between the ladies' legs, Harry Watson averaging six goals per game and the referee perched high over the ice, all heads tilting upward with every blast of his whistle.

It was a delightful luncheon that stretched into the afternoon.

I never saw Frank Carlin again.

GORDIE HOWE
and TED KENNEDY

*The Collision That Almost
Ended Howe's Career*

In the summer of 2009, the world lost two famous Ted Kennedys. One was a long-time American senator, the other was a revered member of the Hockey Hall of Fame.

I knew the latter, not the former.

The Ted Kennedy I knew—through his appearances at many of our annual NHL Oldtimer dinners—was a superb Leaf captain who was handed the C after Syl Apps retired, in 1948. Kennedy guided the Leafs to four Stanley Cups in the next five years.

"We should have won five in a row," he tells a group of us one night. On this occasion, aside from myself, the group includes Sid Smith, another former Leaf captain, and Joe "the Duke of Paducah" Klukay, who enjoyed eight successful seasons with the Leafs and three more with Boston. "I'm sure we would have won five straight," says Kennedy, "if it hadn't been for the Gordie Howe incident."

Ah, the Gordie Howe incident.

He's referring to one of the most controversial incidents of the post-war era, a horrific collision that occurred during the first game of a 1950 semifinal playoff series between the Leafs and the Red Wings, a shocking crash of body into boards that almost ended the life of Gordie Howe, the greatest scorer of his era.

Howe, age 21, had blossomed into a true superstar that season, scoring 35 goals and finishing third in the league in total points, behind teammates Ted Lindsay and Sid Abel. The Red Wings had compiled 88 points, the most in NHL history, and in the post-season were itching to knock off the Leafs, who had humiliated them in playoff action for the past three seasons—Howe's Wings had lost 11 straight playoff games to Kennedy's Leafs.

"Tell me about that series," I say to Ted, "and what happened to Howe."

His pale blue eyes lock with mine. He pauses a moment and sighs. Then he says, "It's late in the first game, and we're winning 5–0. I'm carrying the puck up the boards and I've got a charley horse, so I'm not skating my best. Out of the corner of my eye, I can see big Howe coming. He's coming across the ice in full flight—really fast—and I'm thinking, if this kid ever hits me, I'm going to land somewhere up in the stands. So I pull up a bit. I know I can't outfoot Howe. But I saw George Gravel, the referee, begin to raise a finger. He's going to give Howe a charging penalty as soon as he nails me. So I pull up, and *boom*! Howe brushes by me and crashes into the boards—headfirst!

Klukay, sitting next to Teeder, nods in agreement. "Howe was coming fast," he says. "He lost his footing. I was there. That's the way I saw it."

The crowd gasped as Howe nose-dived into the boards and flopped to the ice, unconscious. Seconds later, he tried to get up but couldn't.

Team doctors called for an ambulance, and Howe was rushed to Detroit's Harper hospital. An early diagnosis indicated he'd suffered a possible broken cheekbone, a serious concussion, a broken nose and damage to one eye.

Later, Howe would say, "I was going to run Kennedy into the boards, and I was leaning forward, head low to the ice, when Kennedy passed the puck to Sid Smith. On the follow-through, Kennedy's stick spiked me right in the eye. The blow didn't do a lot of damage, but it threw me off. I went flying into the boards.

"I'll never forget that horrible ride to the hospital. I felt horribly sick. I remember someone gave me a glass of water and I vomited. The doctors decided to operate right away, and they shaved my head. That upset me, and even though there was an anaesthetist on duty, I recall the shock of feeling the pressure of a drill on my skull. I remember hoping they knew when to stop drilling."

A renowned neurosurgeon, Dr. Frederic Schreiber, drilled a small hole just above Howe's right ear to relieve pressure on the brain. After the operation, the surgeon told Ted Lindsay that if there'd been a 30-minute delay, Gordie might not have made it.

"I hated Kennedy back then," says Lindsay. "Just like I hated Rocket Richard and most of my opponents. But I respected him as a player. He was a great one."

Back at the Detroit Olympia, accusations were flying. Red Wings coach Tommy Ivan and his boss, Jack Adams, denounced referee George Gravel for not calling a penalty on Kennedy. "He butt-ended my guy in the eye," Ivan screamed.

Kennedy offers a theory on the emotional backlash: "What really precipitated it was the fact we knocked Detroit out three years in a row. Four straight! Gone! And there was hell to pay in Detroit. The Detroit organization, particularly manager Jack Adams—who was a very volatile manager, as everyone knows—was livid. In my view, there was so much animosity, so much frustration over being beaten by the Leafs, that they made a real big deal out of it. A very big deal."

"I offered to swear an oath that I had not intended to injure Howe. I didn't even know he was badly hurt until I came back down the ice and saw him lying there. Hell, I considered Howe to be a friend. I'd never do anything to harm him."

"Ted's right," chips in Klukay. "It was Jack Adams who fuelled the flames."

At the time, some of the Red Wings scoffed at Kennedy's comments. Howe's linemate Sid Abel snorted, "Baloney. How in hell can Kennedy claim he didn't hit Gordie?" Red Wing goaltender Harry Lumley called Kennedy "a damn liar."

Howie Meeker, my *Hockey Night in Canada* colleague for many years and Kennedy's linemate with the post-war Leafs, said the injury to Howe in game one cost the Leafs the series. "After Howe accidentally fell into the boards while trying to check Kennedy," Meeker said, "there was a backlash against Teeder and the Leafs for trying to injure Howe. It really affected us.

Some hack writers accused Kennedy of butt-ending Howe, but that was bogus. Still, the injury to Howe gave the Wings motivation. We lost in overtime in game seven when Leo Reise scored the winning goal."

"If we had won the series against Detroit," says Kennedy, "we surely would have knocked off the Rangers in the finals and won the Stanley Cup. That would have given us four in a row, and the next season we came back to win it again. So that's how close we came to becoming the first team ever to win five straight Cups."

To Howe's credit, he never blamed Kennedy for the injury that almost ended his playing days.

●

I ask Sid Smith to tell me about Gordie Howe's renowned strength.

He laughs. "I was checking Howe one night in Detroit, and I tried to run him into the boards. But the guy was so strong, he just lifted me up with one arm and held me there. I was three inches off the ice. Then with the other arm he shovelled the puck over to Ted Lindsay, and the Red Wings scored a goal on the play. I came back to the bench and coach Hap Day said to me, "Smitty, why the hell didn't you run Howe through the boards?" and I said, "Hap, I tried to, but the guy wouldn't put me down."

More recently, I asked Phil Esposito what he thought about Howe. He said:

Old Gordie was something, boy. The toughest old bugger I ever played against. I played in an oldtimers' game on the same side with Gordie many years ago, and some fancy Dan guy was flying down the ice. Gordie leaned over to me and said, "You know, Phil, I think it's time we cut that guy down to size." Two minutes later, the guy was lying on the ice and Gordie's leaning over him, saying innocently, "Are you all right?" Christ, he just speared the guy—right in the balls. It was unbelievable.

I remember one time watching *The Dick Cavett Show*. Gordie was there with his sons Mark and Marty. And Cavett says, "What kind of equipment did you wear?" Gordie says, "I wore skates, shin pads, elbow pads, pants and shoulder pads. And a cup, of course." Cavett says to the boys, "Did you wear the same things?" They say, "Yeah, but we also wore helmets." Cavett turns back to Gordie and says, "You never wore a helmet?" Gordie says, "Nah, I never wore a helmet." Cavett says, "But you wore a cup? Why would you wear a cup but not a helmet?" And Gordie says, "Hey, you can always get someone to do your thinking for you." Geez, I fell right out of bed when he said that.

Then there's the story of Gordie and his two boys playing for Houston in the WHA. One night, a guy jumped one of the Howe kids—Mark, I think. This guy had Mark down and was flailing away at him. Gordie skated over and told the guy, "Let him up." The guy told Gordie to eff off. So Gordie leaned over and stuck two of his fingers up the guy's nostrils and hauled him to his feet. The guy's nose must have ached for a week.

When Pierre Larouche played against Howe one night, he approached him during the warm-up. "Gordie, you've always been my hero. Can I have your stick after the game?"

Gordie said, "Sure, kid."

"Well, in the third period he chopped me for about six stitches in the head," recalls Pierre. "And while I was still reeling, he said, 'Hey, kid, that stick is going to mean a whole lot more to you now.'"

And you know, he was right.

●

In 1975, as the playing-president of the Houston Aeros of the WHA, Howe was suspended by the league after he "bumped" referee Ron Asselstine. Asselstine immediately resigned, stating, "I'm finished. When the man who's supposed to be the craftiest player ever to play the game drives me in the guts, it's obvious I'm not the man for the job."

Even the fans weren't safe from Gordie's quick temper. In Chicago one night, a fan needled Howe—more than once. When he'd heard enough, Howe turned and nailed him with a punch to the jaw. The fan sued, of course, and when the judge heard the case, he asked, "Did you provoke the hockey player?"

The fan admitted he did.

"Then you deserved what you got," said the judge. "Case dismissed."

Perhaps what is most remarkable about Howe's brilliant career is his unmatched longevity in the game. The numbers make your head spin.

More than 2,000 professional games played, more than 1,000 goals scored and more than 1,500 career assists accumulated. A six-time NHL scoring champ, Howe finished in the top five in league scoring for two decades—20 straight seasons. The six-time MVP is a member of 11 different halls of fame.

Howe's final professional game (not including a single shift with the Detroit Vipers in 1997 that allowed him to assert he'd played in six decades) was on April 11, 1980, when the Canadiens eliminated the Hartford Whalers from the playoffs. Grampa Howe was 52 years and 11 days old that day, finishing a pro hockey journey that had begun more than 34 years earlier, when he scored a goal in his first game with the Detroit Red Wings.

In 2014, Howe, 86, was said to be near death in Texas. But the old fellow rallied after stem cell injections in Mexico and on February 5, 2015, his friends and fans were amazed when he said he planned to attend a sports celebrity banquet honouring him in Saskatoon. A few days before the event he learned his younger brother Vic, 85, had passed away in Moncton, N.B. Vic played briefly with the Rangers in the early '50s and scored three goals in 29 NHL games. A grieving Howe showed up as promised. At the sold-out event in Saskatoon, Wayne Gretzky, Bobby Hull, Dennis Hull and Brett Hull were head-table guests and all four lavished praise on Mr. Hockey.

But it was Gretzky, at the end of the evening, who perhaps said it best. Gretzky, the player who replaced Howe as hockey's greatest scorer, stood up and said of his childhood idol and hero, "He is, he was, he will always be the greatest of all time."

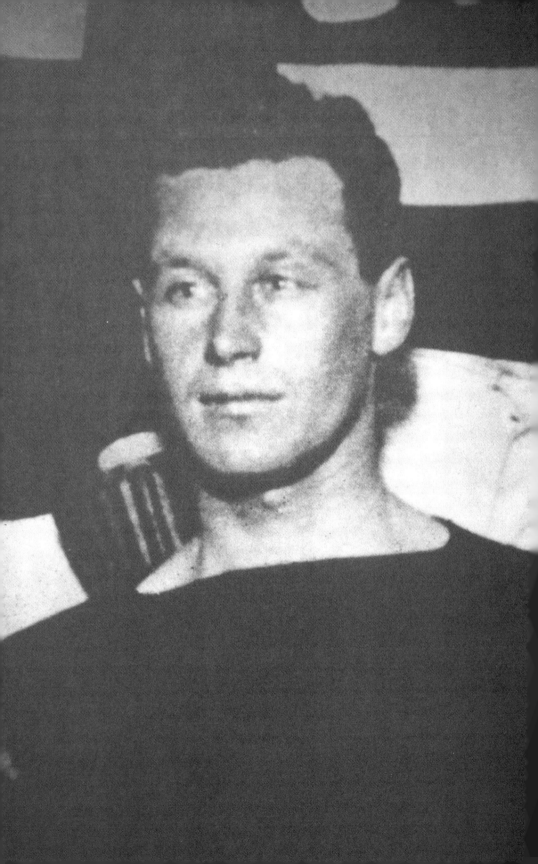

HOBEY BAKER
First American Hockey Hero

In the early 1950s, as a college player with St. Lawrence University, I had the opportunity to play against teams from Princeton University. At Princeton, I recall being curious about the name I saw over the arena entrance—Hobey Baker Memorial Rink—and I wondered about the man to whom the rink was dedicated. I soon learned that Baker was revered as one of Princeton's greatest athletes and one of the world's greatest hockey players. How could that be, I wondered? The man was never a professional. But further research convinced me that Hobey Baker was indeed a superb all round athlete and one of the greatest hockey players in North America more than a century ago.

Long before the New York Rangers and the New York Americans made their splashy debuts in the NHL, hockey was well established not far from Broadway. The 20th century was a little more than a decade old when a handsome collegian captured the headlines with his prowess on ice.

Outside St. Nicholas Arena in New York, its marquee emblazoned with a huge banner proclaiming "Hobey Baker Plays Tonight," a line of limos would stretch along 66th Street, from Columbus Avenue to Central Park West. It was like a night at the opera or the opening of a

Broadway show. Inside the arena, fans dressed in their Sunday best filled every seat, lured by the appearance of Hobart Baker, an American kid, a hockey phenom possessed with extraordinary athletic ability.

"Here comes Hobey!" the fans would shriek, leaping to their feet and cheering as the handsome blond "rover" for St. Nick's circled his goal and began an electrifying dash down the ice. One veteran sports writer, after seeing Baker perform, said, "I have never heard such spontaneous cheering for a player and I never expect to again. Spectators went hysterical when he flashed across the ice, cradling the puck on his stick, swooping and swerving in a most graceful manner. He was an athletic marvel, a phenom on metal blades."

This was not a hardened professional or even a semi-pro he was writing about. Baker and his St. Nick's mates were true amateurs. After games, they found no crinkled bills stuffed in their shoes, a common practice in Canada at the time. The St. Nick's boys paid for their ice time at the arena. They were bankers and brokers and men of substance and influence. Incredibly, several players had their personal valets accompany them to games. After the matches, the valets would assist the players into evening attire—tails and white gloves—and off they would go in the waiting limos with their ladies to a posh restaurant or nightclub where they would dine and dance the rest of the night away.

The St. Nicholas ice surface had long been a winter playground to Hobart Baker. He first played under its lights at age 16, when he was regarded as the best player ever to perform for St. Paul's School in New Hampshire. It was Christmas 1908, and the St. Paul's preppies came to New York to play a pair of schoolboy games at St. Nicholas against Lawrenceville, a traditional rival. Why St. Nick's? Because several alumni of St. Paul's had purchased a nondescript icehouse and converted it into an arena—complete with artificial ice. Artificial ice had been around for a long time. The Glacarium, an arena in the Chelsea area of London, which opened its doors to skaters in 1876, was the first artificial ice rink. By the turn of the century, similar rinks had opened to skaters in Paris, New York, Melbourne and Johannesburg.

On the eve of the Christmas competition on the artificial ice of St. Nicholas, illness struck the Lawrenceville seven, and a team called St. Nick's, composed of older, tougher excollegians, was recruited to stand in. St. Paul's stunned the former college stars with a surprising display of hockey technique, most of it flowing from the strong arms and legs of a blond teenager—Hobart Baker.

Who was this lad with the blazing speed, the deadly shot and the stamina of a Canadian pro? It was revealed that he'd been born in Bala Cynwyd on Philadelphia's Main Line in 1892, son of a former Princeton football star—Thornton "Bobby" Baker. When the Bobby Baker marriage ended in divorce in 1907, Hobey, 11, was packed off to St. Paul's School in Concord, New Hampshire.

At St. Paul's, which he attended for seven years, Hobey (more so than his older brother, Thornton) discovered the joys of athletic pursuits. He excelled in gymnastics, football, baseball and swimming. He could master almost any sport with little or no training. He donned roller skates for the first time and in a few minutes was doing stunts on them, often on one foot. By his 15th birthday, he was regarded as the best athlete on campus, perhaps the best in St. Paul's history.

Hockey was big at St. Paul's, and Baker quickly showed an uncanny ability to play the game. By 14, he was a regular on the school team and skating, even then, as well as or better than most professionals. Throughout his career, he wore a minimum of padding, and never donned a helmet in any of the sports he played—even college football.

After graduating from St. Paul's, he attended Princeton University, where he became the wonder player of college hockey—and football. He captained both teams and became a marked man on the gridiron and on the ice. The light hockey padding he wore made him vulnerable to sticks and fists, and he suffered some brutal beatings in games. He never lost his temper, never retaliated. In his entire college career he received two penalties. His movie star looks made him the idol of the crowds.

On-campus arenas were unknown in Hobey's day. College games were played in big city rinks like St. Nicholas, and huge crowds began to show up for Princeton games—there to see the greatest American-born amateur player of them all.

John Davies, Baker's biographer, writes about his acute modesty. "He was always polite and obliging, except when talk got around to his athletic exploits. Then he could be curt. His exquisite coordination he regarded as some kind of freak power he had been born with and he took no special pride in it. He was deeply embarrassed by the sign 'Hobey Baker Plays Tonight' and sometimes refused to play until it was taken down."

When he joined St. Nick's after graduation, he played against players on various teams who were paid to play hockey. Many were imports from Canada who didn't share Baker's views that hockey was a "gentleman's" game. They used knees and elbows and every conceivable dirty trick to force him to the sidelines. When he'd had enough, he'd answer with some flashy moves, score enough goals to win the game, then offer a smile and a handshake to his frustrated vanquished opponent.

Lester Patrick, the world-famous Canadian player who would later enjoy a brilliant career as coach and general manager of the NHL's New York Rangers, once said, "Hobey Baker is the only amateur player I've ever seen who could have played professional hockey and been a star in his very first game."

What amateur ever received higher praise?

By 1916, Hobey Baker had found a fresh outlet for his boundless energy and enthusiasm. He took up flying and mastered it quickly, to no one's surprise. He was among the first to join a group of American pilots who volunteered for war service in France.

He became a commanding officer of the 141st Squadron at Toul in France and downed at least three, and possibly as many as 14, enemy planes. But the war ended too quickly for Baker, who longed for more combat. With the Armistice he was ordered back to Paris but decided to take one final flight in his SPAD, a two-wing fighter plane painted in Princeton colours—orange and black. But a mechanic suggested he take another plane up instead, one ready for a flight test. Baker agreed and took off through the mist. At 600 feet, the engine sputtered and quit. Baker threw the craft into a steep dive, obviously hoping to gain enough speed to pull the plane up at the last second and glide to the landing field. But he ran out of altitude. Alas, the plane hurled itself into the ground, and Baker was killed instantly. He was buried with military honours at the nearby American cemetery at Toul. A national day of mourning marked his passing. Eventually, family members made arrangements for his body to be returned to Bala Cynwyd for reburial in West Laurel Hill Cemetery. An anonymous poet penned the following for his headstone:

You seemed winged, even as a lad,
With that swift look of those who knew the sky,
It was no blundering fate that stooped and bade
You break your wings and fall to earth and die,
I think that someday you may have flown too high,
So that immortals saw you and were glad,
Watching the beauty of your spirits flame,
Until they loved and called you, and you came.

In 1945, Hobey Baker's name was enshrined in the Hockey Hall of Fame in Toronto—a rare honour for an American-born non-professional.

U.S. college hockey's most prized award is the Hobey Baker Memorial Award, which goes to the top player in university or college hockey each year. Winners who went on to NHL fame include forward Paul Kariya and goalie Ryan Miller. Kariya was a huge star at the University of Maine, while Miller, who played his minor hockey in California, set an NCAA record for career shutouts with Michigan State, with 26. He is one of 10 members of the Miller family (grandfather, father, three brothers and five cousins) to play for Michigan State. He was drafted 138th by Buffalo in 1999 and later signed a five-year extension to his contract, worth $31.25 million. He now plays for the Vancouver Canucks.

Johnny Gaudreau of the Calgary Flames, a Hobey Baker winner in 2014, went straight from Boston College to the Flames and has completed two impressive seasons. He broke in with a bang, scoring on his first shot in his first game.

Former USA Hockey president Walter Bush says proudly, "I was the guy who suggested they name the MVP award after Hobey Baker. They were toying with the idea of naming it the Johnny Mariucci Trophy or the Snooks Kelley Trophy. I said to them, "Have you guys never heard of Hobey Baker? There was no greater college player than him."

Most of them hadn't heard of Baker. But once they learned who he was and what a dazzling legacy he left, they forgot about Mariucci and Kelly. And I like the fact they simply refer to the award as the "Hobey."

ANDRE LACROIX
The Ultimate Free Agent

Andre Lacroix grew up in Lauzon, Quebec, as the youngest of 14 children. Imagine being the youngest of 14 and not having a single sibling share your interest in hockey.

He was never a big star in the NHL, despite his abundant skills. The slim centreman, a junior star with the Montreal Junior Canadiens and the Peterborough Petes, where he twice earned MVP honours, turned pro with the Quebec Aces of the AHL in 1965–66.

With NHL expansion in 1967, he became an original member of the Philadelphia Flyers. After three 20-plus-goal seasons in Philadelphia, in 1971 he was traded to Chicago, where he scored a mere four goals in 51 games.

His future in pro hockey looked dubious, wouldn't you say?

Not at all.

As a pro hockey player, Andre Lacroix was an intelligent, resourceful young man who placed a high value on his services. He always negotiated his own hockey contracts—unheard of today and rare back then—both in the NHL and the WHA. And he never made a bad deal. Never.

With a dozen years of pro hockey behind him, sitting in the stands of the arena in Hartford one day, he told me about his fascinating career.

Let's begin in Philadelphia, when I signed with the WHA Blazers in 1973. I negotiated a five-year contract worth $65,000 a year. The previous season, I'd played for the NHL Chicago Black Hawks—for $30,000 a year. The Blazers had to give me what I wanted, because the team had called a press conference for the next day to announce the signing of their new coach—Fred Creighton. But Fred backed out at the last minute, so they were really stuck for a news story. I became the story. But not before I asked for a big contract and I got it. They really needed me at that press conference. And I made sure there was a clause in the contract that stated if the team was sold or moved I would become a free agent. Also, I demanded a car of my choice—a Mark IV—and I put in a lot of bonus clauses. Well, that season, I went from four goals to 50 goals—and 124 points. And I captured the first of my two WHA scoring titles, and I made the First All Star team. The Blazers had to pay me $40,000 in bonuses alone. I'm sure not too many players have collected $40,000 in bonuses.

Then the team moved to Vancouver, but I didn't have to move, because I became a free agent. I decided to move to New York instead and negotiated another fat contract with the team there. The next thing I asked for was a new Cadillac, and they said, "No problem." So I drove around in my new Cadillac, until I got a phone call from the sheriff. He said, "Bring the car in, Mr. Lacroix. The team can't make the payments on it."

Within days, the New York team moved to New Jersey, and the minute they did, I became a free agent again. The New Jersey team was owned by a construction man—Mr. Joe Schwartz. He said to me, "Andre, we're going to move the team to San Diego." I said, "That's fine, Mr. Schwartz, but I may not go, because if you move I'll be a free agent again. It's in my contract." So he decided to take me to Las Vegas for three days. I stayed in a big suite while we negotiated a new agreement. Finally, I signed a new five-year contract with Joe Schwartz, with all the money guaranteed. And I told Joe I'd like to drive a Porsche as part of the deal. He said, "No problem, Andre." So I drove a big Porsche around until Joe Schwartz ran out of money after a couple of years.

That's when Ray Kroc [then the owner of McDonald's] came in and bought the club and he hired a big-name baseball man, Buzzie Bavasi, as club president. When Bavasi talked to me about signing, he told me, "You know, Andre, baseball players, when they make so much money, don't have bonus clauses." I told him, "Look, Mr. Bavasi, I'm a hockey player, not a baseball player. I must have bonus clauses." And he said, "Okay." I also told him I wanted a Rolls-Royce to drive, one of those $95,000 ones, not a cheap one. Mr. Bavasi said, "No problem, Andre."

Ray Kroc and Bavasi offered me $150,000 a year for five years. I said, "No, I don't want to sign for that. I think I'll go back to the NHL." And I got up to leave the room. But Ray Kroc called me back and said, "Andre, I'm prepared to give you $175,000 a year for six years, with the money guaranteed personally by me." I said, "That sounds okay with me, Mr. Kroc." So I signed a personal services contract with Ray Kroc, not the team or the league. And soon I was driving around in a brand new Rolls-Royce.

It wasn't long before Ray Kroc decided he liked hamburgers better than hockey, so he sold the team. Once again, I became a free agent, and I decided to go to Houston. And if Houston at any time didn't pay me, Ray Kroc was still responsible for my contract. When Houston folded some time later, several of the players opted to go to Winnipeg. I decided not to go. I was a free agent again, and I was persuaded to go to Hartford—to the New England Whalers. The Whalers promised to honour my contract. If they didn't pay me for some reason, Ray Kroc was still responsible.

When I thought about retiring from Hartford in 1979, I still had two years left on my contract. I told the Whalers, "Look, you'll owe me about $400,000 if I continue to play. And I'm not going to retire unless I get my money. So why don't we do this. You can have the advantage of using that money if you'll pay me over a period of time with interest. And they said my idea sounded like a good one. So I agreed to be paid over a period of seven years. When I quit in 1980, I knew there would still be plenty of money coming in. What's more, I'd have some time to look around and see what I wanted to do with the rest of my life. And I didn't have to work for the team to earn any of that money. I thought it was a pretty good deal.

I never had an agent to help me make decisions. Never felt I needed one. I made all my own deals and had good relations with all the owners, general managers and coaches I ever played for—except for Vic Stasiuk, my coach in Philadelphia. I never liked him after he ordered the French-speaking players on our team to speak English only.

I was very impressed with Andre Lacroix during the brief time we spent together. Recently I watched him on video clips on my computer monitor, scoring goals easily and often. Avoiding checks, delivering slick passes, deking the great Soviet goalie Tretiak. And look, he just stole the puck off Gordie Howe's stick! No wonder they called him the Magician. I often ask a hockey trivia question: Name the all-time leading scorer in the WHA. I've heard answers ranging from Bobby Hull to Gordie Howe to Marc Tardif. The true answer is, as you've probably guessed, Andre Lacroix. Andre tallied 100 points or more six times in his WHA career. Only four other pro players surpassed that mark. He finished with 798 points in 551 games.

Following his pro career, Andre launched a second career as an entrepreneur, doing consulting work with several rink facilities in the U.S. In 1993, he settled in Oakland, California, where for 11 years he was director of hockey programs for the Oakland Ice Center. He developed thriving youth and adult hockey programs in the area. He founded the Andre Lacroix Foundation for Giving, which helps raise money for children with disabilities. Recently he moved to Chagrin Falls, Ohio, and became the general manager and director of hockey programs for the Pond Ice Rink in Auburn Township. Even more recently he agreed to coach a high school hockey team in Ohio. Always willing to give back to the game.

BOB MCNEIL
A Story of Survival

Does that name register with hockey fans?

Probably not. Bobby McNeil never made it to the NHL. Never made big money in the game.

But he was a player. Made a living as a pro. I think of him as a golden oldie.

If he was alive today, he'd no doubt say, "Aw, I wasn't a golden oldie, but I was a player. That pretty much says it all. Yeah, I was a player. And proud to be one."

He came close to becoming a well-known player—an NHLer perhaps, like a lot of his hometown buddies in Timmins, where he was born. That was on November 18, 1933. He was one of a few thousand other players who, over the years, caught the eyes of the NHL scouts.

I write about Bobby McNeil now, a few months after cancer claimed him in January 2013, because he was a good friend and teammate for many years. For two decades we played oldtimers' hockey together, along with former NHLers like Peter Conacher, Howie Menard, Bobby Lalonde, Ivan Irwin, Bo Elik, Bobby Baun, Carl Brewer and many more. McNeil, at 79, could skate faster than any of us. And he displayed the same fierce determination to win in a pickup game as he showed when cancer came calling.

"That son of a bitch cancer isn't going to take me," he declared. "I'll play hockey and I'll be rollerblading and I'll be in the Terry Fox Run for a lot of years yet."

But "that son of a bitch cancer," as millions can attest, is a stubborn, unrelenting opponent, and Bobby finally succumbed.

An overflow crowd attended his funeral in Stouffville, Ontario. Everyone in the community knew Bobby. He was an electrician by trade, and a good one.

A few weeks earlier, I sat with my friend and asked him to tell me more about himself. How could I know him so well and know so little of his childhood or how he earned a living from the game? His life story—and that of his brother Ron—was fascinating.

My dad was a Cape Bretoner, and he married my mother, who was from Salem, Massachusetts. They had six kids, and none of us was born in the same place.

I was fourth in line.

It must have been hell for my mother, travelling around from one mining town to the next. At one time she lived in a log house with four of the kids. No running water. An outside toilet. Every day a challenge to find food to feed her kids. Yeah, she had a pretty rough life, my mother.

My dad was a miner, a shaftsman. He used to travel wherever there was a mine starting up. That's where he headed for.

You wouldn't want to turn your head the wrong way—not with him. He was a hard-rock miner and he was a boozer. He loved to drink and to fight. He was quite a scrapper. He gave my mother a few goings-over, and we kids were petrified of him.

This was in Timmins, up north in Ontario. When we were a little bit older and he'd come home from work and we'd be in the kitchen, he'd say to my older brother, "Okay, Don, put the boxing gloves on with me."

He'd knock the hell out of Don until he had him crying like hell. Then he'd say, "Okay, Gene, put the gloves on with Don." And Don would be mad by then and knock the hell out of Gene. Gene would be crying like a son of a bitch. Now he'd say, "Gene, put the gloves on with Bob." And Gene would give me a goddamn lickin' too. And I'd be uptight and Dad would say, "Okay, Bob, put them on with Ron." So I'd beat the shit out of Ron, my younger brother. My dad sort of enjoyed that, I think.

My parents gave up on us for a time. That was a huge decision. We were sent to a home in Kirkland Lake—all six of us. Dormitories for the boys and for the girls, and it was not a happy place. It was run by the French nuns, and we were miserable there. Getting through the nights was the worst part of it. If you wet the bed in the night—and there was a lot of that—they'd haul you out of bed and they'd take the wet sheets off the bed and throw them in a big tub in the corner. Ice-cold water. Then they'd throw you in the tub, right in with the stinkin' sheets. And when they figured you'd had enough, they'd drag you out and make you stand in the corner. You'd be shaking and freezing and blubbering. We were just kids, eh? Scared kids. And then they'd fling the wet sheets over your head and you'd stand there some more. You were supposed to learn some kind of lesson from that. All we learned was we hated it. The worst two and a half years of our lives.

We did a lot of praying. Praying for the day we'd get out of there. And the food—well, I don't remember much about the meals except once a week we'd get dessert, which was molasses mixed with puffed wheat. Sounds awful, but we all looked forward to that.

I remember one day they took us out to a slide in the country, and I was freezing cold. I started to cry, "I wanna go home." Well, they sent two guys for shovels and they came back and dug a big hole in the snow and they dropped me in the bloody hole. I thought they were going to bury me alive.

I think that may be where I got my temper from. I was a pissed-off little kid that day, sitting in a deep hole freezing to death.

Then one day it ended and we were reunited with our parents. We went back home.

Everything we had back then was hand-me-down, odd-fitting clothes and boots. Hand-me-down skates and sticks and flimsy gloves.

How did I get out of that rotten situation in Timmins? By playing hockey,

I was about nine years old, and I got a pair of hand-me-down skates. I was able to skate from the house down to the open-air rink, and I played a lot of hours on that rink. I'd rather be there than at home, waiting for my dad to get off work. I was able to play hockey for the school, and I graduated up the ranks—to midget and juvenile and then to junior. I was the only kid in our family to play hockey.

The organized team was the school team. I remember the rink burning down in Timmins in about 1948. I only played hockey there once—with the school team—and it was the only time my dad saw me play. After the rink burned, we played outdoors until I was about 16, when we played in the McIntyre Arena. That was in Shumacher.

Leo Del Villano (a mailman, and later mayor of Timmins) and Tony Amonte (a friend who was a bit older than the rest of us) were two of the guys who really looked after me. And they looked after a lot of other guys. We all owe them a lot. Without those guys, we would have still been working underground forever. I worked underground for a while, and then I worked on the surface with some of the boys who came back from playing hockey—pro hockey—and they played ball up there, guys like Johnny McLellan, Les Costello and Pete Babando.

Les Costello, who later gave up a big-league career with the Leafs to become a priest, was simply unbelievable. And Ted Lindsay. They were our heroes. I missed my bus one night after a ball game in Kirkland Lake, and Ted Lindsay was coming back home. He had Dick Duff with him, and he picked me up. He was driving a DeSoto convertible, and he could have breezed right by. But he stopped and said, "Hop in." When I met him, I was on cloud nine. Never forgotten it.

I used to watch Costello when he was skating. At the rink, there'd come a time when they'd have men's skating only, the women would all sit down. I'd follow that Costello. I'd be right on his heels, and could that man ever go. I tried to keep up to him, and I did a pretty good job of it. I found out then that I was really fast on my feet. Imagine keeping pace with Les Costello, an NHLer.

When I was 16, I came down to Toronto to play with the Marlies. I spent three weeks there, and I played a couple of games with the Weston Dukes, a Junior B club. The Marlies were going to sign me to a card, and I says, "Give me a ticket back to Timmins. I don't like it here. I keep getting on streetcars and they're going the wrong way all the time." So I went home, and the following year I signed a C form with Chicago. I went down to Galt and I was there for a while and got a dislocated shoulder, and I was traded to Windsor Spitfires for John Muckler, who years later coached Wayne Gretzky in Edmonton. That was in 1952.

I was in Windsor with Al Arbour and Dennis Riggin and Larry Hillman and three or four guys from Timmins. I was with two of the guys from Timmins a year earlier when we were one, two, three in the scoring in that Northern League.

I dressed for seven games with Windsor. We went to Kitchener on a Friday night and we lost. Saturday night we played in St. Catharines and we lost. Sunday afternoon we played the Marlies in the Gardens and we lost. Back in Windsor, there was a meeting. Jimmy Skinner, the coach, went around the room giving everybody a blast. He came to me and he gave me a blast. Well, I think I got on the ice for about a minute and a half in those games we lost, so I said to him, "If you put me on the ice, I might be able to score the odd goal."

Later, he said, "Bob, we want to see you in the office." I knew right then I was history, because if you opened your mouth in those days, you were gone. I was a hot-headed little son of a bitch because I really wanted to play.

Skinner said, "There's a team in Grand Rapids looking for players."
I said, "Grand Rapids? Where's that?"
He said. "In Michigan. It's in the International League."
I said, "I'll go there then."
So I went to Grand Rapids and found myself playing with guys 25, 27, 30 years old. And I was 18 and living in an old hotel all by myself. I played three games and I said, "That's enough of this shit. I'm going home."

So I went back to Timmins and played senior hockey. They gave me a job with the mine, on the surface—with the McIntyre.

Then the junior club came after me, and I played with them—the Porcupine Combines. We won the North, beating out Kirkland Lake and then Sudbury.

Then we went to Ottawa and beat out Eastview–St. Charles. We went on to the Maritimes and beat out the Sydney Franklins team. We went on to Quebec City to play the Citadels, and they beat us three games to zip. They had a hell of a junior club, with Aggie Kukulowicz and Camille Henry. We were away from Timmins for 33 days that spring. It was quite a trip, with a good bunch of guys.

The next season I went back south and played with the Barrie Flyers. I had a pretty good year there. That was the end of my junior career, and the next season I went to Fort Wayne in the International League.

I was paid 45 bucks a week in Barrie, and I had a car there but I couldn't drive it. I played with Don Cherry there, and he was a hard nut on the ice. He's still a pretty good friend of mine.

I had a good year with the Fort Wayne Komets, but we had a sad thing happen at the end of the season. We used to travel in Ford station wagons all the time, barrelling from place to place at 80 miles per hour. The second-last game of the season, our trainer bought a 1954 Buick hardtop and he went out to the arena to get the equipment ready. There was a railroad crossing, and a train was coming. But the land was flat, and I guess he thought he could beat the train in this new car he had. But he didn't. He ran smack into the engine and was killed instantly. After that we decided to drive those Ford wagons at 50 miles an hour—a snail's pace.

I couldn't go back to Fort Wayne, because I would have been eligible for the U.S. draft.

That summer I got a letter from Red Stapleford over in London. He invited me to play for Brighton in the English League. The minute I got there, I loved the place. So I had three years in Brighton, then a year playing in Switzerland. Then I played in Italy and Germany. After that I went back to Brighton.

I met my wife, Sheila, in 1960, when I was on my way over to play and coach in Switzerland. I happened to go in the rink one night before I left for Switzerland, and I saw her skating around the ice. She had beautiful red hair.

I remember asking her if she could teach me how to skate, and that was the start of it. She didn't know anything about hockey back then. But she learned. She's a great woman—the love of my life.

When I played in Brighton, we had some ding-dong battles. The Scottish boys—there were two or three of them—were real head-chasers. And there was one guy—Joe Brown—he was an animal. He was about five-10 and 280 pounds, and he actually took the eyes out of one player over there. He ripped another guy from his ear to his chin with a swipe of the stick, and I saw him kicking guys with his skates. Yeah, he was an animal.

The last year I played there—1964—I was married then and getting into the electrical trade, so I decided to play one more season. The rink had been bought and was going to be torn down, so it came down to the last game. I show up for a game on the 23rd of May, and I'm sailing for home three days later, with Sheila.

I walk in to the rink and Benny, the manager, says, "Bob, you're not playing tonight."

I say, "What do you mean?"

He says, "The Scottish boys have threatened to take your eye out if you step on the ice. They're vicious and they mean it."

I said, "Benny, no son of a bitch ever ran me out of a rink."

So I walk in the dressing room, and I've got two linemates from Scotland. They say, "Bob, don't play tonight. The boys are out to get you before you sail for home."

And I repeated myself: "No son of a bitch is going to run me out of a rink."

So I was pumped, and I got out on the ice and I went around that Joe Brown in the first shift and fired one into the net. I came right back up centre ice and I passed Joe Brown. I put my stick up near his nose and I said, "Joe, you lay the lumber on me once tonight, and I'll kill every Scottie on your team."

We beat them 7–4, and I scored four times that night. It was my last game. They knew the lumber I carried was as big as anybody's.

I was in Germany one time, up in the mountains, and a team in Garmisch wanted me to come down and play for them. So I agreed and came down. They said, "You're not Bob McNeil tonight, your name is now Littner. We're not allowed more than two Canadians. Don't speak to anyone."

I said, "No problem."

So I race in on goal, and a big German turns and whacks me with a two-hander across the arms. So I dropped my stick and threw a punch at him, and the referee gives me a penalty but nothing to the German.

Now I'm in the box and the big German comes roaring up the ice. Well, I reached out and clotheslined the bastard. Geez, did he go down. And that started a bit of a riot. So they threw me in the dressing room and locked the door and wouldn't let me come out for the second or third periods.

The next day, we're playing the same club, this time in Nuremburg, and this same German whacks me again in front of the net. I jumped at him and tried to knock his head off, and the ref gives me a penalty.

I cursed the ref and called him a bald-headed son of a bitch, and he says, "I speak perfect English. That's 10 more minutes."

Yes, there were a few times that tempers flared over there. And I always seemed to be in the middle of it.

Now, you ask me to talk about my brother Ron, and I will, but his story has nothing to do with hockey. Ron was my younger brother by a year. He led a much more interesting life than I did.

I'll start in Temagami, where Ron worked as a young man in the tourist lodges there. He met some wealthy Americans from Yakima, Washington, and they took a shine to Ron. "Why don't you come out to Washington and work on the farms out there?" they asked him.

Ron thought that was a good idea, but when he started home after the summer, he missed his ride, and somebody flew him back in a float plane. That was a huge thrill for Ron. Well, he came in the door and he said, "Mom, that was so exciting. I'm going to become a pilot."

Mom said, "Sure you will. Remember, you never got past grade eight."

By then Ron had decided he was headed for Washington. Now, he had this old car. The doors were wired to the frame so they wouldn't fall off. It was a wreck. But he took off for Newark, New Jersey. Said he wanted to visit some cousins down there. And when he got there and told them he was headed out to Washington, they laughed and said, "Ron, you'll never get there in that old beater."

He said, "Sure I will," and he did. In Washington, he worked in the orchards, picking apples, and all the money he put aside was for flying lessons.

Well, he got his licence, and a few years later he got involved with helicopters, and a fellow who liked him taught him how to fly them. In time, he had his licence to fly helicopters as well. The man told Ron how difficult it was to pass the tests. "I had to write for my licence three times," he said. "When it came to spraying the orchards, there were words on the test a foot long. Chemicals and pesticides I couldn't even pronounce. But I persevered and finally got the licence."

One day, Ron was flying up in the mountains somewhere when the tail rotor broke. The helicopter spun to earth and crashed in a deep ravine. Ron scrambled out and crawled away, fearful that the chopper would catch fire. He walked some distance to a road and flagged down a lumber truck. The driver took one look at Ron and said, "My God. You're some cut up, boy."

He drove Ron to a hospital, where he went into shock and spent the next four days there. Then it was back to flying again.

Eventually, he ended up going to Alaska. And he was in the air on the 22nd of December, 1970. He was following another helicopter back to Anchorage. "My heater quit and I was beginning to frost up," he told me. "I radioed the guy ahead that I was returning to Prudhoe Bay. But he'd changed his frequency and never got my message."

The next morning they took off—the mechanic and Ron. "We flew south and ran into a wicked whiteout, and so we set her down on the top of a hill with the antenna sticking in the snow. We sat there for 45 minutes, hoping the storm would break. But it didn't. So I said to Paddy, the mechanic, 'We've got to get off this hill. We're using up too much fuel.'"

So Ron came off the mountain—took her up, and all hell broke loose. He had to get down again and he wound up on the bank of a river, the Chandler River. "We had no idea where we were, but we had a geophysical map with us. So we pinpointed where we'd landed, about forty miles from the nearest base as the crow flies. But if we followed the river, it would be almost double the distance. We got out of the chopper after the storm broke, walked down to the curve of the river, snow up to our chests, back up the other side and thought we'd be picked up in a day or two. We were able to get a fire going with some small sticks we found, and we had a couple of tins of tuna with us, which we ate because we figured it would be only a day or two before we were rescued. When no search planes came along, we decided to hike it out."

When I was notified and told my brother had been missing for several days, I flew out to Anchorage, and got there on January 1, 1971. My brother Ron had been missing now for more than a week—since the 23rd of December.

When I landed, Mr. Brady, the head of helicopter services, told me bluntly, "Bob, there's no way they could survive. It's 40 degrees below zero, they have no survival gear and they have no food. All we're looking for is the helicopter and two bodies." They wouldn't let me get involved in the search.

The next day was going to be the last day of the search. They'd already spent over 800 flying hours and $600,000 flying in all directions.

So we flew up to Point Barrow and then on to a place called Deadhorse. That's where the search headquarters were. They asked me about my brother: "What kind of a man are we looking for, Bob?"

I said, "Well, Ron's like my old man, a tough Cape Bretoner. If you said the wall was white and he said it was black, then the son of a bitch is black. That man is so stubborn. If he set that helicopter down, then he'd walk clear across Alaska to find his way back."

Three hours later, they radioed in from Anchorage. The pilot and the mechanic had walked into Umiat. The man said to me, "You know your brother, don't you?"

I said, "You're damn right I do."

But when they started to hike out, it was 40 below, and they ran into a storm. They covered themselves with the engine blankets they had and stayed covered over for a day and a half— until the storm broke.

When they started off again, there was a crust on the snow and they'd slip and slide along. Sometimes one of them would slide 30 to 40 feet down to the riverbank, and the other would wait while he climbed back up. One time, Paddy slid down and wouldn't come back up. So Ron went down to get him, and Paddy handed him a .38.

"Shoot me, Ron," he said.

Ron said, "Ain't no way I'm going to shoot you. They'll hang me for murder. Come on. Get up!"

So they hiked out 40 miles or more, and they pulled into Umiat. They went into the control centre at the airport. There was a woman attendant there and she said, "Who the hell are you two?" And my brother said, "I'm Ron McNeil."

She was amazed. She said, "We've been looking for you for a week. We'd given you up for dead."

Ron said, "Lady, I'm far from dead."

She said, "We'll get a plane up here for you right away."

Ron said, "Like hell you will. We're going to take a hot shower and sleep between clean sheets tonight."

The next day, they picked me up along with the search coordinator and a couple of mechanics. We flew over where the chopper was, and I was the first guy to spot it. It was just a sliver in the snow. We landed in Umiat, and I see a guy walking from one building to another, no hat, coat wide open, and I say, "There's my brother."

I walked up to him from behind and I tap him on the shoulder, and he turns and says, "Bob, what the hell are you doing here?"

I said, "I came up to find you, you silly bugger."

We flew up to Anchorage, and a guy comes on the plane and says, "The media is here from all over, there's TV cameras and radio guys. We've had New York calling, San Francisco calling—everybody wants to know how you survived."

It wasn't long after that we heard the mechanic, the guy Ron wouldn't shoot, sold the survival story to the *National Enquirer* for $5,000—and Ron got squat. My brother told me, "Bob, I'd a been outta there the first day, but that friggin' mechanic cried all the time. He gave up. But I couldn't leave the guy."

One adventure like that is scary, but Ron had another one just as bad.

This was in Washington State. A deputy sheriff out there asked Ron to take him up in the chopper. They flew over a mountain and dropped down over a cornfield.

"There it is!" said the deputy. "Lots of marijuana growing in between the corn rows."

Ron flew him back to Grandview, and the cops got a crew together and went back and destroyed the cornfields. Ron figured there was a quarter of a million dollars' worth of marijuana growing there.

So, weeks later, Ron comes out of the tavern one night and four Mexicans grab him and toss him in a car. Two of them hold him down while another big bastard lays a beating on him.

They drive him six miles out of town, into the hills somewhere, and beat him some more. They kicked his head in, kicked his ribs in, stabbed him in the chest with a knife 16 times and leave him for dead.

He comes to about two in the morning. He couldn't see, couldn't walk, but he could hear traffic off in the distance. And he could crawl. So he crawled along the trail until he got to the main road. A driver spotted him but was afraid to pick him up. He thought it might be a setup. The guy drove back and forth four times before he called out, "Hold on, buddy, I'll call an ambulance."

Ron said, "No time for that. I'll never make it."

So the guy hauled him into his pickup and drove him to the hospital in Grandview. Doctors there operated on him until 7 a.m., and he had four broken ribs, 16 stab wounds and a head like a football.

We got word about Ron's condition, and all the brothers and sisters flew out to see Ron in the hospital. I remember thinking it's the first time we've been together since we were kids growing up in Timmins.

Four days later, he came out of the hospital—no insurance, and with a bill for $100,000. A group called Crimes Compensation paid the bill.

They never caught the guys who almost killed my brother. They were probably connected to the field of marijuana Ron helped destroy.

A few years later, he was crop-dusting at a place called Quincy. He was standing there talking to a mechanic when suddenly the eyes go back and he hits the deck and goes into convulsions. His heart stops.

The mechanic jumps on him, gives him CPR, and the heart comes back. But on the way to the hospital it stops two more times. They finally get him into the hospital, and when he comes to, he says, "I'm outta here. I want to fly."

They say, "Ron, you can't fly. You've been dead three times."

Ron says, "Aw, there's nothing wrong with me."

So he went back to his little trailer near the airstrip and my sister called him and convinced him to go back to the hospital. One of Ron's friends had noticed he wasn't the same man at all as he was before. He wore the same clothes day after day, the trailer was a mess, and he wasn't showering or washing himself.

After he went to the hospital, the report we got was not good. There was a tumour on the brain. And they thought he had lung cancer, and they were going to operate on the following Monday. But on Thursday he went into convulsions and they operated immediately, taking a big chunk out of his forehead. He went into a coma.

So the brothers and sisters flew out again, and the doctor told us the prognosis was not good.

I told him, "Don't count that guy out yet. He's one tough son of a bitch. He survived a chopper crash in Alaska, he survived a beating and a stabbing that would have killed a normal man."

Turned out he didn't have the lung cancer. The X-rays were of scar tissue from the beating and stabbings he took.

Ron came out of the coma with his short-term memory gone and with a big hole in his head. There was skin over it, but he was mad at the doctors for doing this to him.

Ron lasted another 10 years, which amazed everybody. But he never flew again. He lived alone in his little trailer. There came a time when his pals hadn't seen him around for a few days. They went in to check on him and found his body in the trailer. They figured he'd been dead for about five days.

Everybody agreed: Ron McNeil was the toughest son of a bitch they'd ever seen.

Well, I knew that.

Years ago, Bobby McNeil was presented with a poster with the iconic image of Terry Fox and Maple Leaf captain Darryl Sittler, taken in 1980. Terry Fox visited Toronto during his historic cross-country trek. In time, Bobby filled the poster with signatures of more than 100 former NHL players, and was seeking Mark Messier's signature just before he died. He planned to auction the poster, with the proceeds going to cancer research.

Recently, Mark heard about the poster and arranged to add the final signature. He even met with the McNeil's daughter Cindy and her two children. "He was so engaging and asked all about Bob's plans for the poster," Sheila said. "Former NHLer Pete Conacher arranged to have the poster framed and it's ready for auction. It should fetch a lot of money."

Keith Acton, a Stouffville resident and Bob's close friend, with over 1,000 games in the NHL, said, "Bobby touched the entire community with his kindness, caring, compassion and generosity. He will be greatly missed."

Former Pittsburgh Penguin Dennis Owchar: "Bob had two hearts—one of a teddy bear and the other of a lion. He was such a fierce competitor, but such a wonderful guy."

Bobby and his wife, Sheila, had been married for 49 years. They settled in Stouffville in the 1960s, where Bobby went into business as an electrician. They had three children, Tim, Cindy and Dan, and grandchildren Brad, Danielle, Mitchell, Braydon, Brett, Blake and Bryson.

Dan was killed in 1992. The car he was in skidded on ice and crashed. He was a player, coming home from a hockey game.

LEO DANDURAND
He Bought the Habs—for 11 Grand

I met Monsieur Leo Dandurand in Montreal in 1964, a few months before his death. It was a privilege to be invited to his posh apartment in Montreal. It was beautifully furnished. He and his wife were dressed immaculately. I showed up wearing the best of my two-suit wardrobe. I remember wishing I'd shined my shoes. The Dandurands oozed class.

Leo Dandurand was a real gentleman. He had stature. I was there to interview him for a feature on one of our CFCF-TV sports programs. I was careful to call him Mr. Dandurand—to show my respect.

For many years, Leo Dandurand was Montreal's greatest promoter. Aside from hockey, he was involved with the race track business, the Montreal Royals baseball club, the football Alouettes and boxing matches.

Imagine this. He and two business partners purchased the Canadiens franchise when it went up for auction in 1921. And they bought it for a pittance—$11,000.

Leo was in Cleveland on the day of the auction, looking after race track business. He appointed a friend, Cecil Hart, to attend the auction and bid on behalf of himself and two partners, Joe Cattarinich and Louis Letourneau.

Hart, who would later donate the Hart Trophy to hockey, topped Tom Duggan's opening bid of $8,000 with Dandurand's bid of $8,500. Then the bidding stopped. There was a week-long postponement while NHL president Frank Calder checked out an Ottawa group's interest in buying the club. When the bidding resumed, Tom Duggan, who had opened the bidding, placed 10 $1,000 bills on the table.

Onlookers were impressed. Cold, hard cash means the bidder is serious. It often means there's a lot more where that money came from—in this case, Duggan's pockets.

Hart pleaded for a few minutes' time, and got it. He ran from the room and phoned Dandurand in Cleveland. Leo had no time to consult with his partners, so he took the initiative. "Go for it," he told Hart.

Hart ran back to the auction room and waved his arm. "$11,000!" he shouted.

There was no response from Duggan. Silently, he picked up his $10,000 and put the money away. Apparently there was no more where that cash came from.

It turned out to be one of the wisest business deals Dandurand and his partners ever made. In 2008, Forbes valued the 100-year-old franchise at $334 million. In 2014, it was revalued at a billion dollars.

In 1924, Dandurand graciously allowed a second team, the Montreal Maroons, to enter his market. Leo figured a strong French-English rivalry between the clubs would be good for Montreal and good for the NHL. And he was right. It's the kind of thinking the brain trust at Maple Leaf Sports and Entertainment would never be able to fathom. Let a second team into our market? You kidding me?

Leo told me of another surprising decision he once made. He suspended two of his own players—a fierce pair of competitors—from a Stanley Cup series in 1923. Appalled at the actions of Billy Coutu (also known as Couture) and Sprague Cleghorn, each of whom launched vicious assaults on two Ottawa stars, Leo banned them from further play. Coutu was particularly violent. He chased after Cy Denneny of the Senators, who had just scored, and bashed him over the head with his stick. Denneny fell unconscious and was lucky to survive the blow. Coutu was tossed from the game. Then Cleghorn lashed out at Ottawa's Lionel Hitchman, cross-checking him in the face, knocking him flat. That ugly blow triggered a near-riot. Referee Marsh was attacked, and debris littered the ice.

Dandurand made a tough—but proper—decision. He suspended his two ruffians for the rest of the series, which was won by Ottawa by a single goal. A similar stance has never been taken by any other manager.

"That was a memorable game," Leo said. "There was a line half a mile long outside the Mount Royal Arena hours before game time. I always blamed Toronto referee Lou Marsh [the Lou Marsh Trophy for Canada's athlete of the year is named after this sportsman] for the debacle that took place that night. The last time Lou Marsh refereed here, he went back to Toronto and said that there had been missiles thrown on the ice and that Dandurand had been responsible for it. In Ottawa for the past two seasons, they have been throwing everything on the ice: lemons, metal pipes, coins and rubber boots. Nothing has been said to Ottawa. Besides, Marsh is hardly the one to talk. Here in Montreal, he was seen striking a spectator one night, and in Toronto he even threw his bell at a fan."

I mentioned that I'd read somewhere about broken beer bottles being thrown on the ice during games of that era.

"It's true. In 1923, newspapers called for fans to cease throwing objects on the ice. But nobody paid any attention. Fans often threw beer bottles at the ref and the players. Some of the more fiendish broke the necks of the bottles before heaving them, so that when they hit a man they might inflict serious damage."

I asked Mr. Dandurand if, considering the Stanley Cup was at stake, he was tempted to change his mind and allow two of his best players to come back in the series.

"Not for a minute. I did not change my mind. Cleghorn and Coutu pleaded with me to lift the suspension, but the decision was made. Coutu was later suspended for life after he struck a game official while playing for the Boston Bruins. He's the only player to receive a lifetime suspension for such a premeditated assault. Cleghorn, on the other hand, enjoyed a Hall of Fame career."

When Dandurand needed a superstar to bring in the crowds, he lured Howie Morenz to his club.

The Mitchell, Ontario native was reluctant at first to turn pro, but he quickly adjusted to life in Montreal and soared like an eagle on the ice, becoming the swiftest and the greatest player in the game.

Dandurand is credited with persuading Tex Rickard, the famous American promoter and owner of Madison Square Garden, to install artificial ice in his new arena and bring professional hockey to New York. Rickard listened. He thought Dandurand had great vision. And he didn't want Boston, granted a franchise a year earlier, to have something New Yorkers didn't have. The ice plant was installed and for the 1925–26 season, the New York Americans, wearing star-spangled uniforms, made their debut and soon had a legion of followers.

Author's note: The Americans were purchased at a bargain price. In 1925, the Hamilton Tigers, an NHL club, went on strike, demanding more pay for more games played. The striking players were suspended and fined and the club was dissolved. The Hamilton players were sold to Bill Dwyer, a New York bootlegger, for a collective total of $75,000. Dwyer brought the Tigers to Rickard and the Garden, named them "Americans" and a year later another team shared the same ice with them—the Rangers.

In 1931, Dandurand announced that a new arena, with seats for 19,000 people would be built in downtown Montreal, at a cost of $3 million. He said the new ice palace would be used as a parking garage until the Canadiens' lease with the Montreal Forum expired in three years' time. It was one of the few promises to Montreal fans he did not keep.

In 1944, he was offered the post of president of the NHL, but he declined the offer, citing pressure from his other businesses. He recommended Red Dutton for the position, and Dutton was appointed.

Dandurand was inducted into the Hockey Hall of Fame as a builder in 1963, a year before his passing. The Hall of Fame induction ceremonies in those days were markedly different than the grand affairs they are today. I attended a couple at the CNE grounds in the '60s and was in the audience for the Dandurand induction in 1963. I remember vividly defenseman Babe Pratt being one of the inductees in 1966 despite having admitted to gambling on the outcome of games when he was a player. What do you think of that, Pete Rose?

Leaf owner Conn Smythe was the presenter at the Dandurand induction. There was no live TV or radio coverage. No ladies invited, no wives and families of the inductees. I remember Mr. Smythe striding to the microphone and beginning his remarks with "Gentlemen—and Frenchmen." It drew a laugh, but I don't think Montrealer Leo Dandurand laughed. Nobody in the media chastised Smythe for his insensitive comment.

LEN THORNSON
Never Got a Big-League Chance

In Naples, Florida, I have coffee every few days with Len Thornson, one of the greatest minor league pros ever. He scored 509 goals in the minors, most of them with Fort Wayne in the International League. He can be proud of ten straight seasons when he scored 100 points or more. But he's a modest guy and I had to prod to get him to talk about his six MVP awards, his two Turner Cups, and his all-time IHL point-scoring record. That was back in the '50s and '60s, when Montreal had superb farm clubs. Len was Montreal property, but he never got a sniff of the Montreal Forum. If he'd been with any other NHL team, well, who knows? A few years after he packed it in, the NHL doubled in size and players less skilled than Thornton were earning salaries that made us gasp.

Here's Len Thornson's story:

I grew up in Winnipeg, among the Icelanders. There was an outdoor ice rink on every corner. I played junior for St. Boniface, and we went to the Memorial Cup in 1953. We lost in six games to the Barrie Flyers and I remember a kid named Don Cherry for them, playing on defense. He was a scrappy guy and scored a couple of goals against us.

When I was a junior—17 years old—the Montreal Junior Canadiens came west every year to play games during the Christmas break. And Sam Pollock, their coach, invited me to play for them. Then he asked me to come east and play full-time for his juniors. But I declined. We had such a good team out west, but when I look back, I might have been better off to go with Pollock. It might have changed my career.

After that, in pro, I played for New Westminster. I was the only rookie on the team, so I didn't get much ice time. And when I did, I made a huge rookie mistake one night that embarrassed me so much I never talked about it. But I will now. It was 1953–54 and I was playing against the famous Bentley brothers in Saskatoon, two long-time NHL stars winding down their careers—and I remember Charlie Rayner was the goaltender, a great former Ranger. I found myself on a breakaway with Rayner bracing himself. And I remembered to look back over my shoulder like a coach had told me to do. You know, to see if someone was catching up. When I peeked back, Rayner sprang from his net and clobbered me. Man, did I get smacked. I heard so many bells I thought I was in a cathedral, not a hockey rink. And Rayner leaned down and said, "You've got to keep your head up, rookie." I thought he'd taken my head off.

Then I moved east to Shawinigan Falls, but it was the same story there—not much ice time. So I went to Cincinnati. Then Indianapolis needed somebody. so I went there. I was traded to Fort Wayne, and that's where I began to blossom. Had a great season. There were more opportunities there than there ever were in Winnipeg. I was in training camp with John Ferguson and Connie Madigan, who later in St. Louis became the oldest NHL rookie, at age 38. Why didn't he make it before that, I wonder?

I went to Cleveland and was the leading scorer in training camp. Ken Reardon wanted me to come to Montreal and play for the Royals. But I got a $10-a-week raise to stay in Fort Wayne. Owner Ken Ullyot said, "Len, if you finish in the top five in scoring, I'll give you a $500 bonus." Well, I broke my leg in the 52nd game and still finished third in scoring. I think that was 1961. We had guys playing for us for $90 to $100 dollars a week.

That club made money. Fort Wayne was named the top minor league city in the U.S. They averaged, playing in the IHL, 8,000 fans per game. A bus league back then—the farthest city away would be about 200 miles. Carl Brewer played in that league, with Muskegon. He and I used to sit in the stands and talk hockey before and after games. He by far made the most money—about 25 grand one season—and we had some good talks. He always carried a briefcase.

Connie Madigan stayed with us for about three years, then he went to Portland. He was the best defenseman in the Western Hockey League. He was a great skater. He was the big Indian guy in the movie *Slap Shot*. But he left [the set] and went home because he thought the Hollywood people were making fun of hockey.

We used to play the Detroit Red Wings and the Leafs in exhibition games. And we would beat them too. We had a lot of guys who wound up staying in Fort Wayne. You play in the minors and they can't afford to let you go. Frank St. Marseille was there and he was a big scorer with us, and when NHL expansion came along, he starred with St. Louis for a few seasons.

In my case, I was owned by Montreal, and they had a team of super-stars back then. Whenever a spot or two opened up, they had about 150 guys to choose from. Montreal did call me up—but not to the big club. They sent me to Buffalo for three games. This was the same year they brought up Jacques Plante. Buffalo had a terrible team, coached by Frank Eddolls. I played with Calum MacKay and Lorne Davis—good players—but the team had a terrible record.

During my 13-year career, mostly in Fort Wayne, the Canadiens won, I think, eight or nine Stanley Cups. If someone had told them I was named league MVP six times and would someday be named the greatest player in IHL history, they'd have yawned and said, "Oh, yeah. Can he do what Beliveau, the Richards, Moore and Geoffrion can do for us?" I knew the deal. I was never bitter. The fact is the Canadiens didn't need me. There were a lot of guys like me, guys paddling like hell but never reaching the Big Time. Cherry was another and he made it—but for just one game.

I lost one eye playing in Fort Wayne when I was 35, and that turned out to be not the disaster you might think. It got me a great job after hockey. This guy's stick came straight up off a faceoff and caught me in the eye. I tried to come back, but I had problems seeing the puck. A shot I normally would duck away from caught me in the face one night and broke my cheekbone. My wife said, "That's it. It's time to quit." But a fan read about my injury in the paper and he came knocking on my door and offered me a job in the insurance business. It turned out to be a great career job.

For years my sight would flicker in one eye. A half a dozen years ago, I heard about a specialist in Indianapolis who was doing some good things. Well, he operated for three or four hours and put a spanking new lens in my eye. I can see pretty good now.

In the off-season in Winnipeg, I used to run a lot. That kept me in good shape. I remember Terry Sawchuk, the great Detroit goalie, running through the parks in Winnipeg like I did. And he always wore a big, heavy sweatsuit.

There were always guys gunning for me when I played. You had to be aware of them, and you always had a little bit of fear. You were crazy if you didn't. The first thing you learn in pro hockey is to play with your head up. Charlie Rayner taught me that. If you don't, you're in big trouble.

But things worked out well for me in Fort Wayne. I have no regrets.

When he retired in 1969, Thornson held team records of 426 goals and 1,352 points as a Fort Wayne Komet. The league record he established, later broken by Jock Callandar, was 1,382 points.

Over coffee, he smiled and said, "That's nice" when I told him someone had written an article naming him as "the best player never to get a shot at the NHL." Another fan had told Len's wife Margaret, "Growing up, Len was my Mickey Mantle."

To be fair, two other minor league stars, Robin Bouchard and Dick Roberge, deserve mention. Let's call them golden oldies. Bouchard, undrafted by the NHL, played with several minor league clubs (mostly in Muskegon) and retired in 2010 with 688 career goals. Roberge, who played throughout the 1950s, 1960s, and 1970s, mostly in the EHL, scored 756 career goals during his 18-year career. He has been designated minor league hockey's all-time scoring champ.

Len, you've got two rivals for that "best player never to make the NHL" tag.

NEWSY LALONDE
Nine Goals in Final Game of 1910 Season

No stranger to violence on ice himself, Edouard "Newsy" Lalonde once named himself coach of hockey's meanest team. This was in 1961, when he selected an "All Mean" team of golden oldies whose hockey halos were severely tarnished.

Newsy's playing career, extending over 21 seasons in professional hockey, from 1905 to 1927, included stops in Cornwall, Toronto, Renfrew, the Canadiens, Vancouver, the Canadiens again, Saskatoon and the New York Americans.

That was after a brilliant career in lacrosse, where he could earn $5,000 per season, almost triple what many hockey players earned.

On March 18, 1910, playing for Renfrew, he yearned to win the scoring championship of his league. But he trailed Ernie Russell of the Wanderers by seven goals with just 60 minutes to play. It was the season finale. Renfrew defeated Cobalt that night by a score of 15–4. Throughout the match, Newsy's teammates unselfishly passed the puck to him, assisting as he scored goal after goal. Fred "Cyclone" Taylor was particularly generous with his passes, rushing to the net with the puck, then tossing it to Lalonde, who banged it in. By game's end, he had potted nine goals, which put him at the head of the scoring list in the National Hockey Association. Ernie Russell's seven-goal lead vanished.

Newsy had begun that season with the Canadiens, scoring 16 goals in six games. He moved on to Renfrew, where he played five games and slammed in 22 goals. How many players have scored 38 goals in 11 games?

For two and a half seasons, between 1932 and 1935, he coached the Canadiens. And his players paid attention. One who didn't, and argued with Newsy, got a punch in the mouth.

After his coaching career, he became a rabid Montreal fan, sitting rinkside at the Montreal Forum. From time to time he accompanied the Habs on road trips. Then, at age 73, he turned to bowling, where penalty boxes are most uncommon.

His scoring skills netted him 441 goals in 365 pro games, and five times he led his league in scoring. He was a genuine superstar of his era. But old-time chroniclers of the game remember him more for the bloody duels he had with many of the toughest players ever to don skates—men like "Bad Joe" Hall, who toiled one season for the Quebec Bulldogs.

Hall nearly severed Newsy's windpipe in Quebec one night. The next game in Montreal saw bloodthirsty fans batter down the gates of the old Westmount Arena, hoping to see Hall get his comeuppance. Instead, they saw Hall carve Newsy again—this time for 18 stitches. But Newsy redeemed himself with the fans. As soon as the doctor wiped the blood off his face and got him stitched up, he returned to the ice and used his stick to shatter Hall's collarbone.

"There was nothing personal about it," Newsy recalled. "When Hall joined the Canadiens soon after that incident, we became good friends and teammates. Poor Joe was a victim of the terrible flu epidemic, which took thousands of lives in 1919. He died in hospital in Seattle shortly after the Stanley Cup series between the Canadiens and the Seattle Metropolitans was cancelled because of the flu.

"So I pick Hall on defense, with the late Sprague Cleghorn as his partner. Sprague was a terror. He almost killed me one night in Toronto and was arrested for assault. Might have gone to jail too, but I pleaded for him in court and he got off with a $200 fine. Sprague disabled three Ottawa players one night—in one game. But his blueline partner Billy Coutu, while almost as mean as Cleghorn, gets only a Second Team berth, in my book."

Eddie Shore gets Newsy's vote for the other All Mean defense position, citing his near-killing of Leaf star forward Ace Bailey. One modern-day player, Lou Fontinato of the Rangers, was selected by Newsy as a Second Team Meanie defenseman on the strength of his league-leading penalty minutes (202) in the 1955–56 season.

Newsy places Paddy Moran of the old Quebec Bulldogs in goal, with this explanation: "Paddy was in a class by himself when it came to chopping toes of opposing forwards who came within range. And in those days, the toes of the skates were soft leather, not hard, so you had to worry about broken toes. Even worse, if a player came in too close, Paddy was an expert at squirting tobacco juice into a player's eye. Tell me that doesn't sting."

Newsy's forward line consists of Bill Ezinicki at centre, flanked by Leo Labine on right wing and Ted Lindsay on left. Labine, he points out, has totalled more than 11 hours in the penalty box and is one of the best needlers in the hockey business. Just ask Rocket Richard.

Lindsay and Ezinicki may have drifted off the NHL scene, but they left a lot to remember them by. Their 1951 brawl is rated a positive "gem" by Newsy. Lindsay, then with Detroit, and Ezinicki, with Boston, were getting along just swell, but then Lindsay gave Ezinicki a shove. Ezinicki replied with his stick and opened a one-stitch cut on Lindsay's forehead. Lindsay retaliated with an 11-stitch bullseye on Ezinicki's noggin. Ezinicki broke loose from restraining hands, ran into a Lindsay right hook and crashed backward onto the ice with such force that he picked up four stitches on the back of his head as well as four more on his already battered puss. He also lost a tooth in the battle. Ezinicki's 19 stitches and the missing molar cost Lindsay a $300 fine plus a three-game suspension without pay.

Newsy's second-string forward line is composed of Cully Wilson at centre, Bill Cook of the Rangers at right wing and Ken Randall of the Leafs and Americans on the left side. At one time, Wilson was the most feared player in Western Canada. Cook, who played three seasons with Newsy in Saskatoon before gaining real stardom with the Rangers, was a master at dishing out punishment, and Randall happily took on all of the league's top scrappers, including Montreal's Nels Stewart.

One night in New York, a sub jumped over the boards to relieve Randall. "Get the hell back to the bench, kid," he barked. "Stewart just came on, and I can't wait to get him."

Randall was once fined $35 by the league and attempted to pay the fine in pennies. The coins, neatly wrapped in paper rolls, were refused when brought to rinkside. But an impish player whacked them with his stick and hundreds of pennies spilled out on the ice.

Newsy's "meanest all star team" looked formidable when he chose the rascals in 1961—more than half a century ago. Since then, dozens of mean-spirited, two-fisted players have graced NHL rosters. Names like Bob Probert, Tie Domi, Tiger Williams and Dave Schultz come to mind. And goalies like Billy Smith and Ron Hextall.

Smith and Hextall kept players at bay with their flashing goal sticks. If they'd known about Paddy Moran's secret weapon, they'd have squirted tobacco juice too.

AUREL JOLIAT
138 Pounds of Might, Muscle and Moxie

"Old-time hockey players like me were the dumbest bunch of athletes in the world," Aurel Joliat once said. "We never got paid what we deserved, and most of us didn't have sense enough to save what money we got."

Joliat, then 85, was reminiscing about the pioneer days of the NHL and his memorable career with the Canadiens. Born in Ottawa, he joined the Habs in 1922 (traded for a fading Newsy Lalonde) and played left wing on a line with Howie Morenz and Billy Boucher. He stayed around until 1938, when he retired as the highest-scoring left winger in history, with 270 goals.

"Retired, hell!" he snorted. "They *fired* me when the Montreal Maroons folded and some of their players moved over to the Canadiens. I'm still damn mad about that.

"And don't say I played with Morenz," he added with a wink. "Although I tried to. Morenz was so fast I had to scoot well ahead of him on a rush or I'd find myself lagging behind him, trying to catch up. Nobody ever played *with* Morenz."

Was Aurel a tough hockey player? As a teenager, he fell off a roof, tumbled 35 feet to the ground and landed on his back. He played 13 seasons in the NHL with two displaced vertebrae, which caused him great pain and forced him to wear an elaborate truss at all times. Then there were the stomach ulcers, which he mostly ignored. He was tough enough to become a football star—a kicker with his hometown Ottawa Rough Riders—at 130 pounds, until a broken leg caused him to think seriously about concentrating full-time on hockey.

"Well, I guess I was tough enough," he once said. "You had to be to survive. But I wasn't the toughest. That muleheaded son of a bitch Eddie Shore was the meanest, toughest player I ever met. I was rushin' up the ice at the Forum one night when my lights went out. Shore hit me with a check that almost killed me. I was what, 130 pounds at the time? And he musta been 190. He dislocated my shoulder, and they carried me off. I remember being in a lot of pain. Then I look around, and Shore is leading a fancy rush. Forget the sore shoulder. I leaped over the boards and intercepted the big bugger. Hit him with a flyin' tackle. Hit him so hard he was out cold on the ice. He had it comin' I'd say . . ."

Joliat led the Canadiens in goals in 1924–25, with 29, played on three Stanley Cup teams and was named league MVP in 1934. That season, fans and teammates paid tribute to Joliat prior to a game at the Montreal Forum. The occasion was his 500th NHL game. The tiny left winger was presented with a loving cup from his mates, and a handsome chest of silverware and a golf bag from his many fans and admirers. A new car might have been a more appropriate gift, but that would have cost a few hundred dollars.

Joliat played 16 seasons in the NHL, all with the Canadiens. Even on a team noted for illustrious names like Vezina, Morenz and Boucher, he stood out. A master stickhandler, he wore his trademark black peaked cap during games. Woe betide any opponent who tried to dislodge it.

In retirement, Joliat coached Verdun and Valleyfield in the Quebec Senior League, opened a grocery store in Montreal and worked as a linesman in the NHL for a couple of seasons. He moved back to Ottawa and wound up as a ticket seller at the Union Station there. Thousands of people purchased tickets from the little man behind the wicket, not knowing that he had once reigned as one of the NHL's most colourful performers. At the age of 80, he played an oldtimers' game out west somewhere, and claims he scored a hat trick.

In 1985, 60 years after he played in the opening game at the Montreal Forum, he was invited back as an honorary member of the Canadiens' "dream team." At age 83, he delighted the fans with a display of vigorous skating and stickhandling. He even took a couple of pratfalls, one of them caused by the red carpet laid on the ice. "The ghost of Eddie Shore must have put that damn rug in front of me," he muttered.

At 85, he could be seen from time to time skating along the Rideau Canal in Ottawa, no doubt looking for a pickup game.

The late Bill Galloway, a hockey historian and one of Joliat's best friends, recalled a time when Joliat, then in his 70s, was invited to Boston for a reunion of living hockey legends. Among the celebrities was Punch Broadbent, another tough customer who had been a thorn in Joliat's side throughout their playing days.

In the press room prior to a dinner for the hockey legends, the two oldtimers became embroiled in an argument over an incident from a game played back in the '20s. Soon they were nose to nose, and their voices, raised in anger, silenced the other conversations in the room. Then punches were thrown and a dandy fight developed. Finally, scratched and bleeding, the two old adversaries were pulled apart by half a dozen bystanders. They were marched off to their rooms and told to cool off and behave themselves. But the fight wasn't over. Moments later, Joliat barged into Broadbent's room and flew at him with clenched fists, and round two was underway. Once again, peacemakers were forced to come running.

NHL president Clarence Campbell was called and persuaded the two legends of the game to call a truce. By then they were so battered and bruised, Campbell barred them from a group photo of the celebrities and told them to forget about attending the dinner that night. "Order room service and we'll pay for it," he barked as he departed.

The following morning, Joliat was seen roaming the hotel lobby. "I'm looking for my old pal Broadbent," he told acquaintances. "I'd like to buy him breakfast, or better still, a few beers, if we can find a bar that's open."

Not long after the Boston shenanigans, Joliat told Ottawa sports columnist Earl McRae he'd like to make a comeback in the NHL. "If a team made me the right offer, I'd come back," he said, straightfaced. "I'd show 'em."

"How long do you think you'd last out there?" McRae asked.

"About five minutes."

"Only five minutes a game?"

"Game? Hell, five minutes a shift!"

Mike Rodden, a former NHL referee who served as sports editor of the *Kingston Whig-Standard* in the late 1940s, was one of many admirers of Joliat. Rodden took issue with NHL president Clarence Campbell's statement that NHL hockey is tops in public appeal and that modern-day stickhandlers are the best. "That's nonsense," scoffed Rodden. "No modern-day player comes close to the stickhandling greats of the past, men like Aurel Joliat, Nels Stewart and Busher Jackson."

I met Joliat in Ottawa one summer day at a golf outing of hockey oldtimers. He spoke that evening to an audience captivated by his hockey tales. I made a mental note to contact him some time later, to drive to Ottawa and put many of his memories on tape. Alas, before I could arrange it, I picked up the paper one day and read his obituary.

The little left winger died on June 2, 1986. He was 85.

CLINT MALARCHUK
A Bullet Near the Brain

Many years ago, Don Cherry invited me to be a guest on his *Grapevine* TV show—it was September 8, 1991—and it was there I met goaltender Clint Malarchuk.

Back then, Don taped two or three half-hour shows in a single day, before a live audience at his Grapevine restaurant in Hamilton. I figured it took him as long to make three wardrobe changes as to do his interviews. And he didn't waste an opportunity. He'd ask a guest from one show to stick around for the next one, and use him briefly in the opening to help introduce his next guest.

When he called me to come up from the crowd, he turned to Clint Malarchuk.

"Did you watch Brian McFarlane on TV growing up, Clint?"

"I sure did. We had a few old black and white TV sets in Grande Prairie at that time. Watched him talking to all the big stars in hockey. He was as important to the game as most of the players."

Hey, nice compliment, Clint, I intended to say. But by then Cherry was into the show, rattling off my bio like he knew it by heart.

Clint left a lasting impression on me that day. You like cowboys?

He was a cowboy through and through. Toothpick bobbing from his mouth, a huge black Stetson on his head. I figured he'd passed on the limo Cherry lined up to get him to the restaurant. Surely he rode up on horseback—or maybe in a buckboard, hollering "gee" and "haw." As much Clint Eastwood as Clint Malarchuk, a guy you'd like to hang out with, affable, quick-witted, a good storyteller.

Aside from being a bona fide cowboy, Clint was an NHL goaltender for almost a dozen seasons. But he's best remembered for what could have been a life-ending moment. It occurred in an NHL game: Buffalo Sabres versus the St. Louis Blues, March 22, 1989.

Years after we met at the Grapevine, he told his story again—with a lot of raw emotion. With a voice that cracked and eyes that grew moist in the retelling, a toothpick quivering between thin lips:

It was late in the 1988–89 season, and I'm right where I want to be, tending goal for the Sabres in the old Buffalo Auditorium. On this night I remember thinking my mom would be watching me back in Calgary. She'd moved there from Grande Prairie. The folks had the big satellite TV back then. No more black and whites. First period flying by, and things were going well. One of the Blues—Steve Tuttle— came charging down the ice, and my defenseman Uwe Krupp—a big German guy as big as Chara—blocked him off as he cut into my goal crease. The guy's leg flew up, and instinctively I pulled my head back, exposing my throat. His skate just—*phtt*—sliced right across my neck, and I hardly felt it but I fell to the ice and suddenly the blood is pouring out. Lots of blood, a bucketful.

In the broadcast booth, the announcers, Ted Darling and Mike Robitaille, knew right away I was in trouble. Big trouble. They told me later there was so much blood, they cringed. "Please take the camera off him," one of them [Robitaille] pleaded. "Oh, my God! I've been around this game since I was three years old and I've never seen anything like that."

And Rick Meagher of the Blues started screaming for help.

You know if you get a throat cut, a jugular vein of a carotid artery, somethin' like that, you've only got minutes, two or three minutes maybe, or you're dead. And I thought, *This is it. I'm about to die.*

Jim Pizzutelli was the Sabres trainer and an ex-army medic. He jumped on the ice and raced over to me. He knew exactly where to put the pressure to stop the bleeding. How would he know that?

He was pushing, pushing, pushing hard into my throat. He said, "Clint, you need a breath?" and I was gasping, "Yeah, I need a breath." And when I grabbed a quick one the blood came squirting. He dug in again, pinching off the blood vessel. "I think I'm dying," I told him, and I remember his eyes getting big as saucers. I said, "My mom is watching. Call her and tell her I love her."

Jim was a chubby guy. Solid hands and fingers. A strong guy. I'll never forget his hands They told me later I lost about a third of the blood in my body. Somehow—don't ask me—they got me to the hospital. I was conscious all the way. In the ambulance I even made a little joke. "Throw a couple of stitches in and get me back for the third period," I told them. Nobody laughed. Surgeons were waiting. They got right to work on me. They needed something like 300 stitches to put my throat back together—the jugular, the carotid. Yep, another quarter of an inch and I was a goner, they told me.

Author's note: Malarchuk was fortunate to be at the end of the rink where the arena's medical room was located. If he'd been at the far end, he might have bled to death before he exited the ice. It was also reported that several fans fainted on witnessing the incident, two more suffered heart attacks and three players threw up on the ice.

"Yeah, I was told that several fans passed out when they saw all the blood," Clint says. "I don't know about any heart attacks."

Of course they wanted me to stay in hospital for a week or so, but I said no, I'm fine, all fixed. Time to get back to my team. I checked out the next day. No, I never should have done it. I know that now. But I was thinkin' of the guys back home. I wanted them to know I was one tough cowboy. Wanted to win their approval. Thinkin' like a dumb hockey player. Or a dumb cowboy.

I came back quick—real quick. Yeah, I came back too quick. I ignored my friends who told me, "Clint, don't rush it. Take time to heal."

Eleven days later, I threw on my gear and was back in my goal net, playing for the Sabres. What an amazing ovation I received from the fans when I skated out that night. Unforgettable.

I should have listened to the doctors who told me to take the rest of the year off. Shoulda listened. Coulda listened. But I didn't.

I found it was hard, really hard, to come back from that injury. In fact, it was devastating. Over the next three years, I suffered from OCD.

The problem became so huge. The depression set in and became unbearable. I could barely leave the house. It became very, very difficult for me to perform on the ice.

No one knew what I was going through. No one.

I knew I was in big trouble. And I knew it was the beginning of the end of my career.

By 1993, I was no longer with the Sabres. I went to the minors, first with a club in San Diego and then with the Las Vegas Thunder. And that was the end of it. I retreated in the off-season to a small ranch in Nevada. And with the meds I was taking, I was getting along all right. Not great, but not too bad. The team gave me horses for my ranch. Part of my contract. But I still wasn't right, and I decided to get away from goaltending. I retired in 1996.

And then I saw the Richard Zednik injury on TV. Richard was with the Panthers, playing against my old team, the Sabres, when he was cut across the throat by a teammate's skate blade. Blood everywhere on the ice. I saw it happen and I just shuddered. It made a huge impact on me. Huge.

That led to a total meltdown, a nervous breakdown. Everything came back to me, everything came to a head. I could no longer function, although I tried to.

I was never a big drinker, but I soon became one. Self-medicating. I became a loner—a big-time loner.

My wife could see things as they were. She saw me headed downhill, getting worse. Knew I was spiralling out of control for maybe about a month.

Clint's wife—his fourth wife—was Joanie Goodley, a figure skater who taught kids how to skate.

She says, "I don't like to talk about that awful day." But she does—briefly. "It was October 7, 2008, and I phoned home to see if Clint was all right. No answer. I called again. Couldn't get a hold of him. I rushed home and got there about 2:30. I walked in the house. He wasn't there. I called his name. Finally, I went outside looking for him. Found him sitting in back of the tack shed.

"'Tell me what's wrong, Clint.'

"He started crying, saying, 'I can't live like this. I don't want to do this anymore.' There was a rifle there—a .22—and he said, 'This is what I want to do. I can't stand being in my head.' He grabbed the rifle, and suddenly there was a shot. Blood was coming out his nose and he looked at me and said, 'See what you made me do.'"

Malarchuk called it an accident. How could that be? He put the rifle barrel up under his chin, pulled the trigger. The bullet, a .22 short, went up through his jaw and lodged in a space above his nose and outside his skull. If it had been a .22 long he'd not be breathing through his nose. He'd not be breathing—period. (Some reports inaccurately state that it was a shotgun Clint used to shoot himself that day. A shotgun blast also would have been fatal.)

"When the gun went off," his wife says, "I had my phone hanging from my hip. I grabbed it and called 911."

Within minutes, an ambulance arrived. Malarchuk was rushed to hospital. Once again, surgeons were waiting, waiting to save his life.

The bullet had shattered his chin, cheekbone and eye socket but stopped short of his brain. Luckily, it lodged outside his skull and above his nose. And there it remains.

"After the surgery and some rehab," he continues, "I knew I had a purpose in life. I'd seen Richard Zednik recover from the dreadful wound he suffered. He'd taken weeks off and made a successful return to the NHL."

Zednik, a Slovak, scored 200 career goals with five different NHL teams. His neck injury, suffered on February 10, 2008, was not as serious as Malarchuk's but he wisely sat out the rest of the season.

Years later, Malarchuk finally got help in his battle with OCD. And with the depression that accompanied it. Rick Dudley, his long-time buddy from the hockey world, helped him get back into the game he played so well. He became a goalie coach and, until recently, tutored goalies in the Calgary Flames system. Now 53, he lives with Joanie on a ranch in Gardnerville, Nevada. He works as an equine dentist, is a mental health advocate and a popular after dinner speaker. He takes his meds and listens to his doctors. He knows that people care for him and support him. He also knows that people afflicted with OCD and depression are prone to commit suicide.

He'd like to pass along a few words of advice.

"If you have OCD, get help. That's my best advice."

Malarchuk reveals the torment, anger, depression and obsessive-compulsive disorder he constantly faced throughout his life in his riveting book *The Crazy Game*. In it, the self-inflicted shot to his head, which he once declared a rabbit-hunt accident, is finally revealed as a failed suicide attempt.

He says, "I was in Edmonton signing at a bookstore and there was a young man there for about two hours taking pictures and just hanging around. He waited until the very last to have his book signed. Then he told me that I saved his life. I asked, 'How's that.' He said when he was in high school he was going to commit suicide. He had written a note and his dad found it before he could end his life. His father had him research me and some of my interviews. He said I changed his life, that he now didn't feel so alone, that he saw a specialist and got well. He was so excited to talk to me. We talked medication and life. We were both so happy to meet."

Hang in there, Clint. You're a tough old cowboy with a purpose—to help others survive.

A final mention goes to a true golden oldie (and one of my boyhood heroes), Rocket Richard. And the contract he signed in pencil with the Canadiens in 1956. While I can't guarantee its authenticity, the agreement, scrawled in longhand on an old calendar, appears to be legitimate. It calls for a salary of $12,000 with a bonus of $2,000. The amount of the stipend is pathetic for a superstar—even in that era when miserly owners and GMs intimidated players and made it clear that agents, lawyers and even fathers were not welcome at the bargaining table. A half bag of peanuts went to the regulars, perhaps a full bag to the superstars. The sympathy we feel for men like the Rocket and Gordie Howe—suckered by their bosses—is matched by our present concern as we witness the incredible swing of the pendulum in the opposite direction.

NOTES ON THE PHOTOS

SPRAGUE CLEGHORN, the most feared man on ice in the early days of pro hockey, was once suspended *by his own team* for the rest of the playoffs after he viciously attacked two Ottawa Senators. [© HHOF Images]

Dozens of NHL stars have been honoured with "Nights" but there was never one like KING CLANCY's, held on St. Patrick's Day on March 17, 1934, at Maple Leaf Gardens. He wore royal robes, a beard and a crown. His main gift was not a new car but a grandfather clock. [Nat Turofsky © HHOF Images]

DICK IRVIN was hugely successful as an NHL coach but his scoring exploits in senior hockey are legendary. In his first two seasons in senior company he scored 48 goals in 12 games. Here he is seen photographed (from L–R) with Maurice Richard, Bill Durnan, team captain, and Butch Bouchard in the Montreal dressing room at Maple Leaf Gardens, Toronto.[© HHOF Images]

EDDIE SHACK is the only NHLer I stood toe to toe with in the Vancouver airport. I called him every expletive I'd ever heard. Something registered because we get along now. We can even laugh about past differences. [From the author's collection]

Coach **BOB JOHNSON** was a rarity—one of those men almost every player hopes to have as a mentor. Photographed is Johnson as Head Coach on the Calgary bench during Game 3 of the Stanley Cup Final on May 20, 1986, at the Montreal Forum. The Canadiens beat the Calgary Flames 5–3. [Paul Bereswill © HHOF Images]

MIKE ROBITAILLE, shown with Sabre superstar Gilbert Perreault (11), built a new life as a broadcaster after a career ending injury. Guts and a good wife got him out of the sandbox. [From the Robitaille collection]

In 1933, **ACE BAILEY**'s fight for survival after an Eddie Shore check was the biggest story in hockey. [Nat Turofsky © HHOF Images]

Canadian fans sneered at the 1948 RCAF Flyers when they left for the World's championships, but thousands honoured them when they returned as champions. [**PATSY GUZZO** From the MacAdam collection]

THREE GOLDEN OLDIES
Hod Stuart dove into chilly waters and never came up. His death at 28 left friends, fans and family heartbroken.

Babe Siebert's life revolved around a paralyzed wife. A drowning victim, he left his spouse and two daughters and a chance to coach the Montreal Canadiens.

Photographed is Howie Morenz, in hospital after breaking four bones in his left leg during a game versus the Chicago Black Hawks on January 28, 1937. When Morenz died in a Montreal hospital in 1937 at age 34, thousands of weeping fans passed his coffin at centre ice in the Montreal Forum. [© HHOF Images]

Rock solid defenseman **BOBBY BAUN** once proved his toughness to his new boss by throwing him on his back. Here he is photographed wearing #8 during the NHL All-Star Game on January 16, 1968, at Maple Leaf Gardens in Toronto [© HHOF Images]

FRANK CARLIN was one of those under-rated hockey managers who mentored future NHLers without looking for praise or applause. [© HHOF Images]

After GORDIE HOWE collided with TED KENNEDY (and the boards) Howe was rushed to hospital where emergency brain surgery saved his life. Pictured is Ted Kennedy skating for the Toronto Maple Leafs during a game at Maple Leaf Gardens from the 1950–51 NHL season. [© HHOF Images]

In early day hockey, Canadians tended to scoff at American players. But HOBEY BAKER turned heads with his brilliant play. He was one of the first nine players inducted into the Hockey Hall of Fame (1945) and the only American. [© HHOF Images]

ANDRE LACROIX, seen chasing Rick Ley, managed his own playing career better than any player I ever met. [© HHOF Images]

I've seen hundreds of players with skills matching BOB MCNEIL's, but few could match his passion, tenacity, or his desire to shake an unhappy past. His brother Ron, a non-skater, had the same kind of determination. [Courtesy of Sheila McNeil]

LEO DANDURAND, a gentleman and sportsman, loved horses and hockey. He and his partners paid $11,000 for the Montreal Canadiens. [© HHOF Images]

LEN THORNSON's minor league stats are amazing. But how could he make the Montreal roster when they were winning five Stanley Cups? [© Le Studio du Hockey/Hockey Hall of Fame]

In 1910, NEWSY LALONDE played in the first-ever game for the Canadiens in the NHA. In his first six games, he scored 16 goals. Loaned to Renfrew he was even more prolific, scoring 38 goals in 11 games to win the scoring crown. [© HHOF Images]

AUREL JOLIAT, one of hockey's smallest superstars, still skated the Ottawa Canal well into his 80s. Photographed is an Ottawa minor hockey team featuring Aurel Joliat (back row, centre), c. 1910. [© HHOF Images]

CLINT MALARCHUK's gripping story of survival in a battle with depression has been an inspiration to thousands. He carries a bullet near his brain as a reminder of how a moment of desperation can be life-ending. [From the Malarchuk collection]

At ECW Press, we want you to enjoy this book in whatever format you like, whenever you like. Leave your print book at home and take the eBook to go! Purchase the print edition and receive the eBook free. Just send an email to ebook@ecwpress.com and include:

- the book title
- the name of the store where you purchased it
- your receipt number
- your preference of file type: PDF or ePub?

A real person will respond to your email with your eBook attached. And thanks for supporting an independently owned Canadian publisher with your purchase!

Published by ECW Press
665 Gerrard Street East
Toronto, ON M4M 1Y2
416-694-3348 / info@ecwpress.com

To the best of his abilities, the author has related experiences, places, people, and organizations from his memories of them. In order to protect the privacy of others, he has, in some instances, changed the names of certain people and details of events and places.

Printing: Marquis   5 4 3 2 1
PRINTED AND BOUND IN CANADA

LIBRARY AND ARCHIVES CANADA
CATALOGUING IN PUBLICATION

McFarlane, Brian, 1931–, author
Golden oldies : stories of hockey's heroes /
written by Brian McFarlane.

Issued in print and electronic formats.
ISBN 978-1-77041-250-7 (pbk)
978-1-77090-772-0 (pdf)
978-1-77090-773-7 (epub)

1. Hockey players—Biography. I. Title.

GV848.5.A1M265 2015   796.962092'2
C2015-902775-6   C2015-902776-4

Editor for the press: Michael Holmes
Cover design and photograph: Tania Craan
Back cover image: KUCO/Shutterstock.com
Author photo: Staff Photo/Sjoerd Witteveen

The publication of Golden Oldies has been generously supported by the Canada Council for the Arts which last year invested $153 million to bring the arts to Canadians throughout the country, and by the Government of Canada through the Canada Book Fund. Nous remercions le Conseil des arts du Canada de son soutien. L'an dernier, le Conseil a investi 153 millions de dollars pour mettre de l'art dans la vie des Canadiennes et des Canadiens de tout le pays. Ce livre est financé en partie par le gouvernement du Canada. We also acknowledge the Ontario Arts Council (OAC), an agency of the Government of Ontario, which last year funded 1,709 individual artists and 1,078 organizations in 204 communities across Ontario, for a total of $52.1 million, and the contribution of the Government of Ontario through the Ontario Book Publishing Tax Credit and the Ontario Media Development Corporation.